CONVERSATION,
LANGUAGE, AND POSSIBILITIES

CONVERSATION, LANGUAGE, AND POSSIBILITIES

A Postmodern Approach to Therapy

HARLENE ANDERSON

BasicBooks
A Division of HarperCollins*Publishers*

Library of Congress Cataloging-in-Publication Data

Anderson, Harlene, 1942–
    Conversation, language, and possibilities : a postmodern approach to
therapy / by Harlene Anderson.— 1st ed.
        p. cm.
    Includes bibliographical references and index.
    ISBN 0-465-03805-0
    1. Psychotherapist and patient.   2. Postmodernism—Psychological
aspects.   3. Intersubjectivity.   4. Constructivism (Psychology).
5. Psychotherapy patients—Language.   6. Psychotherapists—Language.
7. Dialogue.   8. Psychotherapy—Philosophy.   I. Title.
RC480.8.A53   1996
616.89'14—dc20   96-17802
                                                                              CIP

97 98 99 00 ❖/HC 9 8 7 6 5 4 3 2 1

To the memory of Harold A. Goolishian—friend, colleague,
and mentor—who inspired me and so many others,
and to
my conversational partners—in northern Norway,
at the Houston Galveston Institute, and in the therapy room—
who helped make this book possible.

CONTENTS

ACKNOWLEDGMENTS

I first met Harry Goolishian in 1970 and soon began a professional collaboration and friendship that were to last some twenty years until his death in 1991. Our work together centered on founding and building the Galveston Family Institute (now the Houston Galveston Institute) as a vehicle for providing psychotherapy training and clinical services and, central to our shared interests, for exploring the foundations on which theory and practice are based as well as challenging our own and others' ideas as they did or did not fit with our evolving experience and practice.

Invited by Basic Books to coauthor a work on our contributions to family therapy theory and practice, we had not yet put pen to paper when Harry died. In the five years since, the field has continued to change, as have my own thinking and practice. Above all else an intellectual radical and malcontent, Harry would have approved and participated at the forefront of questioning his own and others' ideas, as he did all his life. I acknowledge my profound debt to him and to our collaboration.

The Houston Galveston Institute, my colleagues there, and my colleagues around the world have constituted my primary knowledge system. They have been the conversational partners whose voices have influenced the developing, sharing, questioning, and expanding of my theory and practice. I have been in conversations and relationships extending over years with some and brief chats and passing connections with others, some in the distant past and some more recent. All have been meaningful. I acknowledge Tom Andersen, Paul Burney, Diana Carleton, Gianfranco Cecchin, Dan Creson, Anna Margrete Flåm, Kenneth Gergen, Lynn Hoffman, Kerstin Hopstadius, Arlene Katz, Susan Levin, Sylvia London,

Susan McDaniel, Einar Øritsland, Karen Parker, Peggy Penn, George Pulliam, Jamie Raser, Bjørn Reigstad, Harriet Roberts, Sallyann Roth, Susan Swim, Phil Torti, and Kathy Weingarten. Each has helped me explicate, held me accountable, supported me, and afforded opportunities for self- and other reflections in special and remembered ways. Many others, colleagues, students, and most important, the people I have met in the therapy room, may never know the influence and memory of a question, comment, or challenge they posed at a seminar, on a workshop evaluation form, in a therapy session, or simply talking. I consider myself an inclusive person; I apologize to those I should have but failed to acknowledge.

Several conferences that Lynn Hoffman dubbed the "traveling university" have been pivotal burying grounds for some thoughts and passions and titillating spawning grounds for others: the Institute's 1982 Epistemology, Psychotherapy, and Psychopathology and 1991 Narrative and Psychotherapy New Directions in Theory and Practice conferences, the Houston Galveston Institute Symposiums, the Irish team conferences, and the New Voices In Human Services conference in Northampton, among others. Tom Andersen's North Norway conferences in the 1980s and 1990s deserve special mention. Tom and his colleagues opened the doors of Norway to me, providing multiple opportunities for thought, practice, colleagueship, and friendship—thank you Bjørn, Finn, Anne-Grethe, Inger, Ingrid, Ivar, Kirsti, Liv, Magnus, Anna Margrete, Odd, Pål, Sissel, Steven, Tom, Turid, and all others whom I have not mentioned. My associations in Norway also granted me the privilege of working with colleagues in Sweden and Finland. I extend my appreciation to Kerstin, Matz, Eva and her team, and Jakko and his team.

My special thanks to Lee Herrick and Carole Samworth for their editorial expertise and encouragement. And my thanks to University of Houston Clear Lake graduate students Anne Andras, Ruth Dillon, and Ricka Waldron for their technical assistance.

Most of all, I want to acknowledge the most significant coauthors of my life: my husband, David Shine; my sister, Carol Anderson Ramirez; and my parents, Marjorie and Harry Anderson.

FOREWORD

LYNN HOFFMAN

Once in a while a book comes along that is larger than itself. Harlene Anderson's *Conversation, Language, and Possibilities* gives voice to the unusual achievement of the group of people she has worked with over the years, including the late and much missed Harold Goolishian, her long-time collaborator. Harry never wrote a book by himself, but he is present in this one. So are the many practitioners who contributed to or were influenced by the ideas presented here. Anderson is like a gifted painter who has built a beautiful gallery to house not only her own work but that of an entire community.

At the same time, this book is the unusual achievement of Anderson alone. She has taken on the task of sorting out a dauntingly difficult intellectual movement—postmodern theory—and has shown the links between elements of this theory and the collaborative approach to therapy that evolved in response to it. In this effort, Anderson calls on a larger philosophical conversation that has taken place mainly in academies and only now begun to influence applied fields.

Until recently, the philosophical tradition of Western Europe has considered itself above all other discourses and not a culture-bound palace of thought like the rest. The field of psychology, which evolved from philosophy, has had similar pretensions. Just as medicine has tried to uncover the causal context of physical illness, so experts in emotional illness have claimed to know the causes of psychological distress. It is this tradition of scientific positivism that postmodern critics have faulted, particularly with regard to "soft" sciences such as psychology.

On a human level, Anderson begins with an anecdote entitled "If My Story May Be of Any Help," a mother's heartfelt letter to the professionals who have tried to help her family and its two anorectic daughters. During a workshop in Sweden, Anderson encountered this family's despair of ever finding a professional who would listen to them and take their opinions into account. The rest of the book is, in effect, Anderson's answer to that letter.

It is also an answer to a letter I had been composing in my head for a long time. My own experiences with family therapy (that I now place under the category of "relational therapies") as trainee and recipient often left me feeling paralyzed and incompetent. I used to ask self-mockingly for a Therapy of the Feeble. This discontent eventually led me to the psychologist Carol Gilligan's (1982) concept of women's "different voice." I did not at all believe that this voice, with its emphasis on connection and its mandate for an "ethic of care," was limited to women, but I began to wonder how it might be made available as a valid therapeutic stance in a field to which so many women have been drawn.

Watching Anderson and Goolishian's work over the last decade, I saw that they placed a similar value on connecting with people. They listened intently to those who consulted with them, played back meanings, and asked for confirmation. Often they would listen to one person in the presence of others in the family as if they were speaking with them alone. Interpretations, like interventions, were scarce. Problems seemed to wither away. In their hands, in fact, what I was accustomed to call family therapy began to disappear.

Their ideas about therapy were unusual. They were among the first in the field to call therapy a mere *conversation*. They dismissed the thought that therapists should look for pathology. Most heretical of all, they recommended that therapists come from a place of "not knowing." Although I had been fascinated by the various systems, patterns, and structures that family therapy had "discovered," I had begun to look on these artifacts as fairy tales, to be judged by their usefulness as tactics rather than believing in them in any factual sense. Now I went a step further and wondered whether they didn't do more harm than good.

In setting forth the philosophical context for her collaborative approach, Anderson joins a number of social thinkers who believe that we are moving from a modern to a postmodern paradigm (Gergen, 1994). Dating from the Enlightenment and Descartes, the modern paradigm is based on the belief that a cognizing self can use reason and knowledge to understand and manipulate an objectively verifiable world. The postmodern paradigm abandons the individual–world duality and makes a radical move to a sociolinguistic frame. In the postmodern view, reality—even so-called scientific reality—is woven and rewoven on shared linguistic looms.

The consequences of this shift in psychology's favorite beliefs are immense. Anderson surveys some of the concepts that have been falling like ninepins: that of a free-standing self; that words correspond to things in the real world; the belief in essential traits and foundational truths. With regard to therapy, she shows how this shift in beliefs challenges the expert–nonexpert dichotomy and the hierarchical structure that flows from it; the "client's voice" gains in importance and the idea of therapy as a "conversational partnership" comes to the fore.

The most difficult aspect of this approach for traditional therapists is the proposal that the therapist come from a place of "not knowing," which seems to many to downgrade their skills in an almost ridiculous way. "If therapy is only a conversation," they ask, "how can I take money for it?" This is a serious proposition, however, supported by credible philosophical frameworks. Social construction theory—the idea that reality is not independently "out there" but construed through collective meaning making—was around before the first appearance of a strong postmodern position took shape in the fields of human studies, yet it is the theory most often called on in explaining reality. A theory that fills a similar function is hermeneutics, the art of interpretation, newly excavated from the past. Completing the trilogy is narrative theory, with its implication that human events only become intelligible by being storied.

Looking back and trying to sort out how postmodernism has influenced the relational therapies, I call on three images: the rings, the shelves, and the well. Early on in my pre-postmodern days I used to think of family therapy as a stone dropped into a pond, making widening rings. The first ring of course is the family, and it led to a new professional practice called family therapy. A second ring emerged from an awareness of the professional systems around the family, producing systemic therapy. A third ring indicates the influence of society and its beliefs, from which evolved feminist therapy with its challenge to patriarchy and ideas about the social construction of gender.

A new ring now has appeared that addresses differences among larger cultural groups: third world vs. first world, gay vs. straight, first peoples vs. colonials, and so forth. This ring in particular has been highlighted by the narrative therapist Michael White (1995), who attends closely to the practices by which one culture or group marginalizes another. Given the fact that people who consult with us increasingly will be poor and from nonwhite cultures, we are enormously beholden to an approach that sensitizes therapists to their own myopias in this regard.

But the rings-in-the-pond image seems to imply an ever-widening source of knowledge; the narrative view, being the most inclusive, therefore might be presumed to be the best. Similarly, to suggest that a postmodern view is better than a modern one is to assume a progressive curve that favors the newest paradigm. To avoid such a structural bias, I move next to an image of shelves.

In this instance, a shelf is an outside place to stand that allows you to get a better view of where you used to be. It corresponds to the first order–second order perspective found in the work of the anthropologist Gregory Bateson (Hoffman, 1990). This idea is a purely reflexive one; shelves are nonplaces, like the horizon, or rather, the shelf of this year is the dogma of the next. Family therapy was a shelf from which to see the defects of individual therapy, systemic therapy was a shelf from which to criticize family work, and gender-informed therapy was a shelf from which to see the patriarchal bias of systemic work. Narrative therapy now has found a shelf in the discourses of class, race, and culture, allowing therapists to see the oppressive nature of such discourses and how people are constrained by them.

Harlene Anderson has offered yet another shelf, an epistemological one. By adopting a collectively oriented linguistic paradigm, she has helped therapists move outside the individually oriented realist paradigm in which therapy traditionally has been embedded—no small feat. Walker Percy (1996) ironically describes the problems that arise when you try to make yourself aware of using a linguistic frame as "something like wearing gold eyeglasses and trying to see gold."

An interesting question is why family therapy became so good at developing shelves and consequently mutating—or is it the other way around? My guess is that this field acquired a resistance to its own establishments, perhaps owing to links to innovations in science, the humanities, and philosophy that social thinkers such as Bateson structured our ears to hear. By periodically finding a niche in these outsider conversations, the field may have developed a reflexivity gene that, for whatever reason, keeps unfurling in response to new locations of distress and throwing up new vantage points from which to deal with them.

I now come to my image of the well. It is not easy for us to be conscious of our therapist self; it is even harder to be conscious during therapy of the self that moves in and out of what I call the *shared unconscious* or *common pool*. I had been struggling with this idea for decades and welcomed the notion that knowledge is not a product of the individual nervous system but rather evolves from the living, changing web of meanings in which all our doings are embedded.

I call this activity *collaborative knowing*. I am indebted here to John Shotter's (1993b) description of "knowing of the third kind," a process that is neither in the head nor in the world but takes place in the practical and moral sphere of what he calls "joint action." Shotter uses for an analogy the image of a Ouija board: the answer cannot be predicted or controlled but rather depends on the mysterious trajectory of the little platform under its pile of hands. Another analogy (mine) is the experience of digging underground tunnels at the beach: who does not remember that moment when the final wall of sand crumbles and one set of blind, wriggling fingers touches another?

For me, such analogies point up the reason for a "not knowing" point of view. If, during a therapeutic conversation, our fingers have not touched, there is no channel for exchange. Until now, our field mostly has ignored the importance of this channel and how to create it; the collaborative style that Anderson describes, however, increases the hope that this channel will be attended to. This is what Carl Rogers added to individual therapy (albeit within a humanistic framework), and this is what Anderson and Goolishian have added to the relational therapies.

I would like to mention the political side of Anderson's approach. Not as overtly activist as White and Epston's (1990) narrative model (and it has been criticized on this ground), in practice it corrects for many of the social and cultural biases that permeate traditional therapies. Fairness is never far from Anderson's mind:

> The dominant voice, the culturally designated professional voice, usually speaks and decides for marginal populations—gender, economic, ethnic, religious, political, and racial minorities— whether therapy is indicated and, if so, which therapy and toward what purpose. Sometimes unwittingly, sometimes knowingly, therapists subjugate or sacrifice a client to the influences of this broader context, which is primarily patriarchal, authoritarian, and hierarchical.

A therapist voice that restrains its impulse to control, avoids the imposition of superior understanding, and allows mutually arrived-at solutions to emerge seems to me highly political in nature. Such a voice assumes it can only empower others by being a traitor to its own professional identity—that is, by "shedding power."

I loved reading this book, particularly its "floating islands": the purely philosophical disquisitions sprinkled throughout on the meaning of self, the nature of knowledge, and the question of change. I am especially grateful for Anderson's respectful distancing of the systems metaphor that was such a part of my own professional development. The "onion theory" is how she and Goolishian refer to the normative view of social systems popularized by the sociologist Talcott Parsons. According to this analogy, the individual, the family, and the community are nested together like Russian dolls, with the smaller systems having to adjust to ensure the stability of the larger ones. It is easy to see how such a view promotes a companion theory of pathology that pushes the professional helper to bring dysfunctional persons and families into line.

I am also grateful for the simplification Anderson brings to clinical work. Absent are the analyses of troubled family histories, the study of pathogenic interaction patterns, the scrutiny of maladaptive beliefs. There is no list of questions to follow, a process that always reminds me of sheep dogs herding their charges into the little corral. Indeed, many of the methodological and theoretical superstructures that have long characterized family therapy now seem like historical items. Often I will pull a technique or an idea out of the bag I call Biggest Hits of Family Therapy, explain why it has been considered useful, and offer it; but I try not to forget that I am also, with the encouragement of this book, digging tunnels in the sand.

PREFACE

One of the most important features of life is conversation. We are in continuous conversation with each other and with ourselves. Through conversation we form and reform our life experiences and events; we create and recreate our meanings and understandings; and we construct and reconstruct our realities and our selves. Some conversations enhance possibility; others diminish it. When possibility is enhanced, we have a sense of self-agency, a sense that we can take the necessary action to address what concerns or troubles us: our dilemmas, problems, pains, and frustrations, and to accomplish what we want: our ambitions, hopes, intentions, and actions.

The philosopher Ludwig Wittgenstein articulated this possibility and its actualization as a "change of aspect"—a different way of understanding things—involving a "change of life." By change of life he meant "a plea for personal courage to change one's own life" (as quoted in van der Merwe & Voestermans, 1995, p. 43). Wittgenstein's view of understanding is one of practical understanding from within. Concerned about the ways we relate and respond to each other in our everyday lives, Wittgenstein suggested that we live in a world of events rather than a world of things. He challenged us to "move about around things and events in the world," instead of trying to delineate their essential features or describe them with definitional exactness (van der Merwe & Voestermans, 1995, p. 38). Extending his challenge to our efforts in the realm of behavioral sciences, and specifically to psychotherapy, I wonder, What discourages and what encourages *possibility conversations?* What is language and what is its relationship to conversation? How can a therapist in the social circumstance of therapy participate with another person so that person can realize the possibilities in the circumstances of his or her own daily life? How can we, to use the trailblazing Norwegian psychiatrist Tom Andersen's words, talk with each other and with ourselves in a way that we have not done before? How can we, as creative writers Peggy Penn and Marilyn Frankfurt suggest, create a *participant text* that addresses the questions "How do I want to be with others?" and "How do I want them to be with me?" How can we, as family therapy pioneer Lynn Hoffman wonders, transform our stories about therapy without committing the same authoritarian sins we are objecting to?

I think that conversation—whether in therapy, in learning contexts, or in business consultations—is about helping people to access the courage and ability to "move about around things," to "have a clear view," to achieve self-agency. The encouraging factors and aims are a particular kind of conversation—*a dialogue*—and a therapist's expertise in creating a dialogical space and facilitating a dialogical process—*a philosophical stance*.

This book is an exposition of my current work and the ideas that reciprocally guide and arise from my practice of therapy.[1] It represents a journey, a work in continual process and transformation, a search for more effective ways to understand, meet, and be helpful to the people I see in therapy and in other professional settings (Anderson 1990a, 1990b, 1993, 1995; Anderson & Goolishian 1986, 1988b, 1992; Goolishian & Anderson 1981, 1987a). It is foremost an account and illustration of the way that I conceptualize and participate in conversations and how possibilities evolve from within them. It is about my philosophical stance.

My effort is to extend, to make a contribution to, to add another voice to the emerging postmodern challenge to our familiar psychotherapy discourse, and to advance an alternative view that represents a philosophy of therapy, an approach, not a model. I choose the umbrella word *postmodern* owing to the freedom and possibilities that assumptions associated with it allow; at the same time, I realize that it (or any other designator for that matter, even the word *therapy*) has inherent risks. I approach this task with enthusiasm and hope that my passion does not inadvertently convey tenacious certainty. I offer my philosophy and practice of therapy as one view—one voice—to take into consideration.

I write from my experience, but what my practice looks like in action is difficult to capture. Missing in the written word is the opportunity to experience the practice and capture its essence in the author's presence. Because written words are lineal, conveying ideas and experiences that are nonlineal in a text is difficult and places a burden on both writer and reader. A writer's task is to communicate in a way that invites the reader into a dialogue. As in Mikhail Bakhtin's view, a writer's responsibility is to free the reader from the defense of his or her culture in encountering a text, thereby allowing creative understanding and new meaning to be generated by bridging a familiar and an unfamiliar culture

(Pittman, 1995). The reader's task is to engage in dialogue with the author in a way that generates meaning and beckons to what is not there. It would be impossible for a reader to experience and make sense of my work the way that I do.

To portray a sense of my collaborative approach I intertwine history, philosophical essays (what Lynn Hoffman refers to as "floating islands"), discussions of therapy, and clinical narratives. I find that the voices of others—clients, scholars, and students—often capture the essence of my meaning and inspire my work; I therefore let them speak for themselves. Because my voice embraces theirs, I shift from *I* to *we* as I tell *my/our* story.

There are multiple ways to read this book. It can be read straight through, or one may read the historical and philosophical chapters, clinical chapters, and clinical narratives in any order. I invite you to construct your own narrative, combining the parts and voices with what you bring to them in a way that makes the book significant and useful. The book is divided into four parts: each begins with a clinical narrative. In Part I, to dispel any illusion that my clinical philosophy and practice are objectively presented "floating islands," I situate them in a broader historical, professional, and theoretical context. Next I discuss the philosophical framework central to my approach, including postmodern social construction, hermeneutic, and narrative premises. In Part II, I describe the clinical experiences that influenced my turn to these philosophies and discuss how the therapy system, process of therapy, and therapist's position are conceptualized and actualized. To offer the reader tools to make use of these concepts, I submit "advice" that clients offer therapists who wish to work collaboratively and close with an annotated transcript of a therapy interview. In Part III, I return to the "floating islands" to discuss language, knowledge, and the *self* from a postmodern perspective. In Part IV, I address extensions of and possibilities that lie beyond a postmodern therapy. I conclude with my reflections on writing this book—including its influence on me—and look toward the future.

I am deeply committed to continuously reflecting on my work with myself and others. As a natural consequence, I find myself reflecting on the work of others. As you read, I invite you to think about your own therapy philosophy and practice, comparing and contrasting yours to mine and mine to others. I welcome your opinions, questions, critiques, and challenges and look forward to being your conversational partner.

CONVERSATION,
LANGUAGE, AND POSSIBILITIES

PART I

Creating the Space: The Give and Take of Theory and Practice

CHANGING THE CULTURE OF THERAPY: A PHILOSOPHICAL PRACTICE

My collaborative approach to therapy has evolved from the various flows of the countless "therapy" conversations and conversations about "therapy" that I have taken part in over the years with clients, colleagues, students, and myself as we tried to describe and explain our experiences to ourselves and to others. These conversations about successful as well as unsuccessful therapy have influenced my current ideas and work. In reflecting on them, I kept returning to language, conversation, and relationship as the central parts of therapy. I wondered: What is the difference between a successful therapy conversation and an unsuccessful one? Is there a difference between a dinner conversation with a good friend and a therapy conversation with a stranger? How does what happens in the therapy room make any difference in the person's life outside it? Where does the "newness" that clients often describe as a *sense of freedom* or *feeling of hope* come from? What does a therapist do, if

1

anything, that contributes to that? What kind of expertise does a therapist have? Most important, are these the questions I should be asking?

As I searched for ways to think about our experiences and these kinds of questions I kept turning away from modernism. Something did not fit. I found myself sometimes purposefully and sometimes serendipitously drawn to *postmodern* philosophical assumptions that seemed to fit my experiences and liberate me. In its broadest sense, postmodern thought has provided the springboard for and is the umbrella under which I place my work today, although I realize that there will be something beyond it. Although my approach has become known as a *collaborative language systems approach* (Anderson, 1993, 1995), in this book I simply call it a *collaborative approach*. These terms refer to my conceptualization of therapy: *a language system and a linguistic event in which people are engaged in a collaborative relationship and conversation—a mutual endeavor toward possibility.*

To situate my approach, some thinkers—from the ranks of theoretical, philosophical, social, and feminist psychology and family therapy clinical theory—have created and taken paths that critique scientific authority as the basis of knowledge and have offered alternative criteria for psychological inquiry and intelligibility. I characterize this revolutionary, potentially explosive, and not surprisingly marginalized paradigmatic challenge as *postmodern*—as one that embraces contemporary social construction, and hermeneutic, narrative theories. I have witnessed and participated in this revolution from within family therapy and psychology, although by far my professional growth, identity, and clinical and academic contributions have been primarily within the family therapy movement.

My analysis and critique of psychotherapy in general and my alternative views are rooted in and embody my heritage as a member of the "Galveston group" (formally the Houston Galveston Institute), including this history, context, and colleagueship (Anderson, Goolishian, Pulliam, & Winderman, 1986; Goolishian & Anderson, 1990). The Institute is a private, nonprofit clinical practice, research, and education organization whose roots trace back to the early innovative family therapy research and practice known as multiple impact therapy (MacGregor et al., 1964). The predominant clinical practice at the Institute comprises mandated and failed treatment clients referred by community institutions such as child protection agencies, family courts, women's shelters, and others who have identified them as societally deviant (for example, domestic violence, child abuse). I also have been privileged to be a guest teacher and consultant in other contexts and countries that have allowed unique experiences, backdrops, and enrichments that in turn influenced my practices and ideologies.

These professional settings have furnished critical commonalities: collaboration with inquisitive colleagues who questioned familiar paradigms and explored the frontiers of new ones; teaching environments in which a teacher was also a learner; and an opportunity to encounter people (including individuals, families, larger systems, and organizations) from a broad range of socioeconomic, cultural, and ethnic backgrounds who presented a variety of everyday life and work difficulties.

My postmodern collaborative approach, and this book, are based on these philosophical assumptions:

1. Human systems are language- and meaning-generating systems.
2. Their construction of reality is forms of social action rather than independent individual mental processes.
3. An individual mind is a social composition, and self, therefore, becomes a social, relational composition.
4. The reality and meaning that we attribute to ourselves and others and to the experiences and events of our lives are interactional phenomena created and experienced by individuals in conversation and action (through language) with one another and with themselves.
5. Language is generative, gives order and meaning to our lives and our world, and functions as a form of social participation.
6. Knowledge is relational and is embodied and generated in language and our everyday practices.

These assumptions have profound implications in every human endeavor—and how we are as persons in those endeavors—especially for therapy and therapists, in the way a therapist thinks about human beings and our roles in their lives, the way a therapist conceptualizes and participates in a therapy system, therapy process, and therapy relationship. They separate my postmodern collaborative philosophy and practice from modernist approaches and from others in the "postmodern pack," moving a therapy system, therapy process, and therapist's position along a continuum that implies a move

FROM	*TO*
A social system defined by role and structure	A system that is contextually based and a product of social communication
A system composed of an individual, a couple, or a family	A system composed of individuals who are in relationship through language
A therapist-driven hierarchical organization and process	A therapist-assumed *philosophical stance* that invites a collaborative relationship and process
A dualistic relationship between an expert and a nonexpert	A *collaborative partnership* between people with different perspectives and expertises
A therapist as a knower who discovers and collects information and data	A therapist as a *not-knower* who is in a being-informed position
A therapist as a content expert who is a metaknower of how others should live their lives	A therapist as an expert in creating a dialogical space and facilitating a dialogical process
A therapy focus on top-down knowledge, and a search for causality	A therapy focus on generating possibilities and relying on the contributions and creativity of all participants
A therapist as a knower who is certain about what he or she knows (or thinks he or she knows)	A therapist as a not-knower who is uncertain and regards knowledge as evolving
A therapist who operates from private and privileged knowledge, assumptions, and thoughts	A therapist who is public about, shares, and reflects on his or her knowledge, assumptions, thoughts, questions, and opinions
A therapist as an interventionist with strategic expertise and associated across-the-board skills and techniques	A shared inquiry that relies on the expertise of all persons participating in a conversation
A therapist whose intent is to produce change in another person or member of a system	Change or transformation as evolving through, and as the natural consequence of, a generative dialogue and collaborative relationship

FROM	TO
A therapy with people as contained, core selves	A therapy with people as multiple, linguistically constructed, relational selves
Therapy as an activity that is researched by an investigator of other subjects	A therapist and a client as co-investigators who participate in creating what they "find"

Why and how I think these assumptions change the culture of therapy and what their implications look like is what this book is about. To situate my therapy philosophy and practice, I now offer an account of my view of the changes that have taken place in the psychotherapy field, especially family therapy, and a critique of the currently competing theoretical paradigms and practice models. But first, I pause to tell a mother's story.

"IF MY STORY MAY BE OF ANY HELP . . . "

On a crystalline, nine-degree Sunday afternoon, I was greeted at the airport in Sweden by my gracious Swedish hosts, Gustaf and Kerstin. Hearty hellos were exchanged all around, and quickly the talk turned to the therapists' workshop we would all be participating in the next day. Only during the drive to my hotel did a beat of silence occur—just before Gustaf hesitantly asked me whether I would be willing to meet with a family that evening for a consultation. Their hope was that we could videotape the meeting and use it as a "teaching platform" in the workshop. Never one to decline a good conversation, I agreed. A phone call to the family confirmed the time and place.

It would be two hours before our family arrived. Wanting to be accommodating, Gustaf and Kerstin asked, "Would you care to rest or have something to eat?" Although my body longed for a nap after the thirteen-hour trip, I was—as family therapy historian and clinical theorist Lynn Hoffman says—"poised for action." I chose to eat dinner with my hosts. We ate on a boat docked on a river in the center of town that had been converted to a restaurant. It was Mother's Day. The busy kitchen and the slow service provided a leisurely atmosphere. Over fresh fish and boiled potatoes we talked about Sweden, mental health systems, their work, my work. I asked about expectations: their expectations for the workshop, their guesses about their colleagues' hopes for the workshop, and what they knew of the family members' thoughts about meeting with me.

During our conversation, it occurred to me that it might be a good idea to invite Gustaf and Kerstin to join me in meeting with the family. Not knowing the family's command of English and aware of my nonexistent Swedish, I wondered out loud whether they would be willing to help with any translation difficulties and, most important, to serve as a bridge between the family meeting and the workshop the next day. If my hosts were actually in the room with us, I thought, they would have their own firsthand experiences to share with the workshop participants, creating a far richer "mix" of ideas than my own experience alone. They looked surprised at my invitation. "What would the family think?" "What would our role be?" they wondered. Although they knew the family, Gustaf was worried: "We are not their therapists." But they were intrigued—and they took me up on the idea. I asked them what role they preferred to play. After discussing it with each other they concluded, "We would like to be in the room with you and the family, if it's all right with them. We would like just to listen." I asked whether it would be permissible for me to ask them questions. They readily agreed that it would.

During the drive to the clinic, the car was filled with conversation. I learned that the "family" included a mother, a father, and two daughters, ages sixteen and nineteen. Both daughters had been struggling for two years with anorexia; the older daughter was currently in an adult hospital unit. What remained vague was why this family was chosen and what anyone's expectations were, if any, of our meeting other than as a "demonstration" for the workshop participants.

In the reception area, the family members assembled—all very polite and quite serious. Gustaf introduced me to each person, at which point I asked them whether the host therapists could join us, sharing my reasons and letting them know that this was an idea for discussion not a requirement. All four agreed that this arrangement would be fine. We went into the interview room, where seven chairs had been placed in a circle, and I invited everyone to sit wherever he or she felt comfortable. To the father's left sat the younger daughter, to his right was the mother, and to her right was the older daughter. The parents seemed unassuming and all four perhaps slightly wary. Their voices were soft as they told me where they lived and about their hour-long drive to the clinic. The two daughters' voices were especially hushed, barely audible. Both were small, delicate, and blond. And, although the younger daughter was thin, the elder looked gaunt and lethargic; any observer would not be surprised to learn that she had an eating disorder or some other serious physical problem. The atmosphere in the room felt somber and tense.

But through a somewhat awkward mix of their Swedish English and my Texas accent, we began to get to know each other. I listened carefully and tried to speak distinctly, telling them what I knew about why we were meeting and how I hoped to hear each of their thoughts about being here today. Then, being curious, I asked, "What do you think we should know about you; what would you like us to know about you?" The mother responded quickly, "I have it here." She reached down and took some papers from her purse— two pages, computer typed. She handed the pages to me and I read the capitalized words, "WHY FAMILY THERAPY HASN'T BEEN ANY HELP FOR US." My heart admittedly gave a little jump: My first thought was *"This is going to be the topic of our clinical discussion tomorrow?"* My second thought, the stronger, was "I wonder what she's written?" There was nothing to do but proceed. After a long pause, I asked, "May I read it out loud?"

"Of course," the mother said, and the others nodded in agreement. I slowly read aloud these words on the paper, with bold and capital letters, just as they were given to me.

Anorexia has both a psychological and a physical aspect and it is necessary to treat both sides at the same time. The methods being used towards our girls in order to make them eat better have mostly been misguided, ill-advised, on some occasions even in the vicinity of being ill-natured, and have many times made things worse than they were before. They have caused so much frustration, despair, anguish and resignation that the therapy to a very great extent has dealt with these questions while the other aspects have been neglected.

Much too often our daughters have felt that their opinions were not important, that no one was prepared to listen to them and work through them instead of by way of us [the parents]. It would have cost them, and us, much less pain if more effort had been made trying to *influence their own motivation*, trying to *explain* the dangers with the sickness, not in vague terms but in very concrete manners. *Cooperate* with the healthy part of them, *compliment* them, *don't humiliate* them and don't show them open *contempt*. Be firm; they appreciate that, I can promise, *but not cruel*. Make it easier for their self-respect to grow. If they don't have a very strong wish to recover they won't do it.

I think that a more flexible attitude would have been useful in the approach towards our family. Sometimes it would have been useful to talk with all of us, sometimes with only one member. I am quite convinced that this method would have suited us much better.

The fact that they were both sick at the same time made our situation much more than twice as difficult as it would have been if only one girl was sick with this disease. I think this should have led the medical staff [and therapists] to ponder both twice and thrice if their methods really could be good for our family. I would like to see more humbleness, inventiveness, and ingenuity in the treatment. We have the feeling that they had one theory and wanted to put us into that, no matter how it applied to us, and likewise one method that they tried with rather small alterations when it again and again proved inadequate.

In short, *try to listen to our children*. It is not impossible to talk with them. We are fully aware that in periods it is quite difficult to reach them, but you must try. It pays dividends after a while and at best you may gain their confidence and then much is won.

. . . They must be offered talks with people they can trust, that is, people who regard them as human beings with a sense of pride, justice, integrity and dignity.

Try to listen to us [the parents]. Of course . . . the medical staff never refused to listen and talk to us, that is, until the day our daughter became 18 years of age, and after that day the rest was silence. . . . We have often felt that the doctors only heard what they wanted to hear and disregarded the rest without comment. At best [what was said] was dropped because it was uninteresting, impossible, or . . . was regarded as just rubbish and gravely suspected because the persons who uttered it were incompetent and completely controlled by their daughters, and consequently by the sickness. But we know our daughters more than any other person. We know their reactions and their feelings . . . we know when they can be trusted better than any nurse or doctor.

I have tried. I have seen other people try. Much too often I have failed. I have seen others fail too. But I have at least tried to learn by my failures, but so far I haven't seen much sign of that from members of the medical [and therapy] staff.

That was it: complete, concise, all of it. I silently thought, with a lump swelling in my throat, "This is everything I want to communicate tomorrow." This mother's words simply and eloquently express a plea for an analysis of our therapy traditions: of *the way we are in relationship with* people in therapy, of the way we think about, talk with, act with, and are responsive to them.

I believe that these words could have come from any client, in any country. I did not hear them as condemning nor do I offer them as such. I heard them as an invitation to pause and reflect. This family's experiences are not so different from those many of us experience ourselves: well-intentioned, but with hurried schedules and demanding expectations, we sometimes fail to pause and hear what a client intends and we sometimes fail to pause and share our own inner words.

After another long pause that stretched out in the room's solemn atmosphere, I handed the letter back to the mother and expressed my appreciation for her willingness to share it with us. I slowly began to ask the questions that would help me better understand what she had written. We taped the session. We explored the implications—the challenge and the hope—of her words throughout the workshop the next day.

After the workshop was over, like so many important conversations, I knew that our conversation should not, could not, end there. Her words continued to live in me to spark ongoing internal dialogue long after I returned home. I wrote to the mother to ask her permission to share the letter and the videotapes with other therapists. She responded with an update on what had happened since our meeting and concluded with these words, "If my story may be of any help to therapists, that would be a great comfort to me and perhaps even make me *hope* that our struggles and sufferings have not been completely in vain."

A poignant—and prodding—hope, indeed, here in the latter half of the twentieth century, when one of the major ways people use to solve their problems and enhance growth is therapy. This mother's experience challenges us to rethink our *thinking* about this ritual process—perhaps to place it *inside* the range of normal, everyday ordinary life experience versus *outside,* as a laboratory for the microscopic discovery, analysis, and repair of it. Her words entreat us to reexamine the *relationship* that *is* therapy—a relationship in which the defining elements are crucial. More than answers, her plea invites questions: What do we bring to the relationship? What kind of relationship do we value? Who are we as therapists? Are we experts? Are we teachers? Are we friendly advisers? Are we moral enforcers? And how did we come to be that, anyway?

As important, when "listening" to this mother's words, we are called to examine the factors that influence the way a therapist will hear them. How are we to understand, for instance, one therapist's conviction "The mother is obviously controlling the voice of the family"; another's "Two daughters with eating problems, it's obviously incest!"; another's "Did you notice the father's silence? The mother protects him"; another's "Why was this letter so rich?"?

As a relationship, therapy is as much about who we are as therapists—and who we are in that relationship—as it is about who the members of this family or any client system are, and who they are in relationship to the therapist. It is as much about our self-narratives, the way we define ourselves as persons, and our identities as therapists as it is about the client's self-definitions and identities.

The most important aspect of human relationships begins with the self. That holds as true for us therapists as it does for our clients. What distinguishes all postmodern approaches to therapy is an alternative definition and view of self. Before proceeding to the premises of a postmodern therapy, including its concept of self and the role of self-narratives and the practical implications of these premises, we must first turn to the beginnings from which a shift to postmodern therapy emerged.

CHAPTER 1

Onions and Pyramids

We make our own destinies by our choice of gods.
—Virgil

To understand the current paradigmatic shift to postmodern psychotherapy and how change is taking place, we must trace its historical developments. Here I share my version of this shift and how it was greatly influenced by the evolution of, and within, family therapy. I focus on the roles that cybernetic, social, constructivist, and evolutionary theories have played in its development and in an emerging new shift that overshadows them.

Paradigms, including therapy paradigms, are primarily powerful enterprises for approaching what the proponents of the paradigm consider critical problems. Each paradigm defines what issues are to be seen as problems within it and is designed to address those issues. Paradigms shape problems; problems support paradigms. Currently, in psychology, family therapy, and to some extent psychiatry, some are forging disciplinary self-examinations, searching for the most useful paradigm for understanding and approaching human behavior.

These disciplines, including their dominant theories and practices, are rooted in modernism and empirical scientific methodology. Psychological knowledge, the understanding of the individual

11

in particular and of human nature in general, is arrived at through scientific methods (Blackman, 1994; Buxton, 1985; Robeck, 1964). The object of inquiry, the human subject, is viewed ahistorically and as an unchanging entity that can be observed and quantified (Danziger, 1994), and the essence of the object of inquiry, human nature, is viewed primarily as an enduring universal phenomenon.

The current self-examination of and challenge within each of these mental health disciplines center around scientific realism as informing the theoretical foundations for understanding human behavior and the methods for addressing it. Psychology can no longer be viewed as a science of observing and of knowing human nature—individual behaviors and characteristics. Contemporary debate focuses mainly on psychology's lack of attention to contextuality (Danziger, 1988; Sass, 1992), the irrelevance of psychological knowledge to practice (Hoshmand & Polkinghorne, 1992; Polkinghorne, 1991; Schön, 1983), the individual development of knowledge (Bruner, 1986, 1990; Freeman, 1993; Gergen, 1982, 1985, 1994; Kitzinger, 1989; Lehtinen, 1993), the discipline's commitment to achieving status as a science (Faulconer & Williams, 1990; Messer, Sass, & Woolfolk, 1988; Slife, 1993), and research informed by modern scientific methodology (Jones, 1986; Kvale, 1996; Rosenhan, 1973; Scarr, 1985; Snyder & Thomsen, 1988). Historically, psychiatry has had similar arguments (Chessick, 1990; Fulford, 1989; Kleinman, 1988a, 1988b; Laing & Esterson, 1971; Szasz, 1961). An awareness of how new knowledge evolves to challenge the old and what drives this development is crucial to situating and understanding these self-criticisms. Toward this aim, I consider two perspectives on paradigmatic transformations.

PARADIGMATIC TRANSFORMATIONS

One template for tracking and understanding the revolutionary challenge in psychotherapy is the historian Thomas Kuhn's (1970) perspective on the birth and death of scientific paradigms, and his rejection of the idea that science eventually will discover *the truth*. Science, according to Kuhn, is not a steady, cumulative acquisition of knowledge but, rather, a series of sometimes tense and often nonrational revolutions that interrupt periods of peaceful problem solving. Kuhn defines a "knowledge paradigm" in science as a collection of ideas within the confines of which inquiry takes place. The knowledge paradigm defines which problems, methods, and points of congruence/divergence are legitimate and confer membership in the scientific community, and it specifies which criteria are to be used for scientific inquiry. A well understood set of exemplifications defines a field, determines the rules that govern the formulation of problems, and specifies acceptable/unacceptable and valid/invalid solutions. Such a knowledge paradigm requires the existence of a community committed to similar basic beliefs, common symbolic representation of those beliefs, agreed-upon types of questions to be posed, and acceptability of experimentation results. The knowledge paradigm bears a relationship to the rules and standards of scientific inquiry itself that is similar to the relationship of belief, ritual, and myth to the norms of society and culture. That is, the rules must be in place for *new* concepts to emerge.

Kuhn (1970) suggests that there is a typical process through which all sciences proceed, in which paradigms are created and replaced, and in which there is a shift in professional commitment, language, and values. According to Kuhn, typically this process involves four stages, (1) preparadigm research, (2) normal science, (3) crisis, and (4) revolution, leading back to normal science within a changed paradigm.

In Kuhn's (1970) framework, normal science does not attempt to create new knowledge; rather, it has the basic aim of actualizing the promise of the existing paradigm, and thus forcing nature into the preformed and relatively inflexible box that the tradition-bound paradigm supplies. In this process, *anomalies* that cannot be aligned with the expectations of the scientific community within the confines of the prevailing paradigm are often revealed: there is a logical incompatibility. These anomalies throw normal science into a crisis and over time the existing paradigm is subverted. New bases and agreements for the practice of science emerge; they do not add incrementally to the existing science but, rather, lead in another direction. Scientific revolutions are complicated, lengthy, and difficult processes.

The power in the debate (and, in fact, the ultimate resolution of the debate) always rests on the ability of the proponents of the new paradigm to convince the professional community that it can better cope with the anomalies that arise from the old paradigm. According to Kuhn, a theory or a paradigm is first accepted, then tested. Thus, a new paradigm is judged not on its accomplishments, but on its promise and the community's faith in its ability to perform better than the old.

The social constructionist Kenneth Gergen (1994) offers a critique of Kuhn's analysis of paradigmatic shifts with which I wholeheartedly agree. He points out that Kuhn's view of factual anomalies as unpredictable and independent of the prevailing systems of intelligibilities leaves no room for explaining where they came from. From a social construction view new understandings (or what Kuhn calls "facts") do not appear spontaneously; nor are they discovered suddenly by an observer. Instead, they evolve from and within "socially negotiated forms of meaning" (p. 14). That is, as Gergen suggests, the new understanding precedes the discovery, the creation. Tensions between the old and the new understandings are inescapable.

Gergen (1994) proposes theoretical transformations as a communal process, with distinguishable yet overlapping phases, as an alternative account of paradigm shifts. He suggests that these transformations (or the creation of new knowledge) are changes in reality through social processes, through discursive practices: "matters of evolution in socially negotiated forms of meaning" (p. 14). These negotiated meanings form discursive practices that constitute an "intelligibility nucleus" (p. 6), which, in turn, acts to sustain the discourse. Gergen, relying on the binary nature of linguistic signifiers to support his view, for example, man–woman or hot–cold, argues that the "very formulation of a discursive nucleus simultaneously establishes the potential for its dissolution" (p. 9). In other words, saying what something is inherently implies what it is not. What it is not, that is, differences, emerges through the processes of elaborating what it is and through the tensions produced by the differences within the discourse.[1] Such inquiry, I suggest, may be spontaneously and serendipitously spawned, deliberate and dogged, or some combination. The result is what Gergen calls an "alternative intelligibility" (p. 9). This process of commitment to the discourse and the dynamics of amplifying the discourse sets the stage for what Gergen designates as the

> critical phase of a paradigm shift, in which conventions of negation are employed to undermine confidence in the dominant form of intelligibility. During this phase, however, critique will necessarily employ language fragments from an alternative nucleus, from the range of propositions lending intelligibility to the critique. (pp. 11–12)

Bringing in language from an alternative nucleus is a platform for, and is crucial to, the success of Gergen's (1994) transformational phase (p. 12), in which the discursive implications of the critical phase are elaborated, thus creating a vacuum for the emergence of a new paradigm, a new discourse, a new tradition. He places the transformations in psychological metatheory and methodology that are emerging from the antiempiricist critique within this discursive practice account.

With these perspectives about theoretical transformations in mind, I turn to the issues currently raised in the family therapy field that suggest a need for theoretical and methodological transformation. To do so, we must ask Kuhn's question about which boxes the old paradigm has pushed us into and which anomalies it has encountered, and we must address Gergen's account of the formation of discursive practices.

The Transformation from Individual Therapy to Family Therapy

In Kuhn's preparadigmatic period, family therapy began as a North American phenomenon in the early 1950s and those who were to become its founders were like the proverbial blind men and the elephant, each man describing his experience of some part of the elephant's anatomy without a shared knowledge paradigm. The field's founders blazed their new trail under the banner of individual personalities, discipline persuasions, ad hoc hypotheses, and unique clinical experiences and perceptions.

The move away from the familiar psychoanalytic–psychodynamic paradigms to *family* did not arise because therapists decided the family should be the locus of treatment. The magnet was the frustration with the failure of the familiar psychodynamic and psychoanalytic theories and practices as the modes in which to understand and work with difficult-to-manage adolescents and some seriously disturbed, psychotic individuals. Families initially were brought in so therapists could better understand these patients and their therapies. The focus quickly moved to the family and its members' perceived relationship to the patient's treatment, including its success or failure. As I have said elsewhere,

> clinical circumstances and experiences, combined with the futility of prevailing theories and techniques to translate successfully to those circumstances and experiences, compelled a search for new explanations. . . . A problem and a quest to understand and solve it was the magnet and unifying catalyst that drew the to-be-called family therapists together and provided the arena for collaboration. (Anderson, 1994, pp. 147–148)

Returning to Gergen, I resonate with his perspective on the importance of the introduction of language from external alternative nuclei (Anderson, 1994). In this vein, the early family therapy pioneers were interdisciplinary: from within the psychotherapy discourse, for example, they had roots in psychiatry, psychology, and social work, and from outside the discourse, their various roots included, among other disciplines, anthropology, chemistry, and communications. Almost all were theoretician–practitioners who were trying to describe and explain their experiences, not someone else's.[2]

Family therapy began without a shared belief system or knowledge paradigm that permitted these clinicians to build on the work of others. This influenced the development of multiple schools of family therapy and of divergent descriptions, interpretations, and understandings of the phenomena, although all could be said to be under the same paradigmatic umbrella. In their search for understanding, some turned to and applied familiar psychoanalytic and psychodynamic explanatory concepts for individual behavior to a different social configuration—the family. Others were drawn to explanatory concepts outside the mental health field, for instance, other social sciences, biology, physics, engineering, and philosophy. This latter group, influenced by the cross-fertilization and interactive collaborative nature of their work and inquiry, moved to Gergen's transformational phase. And over these past five decades family therapy, which began as a lonely, radical, on-the-edge discourse, now has its own professional associations and licensing boards, and has found itself in the equivalent of Kuhn's normal science stage.

TWO SIGNIFICANT INFLUENCES
TOWARD A UNIFYING PARADIGM

Significant in this move, two fundamental and intertwined principles organized family therapists' thinking: a negative-feedback, homeostatic cybernetics systems theory and an order-imposing, hierarchically layered social systems theory. Together the two principles became common threads integrally woven into the fabric of family therapy and constituted the overarching theme for the field. The principles mechanistically described and explained a human system as an assemblage of parts whose process is determined by its structure. Both principles brought to family therapy that which distinguishes it from most other theories of psychotherapy: a contextual systems paradigm. *People live and experience the events of their lives in interactional systems.* Problems, in this view, become social phenomena whose development, persistence, and elimination take place within an interactional arena. The emergence of this particular paradigm at this particular time can be appreciated if juxtaposed against the broader cultural discourse of the 1950s and 1960s era in general—a move from romantic notions of the individual to the technology of interrelationships and complex systems—and the cultural discourse in the United States in particular: post–World War II; profamily, stable life-styles; economic growth and development; and technological explosions in scientific methodologies and, eventually, computers.

Cybernetic Systems Metaphor

The more widely acknowledged and more significant of these two developments was the dominance of the cybernetic systems metaphor. This unifying metaphor permitted theoreticians and clinicians the freedom to move from the narrowness and linearity of individual theory toward broader and nonlinear concepts and problem-solving techniques that they found better suited for working with multiple-person human systems, namely, families.

The major breakaway from individually oriented explanatory concepts to the study of human systems that shifted family therapy into the realm of another epistemology came from the seminal work of Gregory Bateson, Donald Jackson, Jay Haley, and John Weakland (1956, 1963) at the Mental Research Institute in Palo Alto, California.[3] Through their study of schizophrenic communication—which focused not on past behaviors, historical events, individual characteristics, and psychic process, but on current observable interpersonal behaviors of individuals within their relationship context (the family)—they were able to move beyond traditional individual behavioral descriptions to *interactional processes* and from linear to *circular causality*. These interrelated concepts of interactional processes and circular causality were key to catapulting family theory to a new epistemological status.[4] The Palo Alto group's research concluded that families are homeostatic, rule-governed, closed informational systems that feed information back to themselves. They also concluded that *all behavior is communication.* Jackson (1965), drawing on Bateson's earlier ideas about learning theory, asserted: "Every message (communication bit) has both a content (report) and a relationship (command) aspect; the former conveys information about facts, opinions, feelings, experiences, etc., and the latter defines the nature of the relationship between the communicants" (p. 8). Their research also led to the concepts of the "double bind" and "family homeostasis" (Jackson, 1957).

In their continuing efforts to find a *language* to describe the multi-level interaction, the Palo Alto colleagues turned first to general systems theory and soon thereafter to cybernetics theory. They adopted a negative, or opposite feedback, model of homeostasis for understanding human behavior, a model that focused on the properties of the family system—a self-contained system—rather than on the individual to describe and to understand individuals within families. The properties were cybernetic in nature and included error- or change-activated, deviation-counteracting feedback. Families, as cyberneticlike energy and feedback systems, were considered a kind of servomechanism with a governor that protected the norm and prevented change. According to the theory, a system with these properties would resist change. In this view, the symptom made sense only within, and as an expression of, the total family context. It no longer represented an individual disturbance, but a signal that a family was having difficulty meeting the demands of stress, change, or natural transition points—difficulty, that is, in moving toward greater complexity. The *meaning* of the symptom was related to the family system's structure and served the function of maintaining the present system's homeostasis: its status, structure, and organization; its stability, continuity, and relationship definition.[5] This cybernetic metaphor of homeostasis—including its central notions of equilibrium, negative feedback, resistance to change, continuous change, symptom functionality, and structural defect—became basic to the understanding of both healthy and pathological family organization.

Although clearly all major schools of family therapy made their unique contribution, this basic knowledge paradigm—the cybernetic principle, or what was to be called first-order cybernetics—became the link between them. And, although the schools all described the paradigm in different terms, the differences among them were simply small variations of the underlying theme of error-activated, deviation-counteracting feedback.[6]

This new cybernetic-based paradigm dramatically influenced the nature of psychotherapy and the therapist's role. The new goal of therapy, to interrupt the homeostasis and thus promote change, required new therapy techniques. The therapist moved to actively intervene to help the family to meet the demands of stress, transition points, developmental stages, and change itself.

Social Systems Metaphor

A parallel, less acknowledged, but no less significant influence on family therapy and on psychotherapy paradigms for individual and family has been the social science theory that views human beings as embedded in *socially organized order-imposing concentric contexts of increasingly complex organization* (Anderson & Goolishian, 1988b; Goldner, 1988; Goolishian & Anderson, 1987a). This dominant view is a permutation of the Parsonian (1951) sociocultural systems theory. In this empirical objective approach sociocultural systems (both macro- and microsystems) are organized according to role and structure, as defined by stability, order, and control. Systems are viewed as cybernetically layered; stability and order are hierarchically and teleologically imposed from above. As in cybernetic theory, equilibrium and homeostasis are critical elements for the system's self-maintenance. To preserve the system's equilibrium or homeostasis, the relationships among its components and the processes within it, and between it and its context, must be such that the system's structure and components remain unchanged.

My colleague, Harry Goolishian (1985), described this as an "onion theory," as each layer of the social system is cybernetically encircled by another layer. Like the core of an onion, surrounded by outer layers, the individual is encircled by the family, the family by the larger system, the larger system by the community, and so forth. In these concentric circles each layer is subordinate to and controlled by the surrounding layer in the service of its own requirements—for maintenance and order. In this view, social systems are objectively defined, exist in some kind of universal way, and are independent of the people involved or of any observers. These externally imposed restrictions of role and structure act as a social harness and produce the social order that we designate as culture and civilization.

This onionlike, cyberneticlike social theory's contribution to family therapy (and family therapy's most significant contribution to psychotherapy in general) is that it contextualizes behavior. At the same time, rather paradoxically, the notion of contextuality risks positing blame, supporting the notion of psychopathology, and thus naming what should be fixed—the social structure and organization. Any problem in this framework is thought to be caused by the system superordinate to the one expressing the deviance. That is, the superordinate system must be inadequately socialized if it is imposing a defective role and structure on the system below. Furthermore, when relationships are considered nested and based on role and structure, implicitly if not intentionally, the duality of the individual and the individual in relationship, such as the relationship with the family, is maintained.

The implication for therapy is that the therapist is an independent external observer of, and thus hierarchically superior to, the system. From this expert position, the therapist diagnoses and repairs the defect in the superordinate system. Therapy informed by this view of boundary-defined systems risks friction or blame between these nested systems as they are defined and as the container of the pathological condition is, so to speak, bumped a level. For instance, individual therapists experience friction with family therapists, family therapists with social agencies, and subordinate systems with superordinate systems. Importantly, from this view, a difference between individual and family therapy is the system within which the pathology is located. The similarity, however, is that both place it *within* a system.

Most family therapists continued to focus primarily on the family ring of the onionlike concentric circles while some began to explore the next outer rings, referring to them in the literature as the ecological system, the larger system, the meaningful system, and the relevant system (Auerswald, 1968, 1971; Goolishian & Anderson, 1981; Hoffman, 1975; Imber-Coppersmith, 1982, 1983, 1985; Keeney, 1982; Selvini-Palazzoli, Boscolo, Cecchin, & Prata, 1980a). All outer ring proponents emphasized the broader human and professional context of therapy, especially the referring person and other professional helpers. At the risk of oversimplifying the essence of this significant emphasis on the context of human behavior and therapy, it was still within the cybernetic and social theory metaphors.

I think it is important to note that cybernetic and Parsonian social theories tend to promote hierarchy and patriarchy—inequalities that unfortunately are normative in our culture whether in intimate relationships such as those of parent and child, husband and wife, or in more detached social relationships such as those of welfare agency and client family, teacher and student. Both theories act to locate, foster, and rationalize inequalities, censorship, subordination, and exploitation—in whatever the domain, be it politics, economics, gender, or race—and view these characteristics as inevitable in human systems. Both disregard the connection between the microdomain of therapy and the macrodomain of sociopolitical life.

RUMBLINGS

Questioning First-Order Cybernetics and Introducing
Second-Order Cybernetics

Although the majority of family therapists continued to subscribe to
the mechanical cybernetics paradigm, a few began to question it.
Most questioning, however, did not arise from discomfort with
hierarchy or the idea of observer-independent systems.[7] Rather, the
challenge was to the principle and contradiction of homeostasis—
homeostasis focused on no change and did not explain change.
Contrary to the homeostatic view, families, like other living systems, were recognized as being unable to avoid growth and change.
The inability of the cybernetics paradigm to handle this living systems problem was veiled with its thought that the slow movement,
or *stuckness*, often seen in families *was* the pathology. The aim of
therapy, therefore, was to unstick the system, to get it moving again
(using whatever technique was associated with the particular
school). The challenge surfaced in a number of creative papers that
appeared within a few years of each other. The sociologist Magoroh
Marayuma's classic article, first published in 1963, "The Second
Cybernetics: Deviation-Amplifying Mutual Causal Processes,"
emphasized that there were two possible types of cybernetic feedback: the familiar negative feedback (morphostasis), which could
account for stability, and positive feedback (morphogenesis), which
could account for change. Early on two family therapists, Lynn
Hoffman (1971) in "Deviation-Amplifying Processes in Natural
Groups" and Albert Speer (1970) in "Family Systems: Morphostasis
and Morphogenesis,"[8] both took the position that something
beyond negative feedback and homeostasis was needed to describe
systems in change such as families and other social systems.

The Palo Alto group in their later innovative work on the concept
of change and brief, problem-focused therapy (Watzlawick, Weakland, & Fisch, 1974; Weakland, Fisch, Watzlawick, & Bodin, 1974)
significantly challenged the idea that one part of a system could
control another part without itself changing. Instead, they offered
an alternative premise, that positive (deviation-amplifying), not
negative feedback (homeostasis) was the basis of problem formulation and maintenance. From this viewpoint, pathology, including
defective structure, was no longer considered a necessary condition for the development of problem behavior and symptoms were
no longer thought to serve a function.[9] The implications for under-

standing human problems and the therapist's role were enormous. This revolutionary about-face in thinking remained, however, within the cybernetic paradigm.[10]

Parallel to the recognition that cybernetic systems could be informed by both negative and positive feedback was the emergence of another distinction that reflected similar challenges in science—Bohm, Einstein, Prigogene—and in philosophy—Derrida, Gadamer, Heidegger, Husserl, Merleau-Ponty, Rorty, Wittgenstein—a challenge to logical empiricism founded on real, existing, and objective data, and a challenge to the notion of subject–object dualism. Einstein's relativity and quantum theory, for example, hold that observation always shapes that which is observed. Observers influence and interpret what they study. The distinctions are not out there but in the observer; the observer is no longer considered to be outside the observed system. What had been thought of as observer-independent systems were now understood as observer-dependent, or what the cybernetician Heinz von Foerster (1982) called *observing systems*. Observing as a reflexive process called into question the idea of objective reality. Observation, therefore, was considered theory-laden and science was understood as a social activity in which the disciplines draw their own rules of practice and evidence.

These developments within the family therapy field became known as second-order cybernetics or the cybernetics of cybernetics.[11] Second-order cybernetics, like the scientific and philosophical challenges, focused on the observer in the circularity of the observer–observed relationship and the creation of what is observed. Once again, within the family therapy field, it was the Palo Alto group that first touched on the question of and insignificance of objective reality (Watzlawick, Beaven, & Jackson, 1967). Bateson himself questioned some of the group's early theory and its implications, referring to the notions of power and the consequences of theory. In the foreword to *The Double Bind* (Sluzki & Ransom, 1976) Bateson's profound reflection warns therapists to become more aware of their active involvement in the phenomena studied and the influence of theory on their observations.

> However well intentioned the urge to cure, the very ideas of "curing" must always propose the idea of power. We were inevitably stupidbound, like the protagonists in a Greek tragedy, to the forms and shapes of processes, which others, especially our colleagues, thought they saw. And our successors will be bound by the shapes of our thought. (p. xii)

Constructivism

Closely intertwined with the development of second-order cybernetics was the resurgence of constructivism (Maturana & Varela, 1980, 1987; Mead, 1968; Segal, 1986; von Foerster, 1982, 1984; von Glasersfeld, 1984; Watzlawick, 1976, 1984).[12] Constructivism is a philosophical theory of knowledge that can be traced back to the work of Giambattista Vico, the eighteenth-century historian, and later appears in the writings of Nelson Goodman, David Hume, Immanuel Kant, George Kelly, and Jean Piaget, among others. The constructivist perspective challenges a Cartesian world and disclaims a tangible, external reality that can be known or described. It disputes the tradition that knowledge is representative and reflects the true and real world, and it asserts that an external objective reality cannot be known (Maturana, 1978; Piaget, 1971; von Foerster, 1984; von Glasersfeld, 1984).

From a constructivist perspective, reality represents a human functional adaptation: humans, as experiencing subjects of the world, construct and interpret reality. The mind constructs or "brings forth" (Maturana, 1978). In constructing, in making an observation, the observer is bringing forth. A constructivist perspective stresses that "knowing is an adaptive activity . . . knowledge is a compendium of concepts and actions that one has found to be successful, given the purposes one had in mind" (von Glasersfeld, 1984, p. 24). In radical constructivism,[13] reality and therefore knowledge are thought to be personally and interpretively constructed; the world we live in is invented, not discovered. That is, according to Ernst von Glasersfeld, a pioneer in constructivist psychology, "all communication and all understanding are a matter of interpretive construction on the part of the experiencing subject" (p. 19) and are "exclusively an ordering and organization of a world constituted by our experiences" (p. 24). Radical constructivism, according to Watzlawick (1984),

> does not create or explain any reality "out there"; it shows that there is no inside and no outside, no objective world facing the subjective, rather it shows that the subject-object split, that source of myriads of "realities," does not exist, that the apparent separation of the world into pairs of opposites is constructed by the subject and that paradox opens the way into *autonomy.* (p. 330)

This shift to constructivism began to translate family therapy in particular into a kind of "lens-correction" process—correcting beliefs, correcting constructions. Family therapy, however, at this point still had not moved very far from the earlier notions of problems and pathology—both were now thought of as faulty lenses. Hoffman (1983, 1985, 1993) referred to the application of second-order cybernetics and radical constructivism concepts to family therapy as second-order family therapy.

Evolutionary Systems

Intertwined with the second-order cybernetics and constructivist metaphors was what Hoffman (1981) referred to as the development of the "evolutionary paradigm" in family therapy (Dell, 1982; Dell & Goolishian, 1979; Elkaim, 1981; Selvini-Palazzoli, Boscolo, Cecchin, & Prata, 1978).[14] The so-called evolutionary direction represented a continued movement away from the concept of homeostasis and causation (both linear and circular). From an evolutionary systems perspective, systems were viewed as evolving, nonequilibrium, nonlinear, self-organizing, and self-recursive networks in a constant state of discontinuous change (Briggs & Peat, 1984; Prigogene & Stengers, 1984).[15] In this perspective system change is random, unpredictable, discontinuous, and always leading to higher levels of complexity. Applying these concepts to human systems implied that neither therapy nor therapists could unilaterally amplify one fluctuation over another or determine the direction of change (Dell, 1982; Dell & Goolishian, 1979). Therapists did not, could not, control the system; rather they were an active part of a mutual evolutionary process. As Dell and Goolishian (1981) stated, "This view of evolutionary systems emphasizes process over structure and flexibility and change over stability. Process—similar to the standing wave pattern at the confluence of two rivers—is determined by the flow of the two rivers" (p. 178). Process determines the structure.

Our Galveston group combined our fascination with evolutionary systems with our interest in language.[16] This turn to language and particularly language as conceptualized in hermeneutic and social constructionist theories eventually enabled us to move away entirely from the mechaniclike cybernetic, onionlike social system, and pyramidlike reality metaphors (Anderson & Goolishian, 1989, 1990a). Conceptualizing human systems as linguistic systems—fluid, evolving communicating systems that exist in language—we developed the concepts of problem-determined systems (Anderson, Goolishian, Pulliam, & Winderman, 1986) and problem-organizing dissolving systems (Anderson & Goolishian, 1988b; Goolishian & Anderson, 1987a).

ONE SPACE CREATED ANOTHER:
NEW PARADIGMATIC RUMBLINGS

Family therapy developed as a foundational ideology focused on the interactions within that system. It is *not* about the number of persons in a therapy room.[17] This now-half-century-old conceptual breakthrough represented a bold leap into the uncharted frontiers of a major paradigm shift to a new understanding of human behavior. The influence of family therapy on the broader contemporary psychotherapy arena—its theory, practice, and research, and the education of its practitioners—is undeniable. Family therapy opened the space for a paradigmatic shift that moved psychotherapy from a foundation of a past-oriented *why* (a unidirectional cause and effect perspective) to a present-oriented *what* (a focus on behaviors, communication, language, beliefs, and beyond). Most would agree that the major impact of this new paradigm, including the development of family theory and practice, both distinct from and within traditional mental health disciplines, has been the recognition of the related concept of the contextualization of human behavior and the individual in relationship to others. This concept represents a shift from viewing human behavior from an intrapsychic perspective to seeing it in the context of systems, with a focus on the interactional or interpersonal framework in which behavior (normal or problematic) occurs. This shift offered a different way of describing, explaining, and locating problems, and thus a different treatment focus. Equally important, family therapy has opened the process of psychotherapy from a sacred secret event to something that can be studied, observed, and shared; this last contribution, "going public," may be its most significant influence on a chain of endless theoretical and clinical transformations.[18]

At the same time family therapy—once seen as radical—was gaining maturity, acceptance, and credibility, critique and skepticism within it began to emerge. This self-criticism coupled with territorial debates around the scope and ownership of family therapy came from several different perspectives. Some of its critics believed that family therapy had come of age, and seeing no differences, they sought integration, unification, eclecticism, and classification (Atkinson & Heath, 1990; Eron & Lund, 1993; Fish, 1993; Held & Pols, 1985).

Others, however, questioned the dominant paradigm itself and noted its limits, paradoxes, and inconsistencies (Anderson & Goolishian, 1988b; Anderson, Goolishian, & Winderman, 1986a; Atkinson & Heath, 1990; Chubb, 1990; Dell, 1980a, 1980b, 1982; Goolishian & Anderson, 1987a; Hoffman, 1985, 1990, 1991; Keeney, 1983; Tjersland, 1990). Others called for rethinking research (Dell, 1980b; Fowers, 1993; Ryder, 1987). Some were critical of the social accountability of therapies that continued to ignore issues of gender (Ault-Riche, 1986; Bograd, 1984; Goldner, 1985, 1988; Hare-Mustin, 1987; Hare-Mustin & Marecek, 1988; Laird, 1989; Luepnitz, 1988; MacKinnon & Miller, 1987; Taggart, 1985) or other cultural and institutional substructures (Doherty & Boss, 1991; Kearney, Byrne, & McCarthy, 1989; McCarthy & Byrne, 1988; Saba, 1985; Weingarten, 1995; White & Epston, 1990). Some criticized its obscure, confusing, and reductionistic nature (Carpenter, 1992; Dell, 1985; Dell & Goolishian, 1979, 1981; Flaskas, 1990; Goldner, 1988; Shields, 1986). Some challenged the usefulness of the system distinction *family* in family therapy as opposed to other systems and the appropriateness of distinguishing *family therapy* within psychotherapy (Anderson, 1994; Anderson & Goolishian, 1988b, 1990a; Anderson, Goolishian, & Winderman, 1986a, 1986b; Erickson, 1988; Goolishian & Anderson, 1987a, 1988, 1990). Some critiqued inconsistencies in theory and practice and confronted the challengers (Colapinto 1985; de Shazer, 1991a, 1991b; Golann, 1988; Speed, 1984). And some asked whether family therapy is a distinct and separate discipline or a subspecialty of another discipline (Anderson, 1994; Hardy, 1994; Kaslow, 1980; Shields, Wynne, McDaniel, & Gawinski, 1994). We are witnessing the challenges and possibilities these seeds hold for future paradigm revolution (Andersen, 1987; Anderson, 1994, 1995; Anderson & Goolishian, 1988b; Fowers & Richardson, 1996; Friedman, 1993, 1995; Hoffman, 1993; McNamee & Gergen, 1992; Penn & Frankfurt, 1994; White & Epston, 1990).

I believe not only that family therapy is in the midst of a revolution, but that it is a revolution within a revolution in the broader psychotherapy arena, as evidenced by a growing number of writers who critique modernist-based psychological theory, practice, research, and academia (Agatti, 1993; Baker, Mos, Rappard, & Stam, 1988; Danziger, 1994; Flax, 1990; Freeman, 1993; Gergen, 1982, 1985, 1991a, 1994; Hoshmand & Polkinghorne, 1992; Jones, 1986; Kvale, 1992, 1996; Messer, Sass, & Woolfolk, 1988; Nicholson, 1990; Polkinghorne, 1988; Scarr, 1985; Schön, 1983; Shotter, 1985, 1990, 1993a, 1993b; Shotter & Gergen, 1989; Smith, Harré, & Van Langenhove, 1995). This self-critique within psychology, although related to the struggles between practitioner interest groups and issues of hierarchy and dominance, has evolved mainly as a challenge to the theoretical foundations of the discipline.

Coinciding with these critiques and skepticisms, and following closely on the heels of and to some extent overlapping the interest in constructivist and second-order cybernetic concepts, other seeds were swelling. Fueled by a combination of clinical experiences and theoretical developments in the social sciences and humanities, some family therapists and psychologists began to argue for a dramatic shift: Current psychotherapy theory and practice across-the-board were simply out of sync with our fast-changing world. What is different about this new rumbling is that it is occurring across oceans. Just as the political and economic world is shrinking, so is the professional and intellectual world. Family therapy is no longer exclusively a North American phenomenon, nor is psychology dominated by our continent (Andersen, 1987, 1991; Elkaim, 1981; Fried Schnitman, 1994; Kvale, 1992, 1996; Leppingston, 1991; Mendez, Coddou, & Maturana, 1988; Reichelt & Christensen, 1990; Reichelt & Sveaass, 1994; Seikkula, 1993; Selvini-Palazzoli et al., 1978; Tjersland, 1990). What is similar in this rumbling to the early family therapy challenge is that those of us who are enthusiastically confronting and boldly leaping from the familiar are finding ourselves in a discourse on the edge and in uncharted territories (Anderson, 1994; Anderson & Goolishian, 1991a).

The dissatisfaction this time is broader than the earlier systems challenge and threatens the very existence of family therapy and psychotherapy as most know it. What is this emerging discourse and what is driving it? Paradoxically, it is the core conceptualization of family relationships that has opened the space for some family therapists to move beyond family therapy and beyond the distinctions of individual, marital, and family therapy (Andersen, 1987; Anderson & Goolishian, 1988b, 1991a; Anderson et al., 1986a, 1986b; Goolishian & Anderson, 1987a, 1990, 1994; Hoffman, 1993). Much of family therapy has naively ignored or intentionally abandoned the individual, losing the individual experience, and separated the *I* from the *You*, losing the relationship in identity.

For some of us, postmodernism moves the individual *and* the relationship to the forefront although they are conceptualized quite differently than in modernism. Postmodern suppositions primarily emphasize the social or relational creation or embeddedness of reality; for example, meanings, patterns, diagnostic categories, and stories are the by-products of human relationships and communicative interactions. This emphasis on the social and relational entails important rethinking of the notion of the self or the individual (whether the subject of inquiry is a single core self or collective multiple selves): self-construction, self-identity, self in relationship, and the connectedness of *I* and *You*.

Rethinking the notion of the individual in relationship to oneself (or one's selves), to others, and to one's historical, cultural, political, and environmental world transcends individual and relational dichotomies inherent in such layered social-system frameworks as individual–family, family–therapist, individual–collective behavior, or biological–mental. It moves beyond defining the relationship focus as two or more intimately related people with a shared history who form a social system, *beyond family relationships*, and beyond privileging one level of a system over another. This new emphasis not only moves family therapy away from a restrictive definition by redefining the domain and focus to be addressed, but threatens the very notion of family therapy itself and its systems theories as the explanatory model of choice.

I believe that individual and family are not inevitably competing constructs; rather, family therapy needs to move away from that restrictive definition and redefine the domain and focus to be addressed. I do not suggest that we abandon the notion of family. What I do suggest is that family therapy's concept of relationship has been too narrow. The in-process paradigmatic shift—the interpersonal focus and the changes in how the individual and relationships are conceptualized—has major implications for the way we think about human systems and the problems they present, our work with them, and our relationship with them. Postmodernism offers a challenge to the familiar culture of psychotherapy, to the *what* and *means* of inquiry—what is examined and described and which means are used for the examination and description. It suggests that the focus is neither the interior of the individual nor the family, but rather the person(s)-in-relationship. It suggests that all explanatory assumptions including revered theories must not be taken for granted, but continuously questioned, as Bateson so aptly warned.

But what is postmodernism? How does it differ from modernism? Where does its challenge extend? What possibilities does it allow that modernism does not? And which postmodern landscape do I favor because it best represents my therapy philosophy and practice at this point in time? In the next chapter I discuss modern and postmodern. I do not want to set a polarizing tone. I simply want to address why I moved from a set of assumptions that I found confining to one that I find less confining.

CHAPTER 2

Less Confining Spaces:
From Modern Traditions to
Postmodern Possibilities

The old family customs and the old family traditions are kept up,
because they are old family customs and old family traditions.
—MRS. WOODS BAKER,
Pictures of Swedish Life (1894)

INDIVIDUAL KNOWLEDGE
AND REPRESENTATIONAL LANGUAGE

BEFORE TURNING TO my postmodern narrative, it seems important to visit other voices in time, voices in the modern discourse, since most of us grew up as therapists and live our daily lives within this discourse. In my interpretation, *modernism* refers to a Western philosophical tradition, an era in time, a monovocal discourse, that embodies the Renaissance ideals of humankind as the center of and dominator of the universe—and the Cartesian rooted social and cultural concepts of objectivity, certainty, closure, truth, dualism, and hierarchy.[1] The modernist tradition refers to that movement of thought which originates with Descartes and which has perpetuated itself up to and into the twentieth century . . . [and] seeks to realize philosophy's traditional goal of achieving a basic, fundamental knowledge . . . of what is . . . by turning inward, into the knowing subject himself . . . where it seeks to discover grounds which will allow for certainty in our "knowledge" of . . . "the external world." (Madison, 1988, p. x)

In this tradition, true knowledge is "a mediated, an archival knowledge, a knowledge that is *educational*, leading man out of the cavernous darkness of time into the open light of eternal presence" (Spanos, 1985, p. 56). Knowledge is representative of an objective world, existing independently of the mind and feelings; is subjectively observable and verifiable; and is universal and cumulative. Out of this knowledge evolve grand overarching generalizable theories; thus, modernism becomes a monovocal discourse in which the "truth" dominates and stability is valued.

The philosopher Richard Rorty (1979) suggested that in this modern tradition of knowledge as representational and "as an assemblage of accurate representations" (p. 163) the mind is like a mirror that reflects nature. The individual is a cognitive being whose mind is a computerlike representational system. The mind acts as an inner mental representation of reality. Reality—that which is—is fixed, a priori, empirical fact independent of the observer. The world in this view, as Professor of Philosophy G. B. Madison (1988) suggests, is one

which is fully what it is in itself and which simply waits around for a cognizing subject to come along and form a "mental representation" of it. . . . If only he [the observer] can string his ideas together in the right way, the result supposedly will be that they will form a true "representation" or likeness of "objective" reality. (p. x)

From this perspective the knower is autonomous and separate from that which he or she observes, describes, and explains, whether of a physical nature like a storm or of a human nature like crowd behavior. The individual knower is the source of and validator of all knowledge. The individual is privileged.

Language, in this modern view, is the medium of knowledge; that is, knowledge is conveyed in language. The function of language (including words and symbols, verbal and nonverbal), like that of knowledge, is to give a correct representational picture of the world and our experiences of it and to refer to that which is real. Language is used by rational human beings as a means to convey thoughts and feelings or as expression (Heidegger as cited in Palmer, 1985, p. 20).

PSYCHOTHERAPY FROM A MODERN PERSPECTIVE

Modernism and its truths provide the bedrock foundation for the humanities and social sciences. Our culture of psychotherapy; our theories, practices, and research, including psychology, psychiatry, social work, and family therapy, are historically based in and reflective of this authoritative dominant discourse that has elevated and sustained the therapist as an independent observer with privileged private access to knowledge about human nature: individual personalities and human relationships, normal and abnormal behaviors, and thoughts, feelings, and emotions. Such knowledge allows therapists to observe, describe, and explain human behavior objectively. By virtue of this entitlement to knowledge and truth, therapists hold a dualistic, hierarchical position in which their knowledge supersedes clients' marginal or everyday nonprofessional knowledge.

From a modern perspective, knowledge, and therefore truth, is pyramidal: it constructs a hierarchy. A therapist, as a representative of a dominant social and cultural discourse, is the knower of the human story and what that story should be. This *therapist knowing*, informed by professional and personal theories, biases, and experiences, acts as a forestructure that pre-fixes knowledge that a therapist brings to a therapy room and supersedes a client's knowing. A therapist becomes a master at observing, revealing, and deconstructing the story as it *really* is and *ought* to be. A therapist's knowledge informs and validates his or her future observations; it acts as "backward referencing" and functions to "project the past into the future" (Giorgi, 1990, p. 76).

The modernist discourse perpetuates the notion of *discoverable, universal metaphors for human description*—monovocal and unilaterally determined fixed truths about universal human nature and individual human behavior. These truths ignore the rapid, ever-changing social, economic, political, and interpersonal world in which we live and they ignore the variations within this world. Similar to feminist philosopher Lorraine Code's (1988) characterization of stereotypes, these truths simply become dogmatic "products of accumulated cultural lore, acquired as part of an acculturation process" (p. 192). These truths lump people, problems, and solutions into homogeneous groupings that mask and ignore nuances and differences.

In the modern perspective therapy constitutes a dominant cultural-truth-informed, *therapist-led endeavor* and yields *therapist-determined possibilities*. These truths determine and actualize a priori, across-the-board diagnoses, goals, and treatment strategies. Such thought and action, in turn, may validate and reify a therapist's preknowledge while missing and dismissing the uniqueness, richness, and complexity of an individual or group of individuals. As this preknowledge forms, as this single voice forms, the ensuing therapist-led thoughts and actions risk dominating and silencing the client's voice. In turn, I believe, familiar metaphors and narratives become self-limiting and consequently minimize a therapist's ability to be creative and imaginative; thus, they obstruct the potential for unknown newness—the possibilities that can emerge when the multiple voices of a client and therapist, and others, are present. Privileging our therapist voices, I strongly believe, risks the perpetuation of institutional inequality, albeit sometimes unwittingly, on both the local therapist–client level and the universal individual–family–society level, for instance, overlooking or supporting generalisms such as sexism, ageism, and racism.

The modernist discourse promotes the *dualistic and hierarchical notion of a client as the subject of inquiry and observation* and places a therapist in a superior expert position. In this discourse, the participants in therapy and what each brings to the therapy endeavor are separate static entities—client and therapist—and not interactive participants in a joint endeavor. The relational aspect or the notion of the individual-in-relationship moves to the background. A client as an unknowing subject of inquiry becomes liberated from the villain problem by a therapist who is a knower of and an expert on human nature and behavior: the hero who liberates.

Psychotherapy language within a modernist discourse is a *deficiency-based language* and is assumed to represent behavioral and mental *reality* accurately. Again, using Rorty's (1979) mind–mirror metaphor, the subject of inquiry (the client) is considered defective, flawed, and dysfunctional. Diagnoses operate as cultural and professional codes that function to gather, analyze, and order the waiting-to-be-discovered data. As similarities and patterns are found, people and problems are fitted into a deficit-based system of categories that are sustained through the language and vocabulary of our discourses. This creates an illusion of generalizable psychological knowledge. The language and vocabularies of psychotherapy are therefore impersonalized and disregard the uniqueness of each individual and each situation (Gergen, Hoffman, & Anderson, 1995). Professional and cultural labels classify and place people; they do not tell us about them. The Norwegian psychologist Jan Smedslund (1978, 1990, 1993) for almost two decades has written extensively about the differences between objective and psychosocial reality, proposing what he calls "commonsense psychology": in brief, those psychological explications that are "regarded correct by all speakers of the language in which they are formulated" (1990, p. 46).

Psychotherapy, from this modern perspective, is a technology: a human is a machine, and a therapist is a technician who works with faulty human machines (Anderson & Goolishian, 1988b, 1991a). In the terms of Rorty's (1979) mind–mirror comparison, if the mind is representational, like a mirror, and if the mind is blemished and inaccurately reflects reality, then the task of the therapist becomes that of "inspecting, repairing, and polishing" the flawed mirror (p. 12). A therapist's role is shaped to diagnose dysfunction or defect (for example, in individual behavior, interactional patterns, beliefs, or stories) in the targeted human system (for example, individual, marital, or family), repair the faulty system (for example, individuals, couples, and families), and restore the system to a normative state (for example, a differentiated individual, a complementary couple, or a functional family). Language, in this view, is the medium through which, and the tool with which, we exercise our entitled position to discover, to explain, to predict, and to effect change.

LIMITATIONS, BOUNDARIES, AND DISILLUSIONMENTS OF MODERN-BASED THERAPY

We have always lived in a world in which change has occurred with some predictability and certainty, though sometimes in a chaotic way. Philosophy has attempted to provide structures for understanding change and for controlling chaos. Presently, as the world around us seems to be changing faster and to be becoming enormously more complex, change seemingly occurs with less predictability and certainty and with more chaos. In the social scientist and innovative management consultant Peter Drucker's (1994) words,

> No century in recorded history has experienced so many social transformations and such radical ones as the twentieth century. ... Work and work force, society and polity, are all, in the last decade of this century, *qualitatively* and *quantitatively* different not only from what they were in the first years of this century but also from what has existed at any other time in history: in their configurations, in their processes, in their problems, and in their structures. ... But it is the social transformations, like ocean currents deep below the hurricane-tormented surface of the sea, that have had the lasting, indeed the permanent, effect. .... The age of social transformation will not come to an end with the year 2000—it will not even have peaked by then. (p. 54)

These social transformations and their inherent uncertainties influence our everyday lives, and our futures, which will include political, economic, and cultural changes and challenges, require a new mind-set and demand changes in the way we understand our world and ourselves in it (Gergen, 1982, 1991a, 1991b). From a social science perspective, modernism lacks the capacity to deal with and meet the complexities and challenges of these changes.

Postmodernism has emerged as an alternative form of inquiry among theoreticians and scholars across disciplines who are in the midst of questioning the metanarratives, the certainty, and the methods and practices of modernism in traditional science, literature, history, art, and the human sciences and who are exploring alternative conceptions and descriptions (Berger & Luckmann, 1966; Gergen, 1982, 1985, 1994; Harré, 1983; Lyotard, 1984; Shotter, 1989, 1991b, 1993a, 1993b; Sylvester, 1985; Vygotsky, 1986). In art, for instance, the critic David Sylvester (1985) compares the essence of modernism and postmodernism and the history of the arts:

> The supreme virtue in the eye of modernism was Purity. So modernism was full of ideas about what it was not permissible to do. ... I think the *essence of postmodernism* is that it takes a less categorical view of history and of aesthetic morals. It dismisses the notion that a Cycladic carving must be better than a Michelangelo because its lines are cleaner. On the other hand, it is not simply neo-traditional, affirming that it is crazy to believe that a Cycladic carving could be as great as one by Michelangelo. It takes the view that both can be great art—and honourable art too. (p. 232)

Modernist therapist–dominated therapies, which assume thera-pist knowledge and expertise regardless of a therapist's theoretical orientation, are, however, largely unquestioned within or without our disciplines. A handful of social theorists and clinicians, how-ever, increasingly have become disillusioned, although for varying reasons, with the limitations and sustenations of psychotherapy theory, practice, and research informed by and as an expression of the principles of the dominant modernist discourse (Andersen, 1987, 1991, 1995a, 1995b; Anderson, 1995; Anderson & Goolishian, 1988b; Atkinson & Heath, 1990; Cecchin, 1987; Chessick, 1990; Dell & Goolishian, 1981; de Shazer, 1985; Flax, 1990; Gergen, 1982, 1985, 1991a, 1994; Hare-Mustin, 1987; Harré, 1979, 1983; Hoffman, 1993; Kleinman, 1986, 1988a, 1988b; Kvale, 1992; McNamee & Gergen, 1992; Nicholson, 1990; Penn & Frankfurt, 1994; Polkinghorne, 1983, 1988; Sampson, 1981; Shotter, 1993a, 1993b; Snyder, 1984; Watzlaw-ick, 1976, 1984; White & Epston, 1990). This disillusionment has influenced an emerging community of ideas that has major impli-cations for psychotherapy theory, practice, research, and educa-tion. But before considering these ideas, let us examine what postmodernism is.

A POSTMODERN LANDSCAPE

In its simplest form, the concept *postmodern* refers to a critique, not an era. It is related to a discontinuous philosophical direction[2] that radically departs from the modern tradition in its questioning of the modernist monovocal discourse as the overarching foundation for literary, political, and social criticism.[3] In some respects it rep-resents a disorienting crossroads where similar and dissimilar tra-ditions meet.

Although rooted in contemporary late existential thought, post-modernism did not gain recognition until the 1970s. With no one identified author and no one unified concept, the postmodern dis-course is a polyphonic chorus made up of interrelated in-motion soundings, each a critique and disruption of modernism. Post-modern thought (often linked with poststructuralism)[4]—usually associated with the writings of philosophers such as Mikhail Bakhtin (1981), Jacques Derrida (1978), Michel Foucault (1972, 1980), Jean-François Lyotard (1984), Richard Rorty (1979), and Ludwig Wittgenstein (1961)—primarily represents a broad chal-lenge to and a cultural shift away from fixed metanarratives, privileged discourses, and universal truths; away from objective reality; away from language as representational; and away from the scientific criterion of knowledge as objective and fixed. In sum, postmodernism rejects the foundational dualism of modernism, an outer real world and an inner mental world, and is characterized by uncertainty, unpredictability, and the unknown. Change is a given and is embraced.

Postmodern thought moves toward *knowledge as a discursive practice*, toward a *plurality of narratives that are more local, contextual, and fluid*; it moves toward a *multiplicity of approaches to the analysis of subjects such as knowledge, truth, language, history, self, and power*. It emphasizes the *relational nature of knowledge* and the *generative nature of language*. Postmodernism views knowledge as socially constructed, knowledge and the knower as interdependent—presupposing the interrelationship of context, culture, language, experience, and understanding (Lyotard, 1984; Madison, 1988). We cannot have direct knowledge of the world; we can only know it through our experiences. We continually interpret our experiences and interpret our interpretations. And, as a result, knowledge is evolving and continually broadening.

French philosopher Jean-François Lyotard suggested that from a postmodern perspective there are no "grand narratives of legitimation" (as cited in Fraser & Nicholson, 1990, p. 22). What might be thought of as a privileged metadiscourse is simply one among many discourses. There is no one better social theory, description, or critique. Postmodern thought, including all its variations, is just one type of social criticism. In social theorist John Shotter's (1993b) words,

> A postmodernist approach to its [the ordinary world of everyday life] understanding requires us, first and foremost, to abandon the "grand narrative" of a theoretical unity of knowledge, and to be content with more local and practical aims. This means abandoning one of the deepest assumptions (and hopes) of Enlightenment thought: that what is "really" available for perception "out there" is an orderly and systematic world (potentially) the same for all of us—such that, if we really persist in our investigations and arguments we will ultimately secure universal agreement about its nature. (p. 34)

This view leads to the criticism of paradoxically throwing out the baby—the large historical narrative—with the bathwater—the philosophical metanarrative (Nicholson, 1990, p. 9). Uncertainty, unpredictability, and unknown, however, do not necessarily equal nihilism, solipsism, or relativism. Dispensing with the notion of truth does not imply that "nothing exists"; taking a position of plurality does not imply that "anything goes." Rather, postmodernism promotes social criticism; from a postmodern perspective everything is open to challenge, including postmodernism. As we enter the postmodern period and objective reality disappears, the accepted organizing theories of science, and in this case the social sciences, are now thought to be no more true than other descriptions or other fictions (Kuhn, 1970).

Although I am interested in the broad postmodern landscape, the concepts of contemporary philosophical hermeneutics and social constructionism, both interpretative perspectives, have become the center points of my conceptual underpinnings. From my perspective, both lead toward a transformation in the culture of therapy.

TOWARD TRANSFORMATION

Contemporary philosophical hermeneutics and social constructionism view human systems as complex entities composed of individuals who think, interpret, and understand. Both question the application of traditional physical and natural scientific explanation to the analysis of human systems and suggest that the "pre-understanding" inherent in such explanations does not adequately allow for these human complexities. Neither implies a "systematic theoretical framework with a corresponding methodology" (Semin, 1990, p. 151); rather each implies an emerging framework for the critique of and provision of alternatives to dominant modernist concepts.

Although distinct, hermeneutics and social constructionism share similarities. Both examine taken-for-granted everyday beliefs and practices: how we produce and understand individuals and social institutions; how we participate in what we are creating, experiencing, and describing (Giddens, 1984). Both share an *interpretive perspective* that emphasizes *meaning*, meaning as constructed, not imposed. For instance, the meanings of words, the meanings that we attribute to the events and experiences of our lives, including our self-identities, are created by individuals in conversation and action with one another and with themselves, and they are always open to a variety of interpretations. Similarly, for hermeneutics and social constructionism, "Meaning must be seen . . . as the co-production of speaker and listener where both share in the same active power of linguistic competence" (Mueller-Vollmer, 1989, p. 14). Thus, for each, language plays a central role, emphasizing that beliefs and practices are connected to, are created in, and occur in language. And both hermeneutic and social constructionist thinkers question whether the mind can reflect, be revealed, or reveal (Gergen, 1990).

Hermeneutics

Hermeneutics is one of the earliest questionings of the Cartesian theory of the dualistic nature of knowledge, of the separation of the observed and the observer. Historically, hermeneutics dates back to the seventeenth century, when it emerged originally as an approach to analyze and ensure appropriate interpretation—the reader discovers and interprets the written word—of the biblical text and later literary texts. In this Enlightenment tradition, the interpreter was much like Hermes, the Greek messenger of the gods, who had to understand and interpret what the deities meant so he could correctly "translate, articulate, and explicate their intention to mortals" (Mueller-Vollmer, 1989, p. 1). The focus in this earlier hermeneutic sense was on the text, not on the interpreter or questioner of the text. By the late eighteenth century, and largely under the influence of philosophers Friedrich Wilhelm Schleiermacher and Wilhelm Dilthey in the nineteenth century, hermeneutics had broken from this text tradition; it had become an approach to interpreting and understanding human behavior and emerged as a "genuine philosophical discipline and general theory of the social and human sciences" (Mueller-Vollmer, 1989, p. ix).[5]

With the emergence of contemporary twentieth-century philosophical hermeneutics usually associated with the views of thinkers such as Hans-Georg Gadamer, Jurgen Habermas, Martin Heidegger, and Paul Ricoeur, hermeneutics began to take a postmodern turn (see Madison, 1988 and Palmer, 1987). Although no definition is universally accepted and no one school of thought is dominant, broadly speaking, *hermeneutics* concerns itself with understanding and interpretation: understanding of the meaning of a text or discourse, including human emotion and behavior, and understanding as a process that is influenced by the beliefs, assumptions, and intentions of the interpreter. Hermeneutics "maintains that understanding is always interpretive . . . that there is no uniquely privileged standpoint for understanding" (Hoy,

1986, p. 399). Hermeneutics is not an attempt to arrive at the *true* meaning or the *correct* representation and should not be confused with causal explanation. If from a hermeneutic perspective all understanding is interpretive, then one can never reach a true understanding; a speaker's meaning cannot be fully understood, much less duplicated by another person. The truth is not revealed; there is no one right account of an event; and there is no one correct interpretation. Each account, each interpretation is only one version of the truth. Truth is constructed through the interaction of the participants and it is contextual. As such, interpreting, understanding, and seeking truth are neverending.

Gadamer (1975) identified the significance of what the interpreter contributes to the interpretation experience: Meaning is informed by the interpreter's forestructure of understanding as well as by what Gadamer called the "fusion of horizons" (p. 272) between reader and text (in the therapy domain, substitute "people involved" for "reader and text") (Gadamer, p. 338). In this fusion, an understanding emerges unique to that encounter that cannot be attributed to either participant. The interpretation may change as it is influenced by history, culture, and time. Gadamer referred to these interpretation forestructure influences as prejudices. He believed that any act of interpreting, of understanding meaning, is infinite; therefore, the questioner is open to questions.

From this hermeneutic perspective understanding is linguistically, historically, and culturally situated; that is, "language and history are always both conditions and limits of understanding" (Wachterhauser, 1986a, p. 6). Understanding is circular because it always involves reference to the known; the part (the local) always refers to the whole (the global) and conversely the whole always refers to the part—what Heidegger (1962) called the *hermeneutic circle*. The current linguistic practices in which we are immersed and the foreknowledge of our pasts, or what Heidegger refers to as our *horizon*, influence (as well as inform and limit) our understandings, meanings, and interpretations. The process of understanding is the process of immersing ourselves in the other's horizon, and vice versa—each being open to the other. This is an active process, an active dialogue.[6] It is not as if there were a fixed horizon. Hermeneutics "assumes that problems in understanding are problems of a temporary failure to understand a person's or group's intentions, a failure which can be overcome by continuing the dialogic, interpretive process" (Warneke, 1987, p. 120).

I do not believe that one person (for example, a therapist) can ever fully understand another person (for example, a client) or arrive at a speaker's intention and meaning, or what social constructionist Kenneth Gergen (1994) referred to as *modernist hermeneutics*—the belief that you can eventually know. There is no *true* meaning since the process of a quest for meaning in itself shapes and reshapes, creates and recreates, for the interpreter something new, something other than. Understanding does not refer to comprehending something that is, that exists; the very act of understanding produces something different from that which one is trying to understand (Gadamer as quoted in Madison, 1988, p. 167): to understand is to understand differently. According to Gadamer (1975), "All understanding is interpretation" (p. 350).

Gergen (1994) critiqued Gadamer's notions of intersubjectivity, shared cultural heritage, and hermeneutics's central focus on the individual and what the individual brings to the interpretation.[7] The implications of hermeneutics extend beyond the individual to joint interactions between people or to people in relationship. I resonate with psychiatrist Richard Chessick's (1990) opinion that hermeneutics suggests that "meaning in a dyadic relationship is generated by [I prefer *in and through*] language and resides not in the mind of individual speakers or writers but in the dialogue itself" (p. 269). Gergen (1988a, 1994) argued that theories of meaning such as hermeneutic and deconstructionist literary theories focus on the written text and advocated moving beyond the written text and the person as text, replacing "textuality" and the individual as the focus of analysis with the social domain, making "communality" and the relationship the focus of analysis (1994, pp. 262–264). Gergen's emphasis on a "relational account" (1988a, p. 49), a "relational theory of human meaning" (1994, p. 264), is central to the social constructionist discourse in the social sciences. But what exactly is social construction?

SOCIAL CONSTRUCTION

The social construction movement in the social sciences usually is traced to the early work of sociologists P. L. Berger and T. Luckmann (1966), who in their classic *The Social Construction of Reality* suggested a relationship between individual perspective and social process and, accordingly, a multiplicity of possible interpretations and the social nature of knowledge. Social construction is more recently associated with social science theoreticians Jerome Bruner (1986),

Nelson Goodman (1978), Kenneth Gergen (1982, 1985, 1994), Rom Harré (1979, 1983), John Shotter (1984, 1993a, 1994), Donald Polkinghorne (1988, 1991), Theodore Sarbin (1986), Clifford Geertz (1983), and Charles Taylor (1989), each of whom offers his own interpretation.

Social construction is about differences. Shotter (1995a) characterizes social constructionists as follows:

> They have become much more concerned with what it is like to be a particular person living within a network of relations with others, who is positioned or situated in relation to them in different ways at different times. It is this "positioning" or "situating" of what we have to say in relation to the activities of a social group of some kind—sometimes "inside" them, sometimes "outside" . . . that typifies the movement in general. (p. 384)

Social construction is a form of social inquiry. Gergen (1985), considered by many its leading proponent, describes social construction as an inquiry that is

> principally concerned with explicating the processes by which people come to describe, explain, or otherwise account for the world (including themselves) in which they live. . . . [Social constructionism] views discourse about the world not as a reflection or map of the world but as an artifact of *communal interchange* [my emphasis]. (p. 266)

Knowledge, including self-knowledge or self-narrative, is a communal construction, a product of social exchange. For Gergen the relationship is the locus of knowledge. From this perspective ideas, truths, or self-identities, for instance, are the products of human relationships. That is, everything is authored, or more precisely, multiauthored, in a community of persons and relationships. The meanings of language, that is, the meanings that we attribute to the things, the events, and the people in our lives, and to ourselves, are arrived at by the language people use—through social dialogue, interchange, and interaction that we socially construct. The emphasis is on the "contextual basis of meaning, and its continuing negotiation across time" (Gergen, 1994, p. 66) rather than on the location of the origins of meaning. I feel liberated by this move away from the notion of individual authorship to the notion of multiple or plural authorship, because of the possibilities associated with it. But how does such authorship occur? My thoughts resonate with what Gergen (1994) refers to as *supplementation* and what Shotter (1993a, 1993b) terms *joint action*.

Supplementation

Gergen (1994) offers the concept of supplementation as a descriptor for the ways in which the coordination of our utterances and actions engenders meaning. *Supplementation* is the reciprocal process in which one person supplements or responds to another person's utterances or actions. The *potential* (Gergen's emphasis) for meaning in the dyad develops through the supplementation process. The response may be one word or an expanded conversation. Each person of the dyad is immersed in a range of other relationships—previous, present, and future—and the multiple contexts of those relationships influence the supplementations and meanings developed within the dyad. And, conversely, the influence of the supplementation within the dyad carries over (or has the potential to carry over) to outside the dyad as part of an expanding reciprocal process. Thus, meanings are not permanently fixed but are continuously influenced, constructed, and reconstructed over time.

Joint Action

Similar to Gergen's analysis of social construction are the ideas of Shotter (1993a), who refers to his account as a rhetorical–responsive version. He suggests that common to all versions of social constructionism is "the dialectical emphasis upon *both* the contingency *and* the creativity of human interaction—on our making of, and being made by, our social realities" (1993b, p. 13). The central focus of concern is "the contingent flow of continuous communicative interaction between human beings . . . a self–other dimension of interaction" (1993b, p. 12). Shotter, who is historically influenced by the later work of Ludwig Wittgenstein and the ideas of Michael Billig, Mikhail Bakhtin, L. S. Vygotsky, and V. N. Volosinov, is particularly occupied with the self–other relationship and the ways in which people spontaneously coordinate their everyday mutual activities, in "how speakers and listeners seem to be able to create and maintain between themselves . . . an extensive background context of living and lived (sensuously structured) relations, within which they are sustained as the kind of human beings they are" (1993b, p. 12). Shotter defines joint action as follows: "All actions by human beings involved with others in a social group in this fashion are dialogically or responsively linked in some way, both to previous, already executed actions and to anticipated, next possible actions" (1984, pp. 52–53). Shotter's *joint action* is similar to Gergen's notion of supplementation.

Confusions

I often find that people confuse social *constructionism* and the closely related *constructivism*. At its core, each philosophical position rejects the notion of knowledge as reflecting an ontological reality and argues that knowledge is a construction. Social constructionism and constructivism both reject the notion that the mind reflects reality and advance the idea that humans construct reality. Both would agree with philosopher Richard Palmer's (1985) assertion that "one's view of man (person) is a function of one's assumptions about reality" (p. 16). Although there are similarities, for me there are critical distinctions. In my opinion, the primary difference is in how each arrives at and views this construction.[8] Constructivism and social constructionism arose from different intellectual traditions. Early constructivism was associated with the works of the developmentalist Jean Piaget (1954) and the personal construct psychologist George Kelly (1955). Later constructivism, often called *radical constructivism,* is primarily associated with the physicist Heinz von Foerster (1982, 1984), psychologists Ernst von Glasersfeld (1987) and Paul Watzlawick (1984), and the biologist Humburto Maturana (1978). All share an identity as cyberneticians. Radical constructivism regards reality as the construction of the mind, emphasizing the autonomy of the self and the individual as the meaning maker. In von Glasersfeld's (1984) words, "All communication and all understanding are a matter of interpretive construction on the part of the experiencing subject" (p. 19). An experiencing individual's biological cognitive structures and processes are critical to constructivism, for instance, the relationship of inner mental processes to experiences of the external world. Von Foerster (1984) talks of cognition as "computing descriptions of a reality" (p. 47). In all views of constructivism, the emphasis is on the individual constructing mind.

Constructivism, Gergen (1994) warned, is "lodged within the tradition of Western individualism" (p. 68), whereas social constructionism moves away from the idea of the individual constructing mind and challenges the notion of the autonomous individual. The individual is no longer the discrete object of understanding nor the creator of meaning. Mind does not create meaning; instead, mind *is* meaning.

Social constructionism emphasizes the interactional and communal context as the meaning maker—the mind is relational and the development of meaning is discursive. This emphasis is what Shotter (1993b) referred to as "conversational realities." Social constructionism moves beyond the social contextualization of behavior and simple relativity. Context is thought of as a multirelational and linguistic domain in which behavior, feelings, emotions, and understandings are communal. They occur within a plurality of ever-changing, complex webs of relationships and social processes, and within local and broader linguistic domains/practices/discourses. I mention my personal distinction between social constructionism and constructivism because emphasis on social processes and emphasis on the individual constructing mind have different implications for psychotherapy theory and practice.

MY POSTMODERN PICTURE

I do not wish to imply that the postmodern picture that I have sketched represents all the colors of postmodernism. It does not. My picture is only a small sketch that summarizes and represents those postmodern hues that I have currently chosen to adopt in my work. Two, although of course not completely separate, postmodern paths are delineated: One leads to a landscape of the "already spoken"—the existence and impact of cultural discourses, narratives, and conventions. The other leads to the "not-yet-spoken"— the newness to come in dialogue. To date it is this latter landscape—the postmodern premises of contemporary hermeneutics and social constructionism, with its emphasis on the interrelated relational nature of knowledge and the notion of self as linguistically constructed and transformed through dialogue—that serves as the centerpoint of my conceptual underpinnings and provides the predominant hues in a *collaborative language systems* approach. These hues make my experiences intelligible, correspond with my experiences, and inevitably have shaped my experiences. Currently, my thoughts and actions as a therapist and the questions I have about therapy that are influenced by the latter palette center on therapy as a process of internal and external dialogical conversations. I am interested in how change or transformation occurs through this process: how knowledge is created, how newness emerges in the therapeutic encounter through dialogue, how a therapist participates in this creative process, and how a therapist is in relationship with a client.

If you want to continue at this time with the dominant hues of knowledge, language, and *self* in my postmodern landscape please fast-forward to Part III. If you are eager to move into how I conceptualize my collaborative approach to therapy and what it looks like in practice, please continue to Part II.

PART II

Creating Collaborative Language Systems, Relationships, and Processes: Partners in Dialogue

"SABRINA"

Once in a conference demonstration interview I met with a therapist, whom I will call Jane, and her volunteer client, whom I will call Sabrina.[1] Before meeting them I did not know anything about Sabrina, why Jane invited her, or what their agendas would be. As I recount and reflect on our conversations, I use as many of their words and phrases as possible. As you read and interact with my narrative of this interview, I would like you to be aware of the curiosities, questions, and critiques that you develop.[2x]

Minutes before Sabrina's arrival Jane and I had a brief conversation in which my initial curiosities were, Why had she and Sabrina volunteered to talk with me? What were their expectations of the interview? What would she and what did she imagine Sabrina would like us to know to be able to address their agendas and

47

hopes? I could have asked the questions with Sabrina present; however, the "pretalk" was a request of our conference host.

Given the awkwardness of the public circumstances—200 people watching in an auditorium with stage and bright lights—there was only a slight nervousness in Jane's voice as she hesitantly began.

> I chose Sabrina because she is so eager to explore and make some meaning of her life and look at everything with fresh eyes. She was willing to share with you and was available to come . . . and I thought she'd be comfortable since she is an actress. I don't think either of us has any expectations. We are very open to whatever may go on; perhaps you can shed some new light, maybe offer some new possibilities.

Jane told us that Sabrina was in her twenties, in show business, and a fairly new client who had been in therapy before. Jane expressed one concern, Sabrina's "relationship with her father," including the possibility of "sexual abuse." She was not specific as to whether it was her, Sabrina's, or both their concern. The father, Jane said, had "touched her," "wrestled with her," and "once put his tongue in her ear." Then, almost interrupting herself, she said, "I'm not very happy with how quickly the words 'sexual abuse' popped right out of my mouth" (referring to a previous conversation with Sabrina). I asked, "So the two of you have been talking about it, those words that came out of your mouth?" Jane said that she had mentioned to Sabrina that she might tell me this and that Sabrina said it was fine if she did. On that note Sabrina arrived. Whether or not the two of them had been talking about sexual abuse was left hanging, but it sounded as if they had not.

We met with Sabrina in a small room offstage that had been set up for professional videotaping, including three video cameramen and more bright lights. When we walked into the room, Sabrina was already seated with her water bottle by her feet. She smiled and said hello. She had a casual manner, remaining seated when I introduced myself and shook her hand. The chairs were in a slightly curved row. I sat in the chair next to her and Jane sat on the other side of me. Sabrina was affable and animated, and she gestured as she began to talk.

I thanked Sabrina for agreeing to join *us* (Jane, me, and the audience participants). I told her what I thought *our* dual agenda was from my brief conversation with Jane: one, that people were interested in seeing "how I talk with clients" and, two, that I hoped that *"our* talking would be of help to her and Jane in *their work together."*

"Let me begin by telling you what I know about you," I said. I shared what Jane had said, including that she had "let some words slip out of her mouth." I gave Sabrina the opportunity to modify or correct what Jane had told me about her and our agenda.

Comment: Central to establishing a dialogue is creating room for and inviting all voices. This entails showing interest in and respect for what the other person wants to say. It also entails being public and avoiding secrecy. Toward these ends, I am curious about Jane's and Sabrina's agendas, I let them know what my knowledge of the agenda is, and I let Sabrina know what I learned about her and invite her input. I use collective language: *"our agenda," "our talking," "their work together."*

"I don't know anything about you," Sabrina remarked. I told her where I was from and what I do, ending, "Is there anything in particular you would like to know about me?"

"No," she answered.

I continued, "I really don't know what brought the two of you together, what you and Jane have been talking about, what your expectations are for today."

Sabrina's response was "So what is your specific question? Seems like you just asked me a lot of questions."

"I did. I asked you three very complicated questions."

"Which one do you want me to answer?" she asked.

"Why don't we start with your coming here today."

Comment: Some might view Sabrina's questions as a challenge, as a struggle over who will be in control, or as a representative example of a variety of personality characteristics. I simply viewed her question as part of learning how to talk with each other, part of my adjustment to her rhythm.

"I love the process of therapy. I think it's fascinating. So I was curious to find out what that entails and even though I've been working with Jane for a short time I respect her and admire her work so much that if she thought I'd enjoy coming and that it would be interesting and helpful, then I give that a lot of credit. I thought I'd be good at it, a good victim."

"Well, let's hope you don't leave here feeling like a victim or that any of us does," I continued. "So, what have the two of you been talking about?"

Sabrina began to tell her story. "I think when I first came to Jane I wanted to improve relationships in my life and Jane said something like 'Well, isn't that what therapy is about?' And it was specifically because I was having trouble with intimacy in a romantic relationship."

"A particular relationship?" I wondered.

"And also generically," she added and continued, "I felt I had been out of therapy for a year and that it was time to work with someone who was better than I was at it again. I had done as much as I could on my own and with my friends."

"And your previous therapy, was that about relationships also or something else?"

"Yes."

"So, in talking about relationships, what are some of the things the two of you have been talking about?"

"My father," she slightly chuckled, "he's a good one."

"Who is [having learned that she was from New England, I was going to ask, Who is back in New England?]—"

Sabrina interrupted, "I also know that Jane may have or may not have mentioned that to you prior to speaking with me."

Jane volunteered, "I did."

"Those were the words I didn't expand on," referring to my earlier mention to Sabrina that Jane told me some words had slipped out of her mouth.

Sabrina said, "Yes, not yet, but I assumed that Jane would tell you."

I learned that Sabrina's father was in New England and found out who the other family members were. I questioned, "So, you're [referring to Sabrina and Jane] talking about relationships in general and your current romantic relationship has led to your talking about your father?"

Comment: I am interested in our conversation's enhancing Sabrina's freedom to tell her story. It becomes a three-way conversation as Jane and I participate in the unfolding story that Sabrina leads. There are a different tone in the telling and a different rhythm when the client leads. Earlier I had been curious about Sabrina's father—where was he?—but when she interrupted my question I followed her. My question was not about a hidden agenda or assumption. It was not asked to obtain a fact or verify a hypothesis. It was simply a curiosity at the time, a way of grounding myself, a way of helping me grasp her story. I did not interpret her interruption as a signal of control, avoidance, or denial. If she wanted me to know about her father, she would tell me, and she later did when talking about her family and life in New England. This, in turn, brought us full circle back to the words *sexual abuse.*

Jane joined in, "Can't remember which came first?"

To which I said, "The words that came out of your mouth were *sexual abuse?*"

Sabrina interjected, "Didn't I bring them up first?"

Jane puzzled, "My recollection is that I opened my mouth and there they were, as you were describing the different behaviors that your father had . . . over the years since you were a teenager."

Sabrina remembered it differently. "I thought I had asked you to define it for me: '*Is it?*' '*Was it?*'"

Never figuring out the sequence, Jane concluded, "Anyhow, there it was."

I then asked, "But let me back up just a moment; in terms of your thinking about relationships and deciding at this point in time that this was the time to talk about relationships and puzzling over them and figuring out what that's all about, what are some of the dilemmas or challenges or disappointments or problems that you experience in relationships?"

Sabrina: "Fear of intimacy and commitment, trying to find healthy independence and dependence in a relationship."

"Trying to strike a balance?" I wondered. "And so people mean a lot of different things by intimacy and commitment; what do those words mean for you?"

Comment: I do not want to assume that I know or understand what another person means. I want to try to learn Sabrina's precise meanings, what she is talking about and wants me to hear.

Sabrina began to share her thoughts and dilemmas about intimacy. "How long have you had difficulties with relationships?" I asked.

"At least since I was twenty-one."

I wondered out loud how others, for instance, friends or the man with whom Sabrina is in a relationship, would experience and describe her in relation to intimacy and commitment. She told a little about her current relationship and said that the man did not know that she has these problems because she had "decided to try to be better at it" and act differently in this relationship. She said that she was "surprised" that she could actually be "better at it than I thought."

Comment: I share my private thoughts, offering them in a tentative manner as something to talk about if a client so chooses, not as questions to answer.

"So, what kind of opened that door for being better at it than you thought?"

"My will."

"Is this characteristic in your family, strong will, that you put your mind to it and off you go?"

"Yes."

Comment: When I am talking with one member of a system I often wonder what others are thinking. What is their interior silent dialogue about the exterior spoken conversation? If they are not present, I might ask, "If your therapist [father, mother, or boyfriend] were here now, what thoughts do you think he [she] would have about what we have been discussing?" Here, I simply turned to Jane and asked, "So, what are you thinking as Sabrina's talking about this?"

Jane said that she had not known about the strong-willed part; it was a surprise. She added that they had also been talking about Sabrina's career.

Comment: We turn in the direction of Sabrina's career. I did not see this as a diversion from or defusing of a "touchy" topic. Again, conversations are not linear: they touch on this and that, topics crisscross, some pieces are expanded on, and some pieces fade and disappear, some pieces appear again. Conversations proceed moment to moment and cannot be determined ahead of time.

"So, the career is an important part of this independence/dependence?" I wondered.

"Absolutely!" Sabrina quickly and emphatically replied.

"Tell us a little more about your career, if you don't mind."

She told about her frustrations and fears; she said that she was "scared to death," usually had low self-esteem, but was pretty confident right then about putting herself "out there on the line."

I checked with her to see whether I was hearing what she wanted me to hear: "You're talking about the hard work, the disappointments?"

Comment: I do not want to misunderstand.

"A product."

I again checked out what she said so that I did not misunderstand: "Feeling as if you're treated as a product, almost a nonperson?"

"No," she replied.

Comment: Here my curiosity about the hard work and disappointments led us momentarily in what might seem to be another direction but I simply returned to something Sabrina had mentioned earlier.

I returned to learning about what had been hard. She talked about the process of dealing with success and failure, and her feelings about her career. "I'm a good product and you should buy me." She continued that around the age of eighteen to twenty-one, "things got really messy." She said it was the first major shift in her life, referring to the fact that until then her behavior had matched everyone's assumptions that she would stay in the New England village where she grew up.

I wondered, "So, it is kind of a struggle in terms of who other people wanted you to be and who you wanted to be; is that one way of putting it?"

This led us back to a discussion of relationships, her lack of self-esteem, her putting other people's needs, or what she imagines to be their needs, first. She said they don't demand it but she always wants to please. And this naturally led us full circle back to her dad.

Comment: Anything can be talked about or not talked about. I do not want to value one thing over another. If you follow a client's lead, you will be led where you need to go. During this encounter, I am aware of the circumstances of our talking: a public, live interview demands a great deal of respect of both a client and a therapist.

"Say a little bit of how your dad fits into all of this. How would you place him into your struggles with relationships?" I asked.

Sabrina talked about her family, her father and mother's divorce, and her role in the family (these were some of the "messy" things that she mentioned earlier). She talked about issues of power and abuse. Awkwardly and to her own surprise, she exclaimed, "Wow, I'm using the word *abuse.*"

I offered, "You don't have to say anything or any more than you want to say, that you're uncomfortable with. Sounds like you might be wanting to talk further with Jane about . . . "

She did not know whether she wanted to or not. She agreed it was an ongoing, unpredictable question.

Comment: To talk or not talk about it is her choice. I could have asked about what influences this choice or what would need to be different for her to be able to talk about it. Such questions could indicate that I value talking about it. I made another U-turn back to something I remembered—the strong will. When you pay careful attention to and are genuinely interested in what the other person says, you develop a good memory. Things heard earlier in a conversation or in previous talks often surface. It is not, however, as if they have been tagged to resurface.

"I'm still curious about this strong will," I said. This led us back to the relationship between "will" and "changes," and I wondered whether there were similarities in the ways she handled her relationships and her career.

Earlier in our conversation Sabrina had alluded to the helpfulness of her current therapist, so I asked her what had been helpful. She said that Jane had helped with her career. She told the story of an audition she had agonized over, not sure how to prepare her resume or how to get ready for the audition. She rather matter-of-factly repeated what she had said to Jane, "I could give them a resume: I'm twenty-eight, from Boston and etc. That's really boring . . . doesn't say anything about who I am." Jane had asked her what she would want them to know and suggested that she tell them what *she thought* they needed to know rather than what they wanted to know.

Very confidently, pulling up in her chair, Sabrina said, "They need to know that I'm a phenomenal actress, what kind of roles I see myself playing, what my range is, the fact that I understand the business, and I can sell."

She returned to her earlier remarks about being a person, not just a product, and talked about the importance of "getting beyond the descriptive things such as age and where you're from" and letting herself "come alive in the room." Jane added about Sabrina's new positioning in her relationships, "instead of what you thought they wanted you to do, it was important for you to convey . . . "

I commented, "Sounds like your work with Jane is progressing in the direction you want it to."

"She asks great questions," Sabrina quickly replied.

Comment: I did not ask Sabrina to elaborate on Jane's question since she had just given us an example of Jane's questions. Instead, I remembered and asked about something Sabrina had mentioned earlier about therapy. When she mentioned it, I did not develop a plan to return to it. I do not enter with or maintain a list of questions that I want to ask. This question, like others, arose from that moment in the conversation and a simultaneous thought about our conference observers.

"Let me go back to something you said earlier about why you're here. You said you're curious about the process of therapy. As you know a lot of therapists are watching us talk, and they are also very curious about the process of therapy, what happens in the relationship between the client and the therapist? Do clients come because they have a problem or dilemma? Do they come because they're seeking a solution? Would you mind commenting on your experience with Jane? And you've been in therapy before?"

Comment: Again, I posed multiple questions as I did in the beginning of our talk, but this time we seemed to be more in sync with each other, and Sabrina simply responded sans repartee.

> The process of therapy seems to be coming in with a problem and going deeper with it, kind of backtracking, seeing where else it branches out and infiltrates. What kind of language I use to describe this also fits other areas of my life. That's a very hard question for me to articulate. It depends on who the therapist and client are and who the therapist's last client was. How good I am depends on how good the therapist can be . . . where she is that day. . . . It is definitely a partnership.

Comment: Again, Sabrina triggers my memory of her earlier mention of previous therapy.

I asked her about it: How would she describe her experiences; what did other therapists do that was useful; did anything happen in therapy that wasn't useful?

Comment: She began talking about her sensitivity to "border infringements." She talks about the importance of "fit" and "connection." She said because she's the kind of patient that "will ask personal questions," that it takes a really good therapist to deal with that in a professional way:

"I want to know and I care and it's important for me as a patient to know a certain amount about who I'm dealing with or otherwise I can't connect."

She talked of the meaningfulness of having some sense of who a therapist is, as a person beyond academic background, as a human being. She called it a "sense of peership."

I wondered out loud if Sabrina had any questions she wanted to ask Jane. She said she was curious if Jane were married, what kind of relationship she had? I then asked her if there is anything she would like to ask me at that time.

Comment: Remember Sabrina's first comment to me, "I don't know anything about you"? I think most clients, as Sabrina indicates, want to know something about therapists as people. We should grant them this right.

"You don't know a whole lot about me. You're sitting here listening. What's going on in your head? How do you work? Are you listening to the words I'm saying? What are you picking up on? What do you want? Where are you trying to take this session? What are you trying to demonstrate to all of them? What are you mastering here?"*

---

* Sabrina is referring to the fact that the conference interview was announced as part of a "Master Series."

I shared some of my thoughts with her. "I'm curious about you and Jane, your agenda for meeting today, what might be helpful to you." I then told her some of what I value as a therapist.

She commented, "Like running side by side with your client, rather than saying 'come on, you can do it,' [gesturing a 'come to me' with her hands] or 'go ahead' [gesturing a push with her hands]."

Sabrina said she thinks that therapists should "make the environment comfortable enough so it feels safe to talk about it," and that the context and circumstances of the moment influence what can be talked about and how.

Although our three-person conversation ended here, as each conversation is a springboard for others, this one folded into my conversation with Jane and the conference participants, and into future conversations between Jane and Sabrina, and on and on.

We went back into the auditorium and the observers were abuzz. Their comments and questions ranged from: "Not a lot happened"; "If I were your supervisor . . . "; "Client led the session"; "I thought you handled the whole situation with artful respect and skill"; and "Masterful." Their experiences of the interview seemed to be divided around whether or not I should have talked about the "sexual abuse." Some thought she was manipulating me not to talk about it, while some thought she was inviting me to confront the issue. Some thought she was crossing boundaries by asking me questions about myself and my therapy biases. I told them that I believe clients have a right to ask me any question and that I am responsible for responding. I told them that if a client wants to know what I'm thinking, I tell them.

On the airplane home I reflected on the familiar: people experiencing the same event in different ways. I remembered other occasions when the observers of a conversation had markedly discrepant perceptions of it than those intimately involved. From my position I wanted to honor Jane's and Sabrina's agendas: "I don't think either of us has any expectations. We are very open to whatever will happen. Perhaps you can shed some new light, maybe offer some new possibilities." I wanted to honor the public circumstances of our talking: a demonstration interview that was being taped for distribution and observed by a number of therapists. I wanted to honor and protect Jane's and Sabrina's integrity. Sabrina led. I let her take the lead.

The following week Jane left a message on my answering machine quoting a colleague who had observed the conference interview: "Sabrina didn't come with a problem; she came with a solution and her solution was 'I want boundaries, I want contact and I want to feel good about myself. Harlene's respectful approach allowed her to demonstrate that solution.'"

Two months later I received a letter from Jane telling me about her and Sabrina's review of the videotape at their next meeting.

> I've viewed the videotape of the session with Sabrina which was immensely productive. According to her, she felt very competitive with you, assuming that you were purposefully positioning yourself so that the camera showed you full-face and the back of her head. In fact, on viewing it was clear that the camera showed her very clearly and we discussed her assumption that everyone was as competitive as her family is. Sabrina asked herself after the session, "Sabrina, why are you being so critical of Harlene?" and answered herself, "It's because you're so critical of yourself." Once having realized that she re-evaluated the session. I didn't realize either, that an actress may be more used to the lights and the camera but have performance issues that were even stronger than those of a non-actress.
>
> Another topic of discussion was the behavior of the therapist who crossed boundaries which was very beneficially talked over after the viewing. You had brought out the issue that Sabrina spins things around constantly in her head and wants to do more thinking in therapy and less outside. On questioning her about that problem, Sabrina said that she had stopped that behavior (spinning things around in her head) a couple of days after the session with you.

Six months later I received another letter from Jane.

> I recently had a chance to show the video with you and Sabrina to a graduate class in marriage and family therapy. . . . As you know, I was chagrined that Sabrina was so uncooperative [at the time] but I saw it in a different light after she and I talked about it. . . . Sabrina gave me permission to tell the class about her feelings of competition with you and what she learned through the experience. . . . They [students and visiting faculty for that class] thought your work was very respectful and sensitive to both Sabrina and me.

CHAPTER 3

Setting the Stage

*The road was pretty and flowery when the light came in, and we
gradually began to open our eyes. . . . When I say the road, you
do not, I trust, imagine us riding along a dusty highway. I am
happy to say that we are generally the discoverers of our own
pathways. Every man his own Columbus. Sometimes we take
short cuts, which prove to be long rounds;*
Over hill, over dale,
Through bush, through brier;
*through valley and over stream; and this kind of journey has some-
thing in it so independent and amusing that, with all its fatigues
and inconveniences, we find it delightful—far preferable even to
travelling in the most commodious London built carriage . . .*
—LIFE IN MEXICO: THE LETTERS OF FANNY
CALDERON DE LA BARCA (1894)

I thank Elena Fernandez for introducing me to Fanny Calderon de la Barca
in her "Stories of Mexico" that she prepared for the Galveston VI Sympo-
sium, Guadalajara, Mexico, October 1995.

SHIFTS IN CLINICAL EXPERIENCES

AS I HAVE reflected on my clinical experiences—those that piqued my curiosity and occasioned my immersion in postmodernism—I have created an account of their influence on my philosophy of therapy and on their distinguishing features: all had language as their centerpoint and combined to set the stage for thinking about human systems as linguistic systems and a collaborative approach to working with them (Anderson, 1995). What follows might be thought of as an "oral history," a narrative of shifts in my own clinical thinking that occurred through dialogue in a collaborative context with clients, colleagues, and students—a narrative of change.[1]

From Rhetorical Aims to Collaborative Inquiry

Interest in Language

My early focus was on speaking a client's language (metaphorically and literally) to learn about his or her values and worldview, words and phrases.[2] The aim was to converse within a client's everyday ordinary language and use that language rhetorically as a strategic tool of therapy, as an editing tool to influence a client's story, and as a technique to invite cooperation in effecting change. A client's language provided clues to developing problem definitions, treatment goals, and interventions (whatever form they might take), for example, revising faulty beliefs or improving on faulty attempts at solutions. We believed that if these were in a client's language, that client and the therapy would have a better fit. And, as a result, (a) a client would be more amenable to a therapist's diagnosis and intervention, (b) resistance would be less likely, and (c) therapy would have a greater prospect of success. Toward these ends we paid careful attention to our own language and, like chameleons, adapted to a client's point of view, a family's beliefs. Over time, however, we experienced several interrelated shifts in clinical experiences as we carefully tried to learn, work in, and use language in this manner.

Genuinely Fully Engrossed

We experienced that when we listened carefully to clients we actually became interested in what they were saying. Thus, we found ourselves fully engrossed in their unique stories and earnestly inquisitive about their views of life and their dilemmas. We became more focused on maintaining coherence within a client's experience and committed to being informed by his or her story. What began as a purposeful conversational technique became a natural curiosity and a spontaneous way of talking with people and being in relationship with them.

An Individual Language

We noticed that, rather than learning a family's language, we were learning the particular language of each member of a family system. The family did not have a language, but its individual members did. And each member's language was distinctive. Each had his or her own description of the problem and its solution, as well as his or her own descriptions of the family and of therapy. We were fascinated by these differences in the members' experiences, explanations of, and meanings attributed to the same event, the same family, and each other. Somehow sensing that these differences were valuable and could be fruitful, we no longer wanted to negotiate, blur, or strive for consensus (for example, in problem definitions or imagined solutions) but to maintain the richness of differences.

This is not to say that I do not think that family members share beliefs, values, goals, and histories. Of course they do. These are some of the elements that hold families together and give them continuity. But a family is not an entity. It does not think or breathe; individuals do. Thus, we realized we were not working with *a* problem, with *a* family, or toward *a* solution.

One at a Time

Our intense interest in each person and in each version of the story led us to talk to the individuals one at a time and in a concentrated manner. We discovered that while we were talking intensely to one person the others seemed to listen in a way that we had not observed before. They were less likely to correct and interrupt each other. It was as if they were listening undefensively. My interpretation of this is twofold. One, we conveyed in our words and actions that we were sincerely interested in what each person had to say, respected what each had to say, and would give each the time to say it. Thus, the teller did not have to work so hard to try to get us to understand or to convince us of his or her version of the story. Also, the listener was less likely to interrupt, correct, negate, or add to what the teller had to say. Two, the familiar story was being told and heard differently than it had been. The content was the same but the pieces were assembled differently; they now fit together in a way that allowed for an alteration in the sense people made of things and the way they experienced each other.

Everyday Ordinary Language

When we talked about our clients outside the therapy room we identified them by and shared their self-told stories as they had narrated them to us. For instance, in hospital staffings or school consultations we described and explained clients in their words and their phrases. In doing this we found that we were using more of their everyday ordinary language than of our professional language and jargon. Telling a client's story (or a fragment of it) as it had been told to us captured the uniqueness of each client and made each come alive. Colleagues became more engaged with us, and with a client, in learning about the client's particular situation, what it was like for him or her, and the essence of the way each client viewed himself or herself. Students often commented that clients no longer seemed to be the sterile, lifeless lookalikes created by professional descriptions, explanations, and diagnoses such as "passive aggressive," "bipolar," or "bulemic." Rather, they seemed more real; they came alive and the sameness that professional language produces receded when we told a story about them and used words and terms of significance for them, their self-descriptions, such as the bicycle family, the country clothes–city clothes children, or the napkin lady. We began to see the uniqueness of each client and his or her circumstances, the uniqueness of each clinical situation, and the uniqueness of each therapist–client relationship. As important, not only did clients become human through use of ordinary language; so did therapists.

Interventions

As we centered on and learned about clients' language and meanings, we began to relinquish our expertise on how people ought to be and our in-session or end-of-session interventions that relied on the expertise of a therapist. When we examined what we thought were novel, carefully strategized, and individually tailored therapist-designed interventions, we discovered that they were not interventions at all in the usual sense (unilaterally therapist-designed, often outside the therapy room, and driven by a therapist's expertise). That is, although we thought we were doing "interventions," we were not. The ideas and actions we then still called interventions emerged from the local therapy conversations; a client participated in their conception. They were coherent with, logical to, and unique to the family and its members. What was once flashy, entertaining, designer intervention therapy began to look somewhat parsimonious, ordinary, and boring to others. Some critical colleagues declared it "doing nothing," "bow-wow," and "nondirective" therapy. Some called it "imperceptible therapy." Some referred to our clients as "boredom-generating machines." To us, however, our therapy and our clients became more exciting.

Suspending Preknowledge and Focus on Client Expertise

As our interest in and value of the other person's knowledge continued and grew, our own knowledge became less important. With this ebb we found ourselves spontaneously and openly suspending our preknowledge—our stories, our biases, our opinions about how families ought to be, how narratives ought to be constructed, what were more useful narratives, and so on. By suspend I mean we were able to leave our preknowledges hanging in front of us for us and others to be aware of, to observe, to reflect on, to doubt, to challenge, and to change. The more we suspended our own knowing the more room there was for a client's voice to be heard and a client's expertise to come to the forefront.

Shared Inquiry

We found that the more we became immersed in our clients' language and meanings and positioned ourselves as inquiring learners, the more we acknowledged, encouraged, and heard their voices. We found that our learning position began to naturally and spontaneously invite a mutual or shared inquiry. They became engaged with us in a partnered process of coexploring the problem and codeveloping the possibilities. Therapy became a talking with rather than talking to. Client and therapist, and any others involved in the conversation, joined together in a give-and-take process, an exchange, a discussion, a looking at, and a criss-crossing of ideas, opinions, and questions. It was a two-way conversation that we began to think of as a dialogical process—one in which a therapist was no longer a narrative editor of a client's story who used language as an editing tool. The therapist was only one of the multiple authors of the new stories generated in language and through the relationship. The dialogical process of therapy and a therapist's role in creating it became our focus and the importance of our knowledge, and thus, content, faded.

Uncertainty

All of these experiences combined to leave us in a constant state of uncertainty as we realized that the outcome and consequences of our therapy conversations could not be determined ahead of time or predicted. We began to appreciate and value this sense of unpredictability, which in a strange way provided feelings of both comfort and freedom. We had the freedom of "not-knowing" (Anderson, 1990b; Anderson & Goolishian, 1992), of not *having* to know. Not-knowing freed us from needing to be experts on how clients ought to live their lives, the right question to ask, and the best narrative. We did not have to be content-knowing experts. This freedom to not know, in turn, led to an expanded capacity for imagination and creativity. Not-knowing became a significant pivotal concept in a collaborative language systems approach; it marks a significant difference between my ideas about therapy and the therapist's position and those of others.

Influence of Student Voices

The awareness of these distinguishing features was triggered, to a large extent, by students' remarks, questions, and critiques that forced new ways of understanding, describing, and explaining our work. Students often commented on the positive way we spoke about our clients, describing our manner and attitude as respectful and humble. They were amazed at our excitement about each client and astonished that we actually seemed to like those clients whom others might deem socially detestable. They were surprised by how many of our mandated referrals not only came to the first session but continued. In an effort to describe our approach to therapy, a student once wondered, "If I were observing and did not know who the therapist was, I wonder if I could identify them."

Practice and Teaching as Reflexive Processes: Going Public

These experiences in the therapy room and our conversations with others about them influenced our team work and teaching. For the most part family therapy teams are traditionally organized in a hierarchical and dualistic arrangement. The team members behind the one-way mirror, for instance, are granted a metaposition and credited with being able to see more correctly and quickly—as if they are "real and objective knowers." The mirror is thought to give the members protection from being swooped up in the family's dysfunction and faulty reality. Arriving at the better view involves a private closed door process that leads to a synthesis or consensus of the multiplicity of ideas. Whether a therapist is involved in the discussion or not, often the implicit agenda is that he or she is merely a voice of the team's metaview. The team determines what is most fruitful for a therapist and a family—the best idea, hypothesis, suggestion, question, or opinion—and funnels it to a therapist. This process influences a therapist's subsequent actions and thoughts in the therapy room. In this process, what is taken back to the client is preselected by a team and therapist, and it loses the richness of the multiplicity of perspectives. That is, the richness of the original ideas and the discussion among the team members is lost. Clients do not have access to the multiplicity of ideas. They are only left to choose or discard a team's preselected idea as translated to the therapy room by a therapist.

We began to realize how much of the richness of diversity was lost and how we could not preselect what clients might be most interested in when clients began to be inquisitive and in some instances demanded to meet the team "face-to-face" and hear what each of them had to say. At first we experimented with writing every thought, question, and suggestion so that a therapist could take these into the therapy room. This proved time-consuming and cumbersome. So, we would have the team meet with a therapist and a client in the therapy room. Each team member had an opportunity to say what he or she wished, then return to the other side of the mirror, leaving all voices hanging in the air for the family members and the therapist to deal with together. We were often surprised at what the family members were most occupied by and what they ignored. The choice, however, was theirs, not ours. The therapist was no longer an agent of the team hiding behind the mirror, but could now join with the family members in spontaneously and genuinely puzzling over the team's offerings. Family members and the therapist felt permission to ask a team member for clarification or to disagree with a decision. This began to make all thoughts more public and to collapse the artificial theoretically and professionally imposed boundaries among team members, therapist, and family. It also began to give back responsibility to the client and move therapy in the direction of joint therapist–client responsibility.

In learning situations, we often formed two-person student therapy teams. We encouraged both students to be in the therapy room because we found that if one were in the room and the other behind the mirror, often the student behind the mirror felt or at least acted as if he or she knew more. The student in the therapy room often felt discounted, awkward, and ignorant. We encouraged the students to talk with each other, share their ideas, and question and disagree with each other in the client's presence. If they felt more comfortable doing this outside the family's presence, however, they were encouraged to give a summary of their conversations to the family. This part of our history is compatible with Tom Andersen and his colleagues' development of the highly innovative reflecting team concept and practice (Andersen, 1987). Both approaches place an importance on the integrity of the other; both invite multiple voices and allow a therapist to share his or her thoughts publicly.

Beyond Family and Family Therapy

Coinciding with these clinical shifts, "family" became a restricting concept. It implied a priori who should be seen and why, without regard to the unique situation and the individuals' communications with each other, and with us, about the "problem." We began to think in terms of the people we talked with in therapy as part of a system that had coalesced around a problem, which we called *problem-determined systems* (Anderson, Goolishian, & Winderman, 1986b) and *problem-organizing, problem-dissolving systems* (Anderson & Goolishian, 1988b, p. 371). The persons we saw in the therapy room and those with whom we had telephone conversations were determined by who was talking with whom about the problem, and not by their social role and place in a client system structure such as parents, couples, siblings, or school counselor. Said differently, as the conversation of each session informed the members of the next, the "problem system" itself had a shifting membership. Consequently, we were less inclined to see or consider it necessary to see whole families. Much of our work was done with individuals, parts of families, and members of the larger system. We no longer distinguished therapy by social role or organization or by who was in the therapy room.

Historically, for many, the concept "family therapy" had come to indicate a modality for treating a particular social configuration rather than a paradigmatic shift in the conception of human systems and their problems. "Family" took the place of "individual" as the locus of pathology and as the focus of treatment. Family therapy, like individual therapy, for some became a method of social control; child protection agencies and juvenile courts, for instance, began mandating family therapy. It risked obscuring the broader applicability of a systems model to human associations other than families, for example, individuals, work groups, age groups, or larger social systems. As our efforts moved toward nonpathology and client expertise, terms like *therapy* and *therapeutic* were counterproductive to our attempts to move away from the ideas and implications of concepts such as pathology, normalcy, and therapist-as-expert on how others should live. In attempts to deal with the contradictions and changes in our way of conceptualizing therapy—its process and our position were the same regardless of the roles or numbers of people in the room—we denounced ourselves as family therapists, referring to ourselves at times as consultants or describing what we did as "just talking with people."

Conversational Partners

In summary, client and therapist were now conversational partners as we combined a client's expertise on his or her self and our expertise on a process, creating new knowledge, understandings, meanings, and possibilities for all. Our relationship with our clients and the therapy process became more collaborative; consequently, the dualistic, hierarchical nature of the therapy relationship and system began to blur and dissolve. As this collaborative effort developed, responsibility for therapy and its outcome became shared.

CHARACTERISTICS OF AND IMPLICATIONS FOR CLINICAL PRACTICE

Circling back, the philosophical premise that knowledge and meaning are the products of the generative process and social discourse, therapy may be viewed as a special kind of social discourse and best described as a purposeful conversation, whose aim is to create an environment facilitating a process in which cogeneration and coconstruction of meaning by therapist and client lead to new narrative and thus new agency. Through dialogue new possibilities evolve.

If a therapist translated this basic philosophical premise to the therapy domain, what would therapy look like? What would the attributes of such therapy be?

I present here the practical perspectives, the application of these concepts to therapy, by looking at therapy in terms of a schema, one that evolved through my own study and teaching of psychotherapy theories. Any theory of therapy can be described, analyzed, and compared or contrasted to others in terms of how its theoretical premises inform three basic characteristics: the therapist's position, the therapy process, and the therapy system. For example, in the *therapist's position,* one examines a therapist's role and a therapist's intent; in the *therapy process,* one looks at what occurs and what is required for transformation; and in the *therapy system,* one looks at how the theory determines the target of treatment and identifies therapy's membership. As you review these characteristics of the collaborative approach, you may want to compare and contrast them with characteristics of theories of your own and those of others.

One can examine how a theory of therapy informs the *therapist's position,* including defining that position, describing what a therapist does, and identifying therapist characteristics. The theory of therapy will inform the way a therapist talks and acts and the intentions underlying this talking and acting. Questions to address when analyzing a therapist's position that might be germane to a particular theory include, What is a therapist's intent? What is a therapist's expertise? What is a therapist's responsibility? How does therapy affect a therapist? Can a therapist be neutral? How is the relationship between a therapist and a client conceptualized and described? Are multiple therapists used, and if so, toward what aim? How are confidentiality and self-disclosure considered? What is ethical? What is a therapist's responsibility?

One can examine how a theory of therapy informs the *therapy process,* including defining the aim of therapy, describing the interactions between client and therapist, explaining what occurs in the process and how long it takes. A theory of therapy has embedded notions about the process and about change. This includes how the theory conceptualizes the purpose of therapy and what is required to achieve that purpose. How would the theory respond to such questions as the following? What is the goal of the therapy? How are issues conceptualized and addressed? How is change conceptualized? What is required to assure change? How is the therapy process related to change? Who decides when the goal has been achieved or when change has occurred? What amount of change is sufficient? How does what occurs in the therapy room translate outside the therapy room? And, which of these questions or others are considered relevant questions within the theory? Some theories hold extremely complex explanations; others are rather simple.

One can also examine how a theory of therapy informs the *therapy system,* including defining membership, determining boundaries, and selecting the target of treatment. A theory of therapy inherently mandates how to define the membership and how to set the boundaries of the therapy system. The theory determines who constitutes the therapy system (who is involved in the sessions and when), who or what is the focus of treatment, and who makes these decisions. Or, as Tom Andersen says, "Who should be talking with whom, when, where, and about what?" (Andersen, 1991). How would the theory respond to such questions as the following? Is the therapy system bounded by a client? Does the therapy system comprise a family? Is a therapist considered a member of the therapy system, and, if so, in what position? Does the system include others: extended family members, friends, or other professionals? What is the relationship of a client's and a therapist's larger system contexts to the therapy system? Does the theory take into account a client's and a therapist's local contexts? Does the theory acknowledge the broader sociopolitical contexts? Each theory of therapy informs, implicitly or explicitly, whether these are relevant questions, and whether and how they are addressed.

Here in Part II I elaborate on these characteristics and implications by addressing the therapy system, the therapist's position, and the therapy process. To illustrate how they translate into action I present (in my words) guidelines offered by clients (in their words) who gave their interpretations of their therapy experiences. I also include an annotated transcript.

CHAPTER 4

Therapy Systems as Language- and Meaning-Generating Systems

Structure . . . is an incidental product of interacting processes.
—ERICH JANTSCH (1975)

THE DISCOURSE OF therapy and the system it forms exist within and are circumscribed by both broader cultural, social, political, and economic contexts and local therapy contexts, including layers of perceived professional expertise (medical/nonmedical, doctoral degree/nondoctoral degree) and practice arenas (public/private, inpatient/outpatient). Therapists, however, often do not acknowledge or take into account the contexts and cultures in which local therapy discourse and universal discourses about therapy take place and in which the client and the therapist live and work.

Historically, in our society therapy has been a luxury of the middle and upper classes. In the last couple of decades, however, this has changed as increasingly therapy has been used as a social harness. Therapists, as well as those who design and administer therapy systems, for the most part have had privileged backgrounds characterized by values and experiences different from those of their clients. Determinations of what constitutes a problem and decisions about the indications or contraindications for therapy are influenced by multiple factors, for example, socioeconomic circumstances, court decisions, and prevailing psychological theories. The dominant voice, the culturally designated professional voice, usually speaks and decides for marginal populations—gender, economic, ethnic, religious, political, and racial minorities—whether therapy is indicated and, if so, which therapy and toward what purpose. Sometimes unwittingly, sometimes knowingly, therapists subjugate or sacrifice a client to the influences of this broader context, which is primarily patriarchal, authoritarian, and hierarchical.

The local therapy culture and the organization context in which a therapist practices also prejudice the composition of a therapy system. All helping systems, whether public or private, whether community mental health outpatient clinics, women's shelters, or group private practices, have traditions and beliefs that create space-defining parameters that define the role in which a therapist thinks and works. These parameters influence the therapist's view of the members of the treatment system as well as whether a therapist is considered a member of that system, and in what position. These same factors also influence the frequency and length of therapy.

A collaborative language systems approach challenges the modernist notions of objectivity, dualism, and universal narrative common in the psychotherapy field; their influence on the ways we think about and participate in human systems; and the aspects of those systems that we interact with in therapy. This perspective influences a therapy system that encourages *collaborative therapist–client relationships*, which tend to be less hierarchical, authoritative, and dualistic and more horizontal, democratic, and egalitarian. Such a collaborative therapy system is like a *conversational partnership* in which therapist and client mutually define membership, determine boundaries, and select the target of treatment.

This same collaborative conviction extends to the importance of our being aware of who is in *relevant* conversation with whom about the problem outside the therapy room. As therapists we must respect system members' ideas about *what* is germane to the therapy conversation and *who* should be included in it. All decisions about who should be involved in sessions, when, and what is talked about are determined collaboratively session by session, conversation by conversation. This conviction about mutuality is a distinguishing feature of my approach.

SOCIAL SYSTEMS AS LANGUAGE SYSTEMS

Based on the idea that social action as the force that constructs, in language, the relational networks that comprise a system, I conceptualize human systems as language systems (Anderson & Goolishian, 1988b; Anderson, Goolishian, Pulliam, & Winderman, 1986; Anderson, Goolishian, & Winderman, 1986b; Goolishian & Anderson, 1987a).

Social communication and discourse produce and define social organization and sociocultural systems. Human systems are relational systems based on language interaction. Through language— spoken and unspoken conversations and interactions with others and with the self—we generate meaning together. Meaning is an interactive and interpretive process (Gergen, 1982); the meanings of *system, family,* and *problem,* for instance, "only 'make sense' as they are developed within the conversation" (Shotter, 1995b, p. 67). Social systems and units form as people coalesce in relationships around issues that have particular relevance to them.

From this perspective, a therapy system is one kind of relational language system in which people (at a minimum, a client and a therapist) generate meaning with each other. A therapy system, like other human systems, is not a product of social organization. Therapy systems form and are distinguished at any time through their communicative relevance (usually thought of in terms of "problems"). In this view, the systems with which we work in therapy are the products of the linguistic domain of existence, and they exist only in our descriptions, only in our language. They are the narratives that evolve through conversation. A therapy system, therefore, is engaged in developing language and meaning specific to itself, specific to its organization, and specific to its "dis-solution" around the problem.

In contrast, in conceptualizations of human systems based on social structure (for example, Parsonian social theories) people are defined as members of social systems in terms of roles and structures and are perceived as cybernetic, onionlike layered social units (for example, individuals, couples, families, communities). This conceptualization is also in contrast to punctuating systems (for example, families) as creating problems.

PROBLEMS' EXISTENCE IN LANGUAGE

Defining a Problem

People enter therapy for many reasons, usually because they have reached a point where they, as individuals or as members of a family or another relational system, are in conversational breakdown and lack a sense of self-agency. They have lost the ability to be in dialogue and to believe that they can take effective action to deal with a problem: a sense of self-competency or self-mastery. Current meaning, narrative, and story preclude the freedom to handle a problem; rather, they inspire a sense of impoverishment and hinder self-agency. Most people say they seek therapy because they have a "problem." I put the word *problem* in quotation marks for several reasons: I do not want to suggest that I privilege problem over "solution," which I place in quotation marks for similar reasons. I do not distinguish between "problem talk" and "solution talk" because I do not consider one category useful conversation and the other nonuseful. Either focus can be dialogical or monological. The distinguishing factor is the way something is talked about, not its problem or solution focus or content. I do not especially like either word because of the meanings they have developed in therapy discourse: I actually prefer *dilemma* or *life situation* to *problem* and seldom use the word *solution* because I do not believe that problems are solved; rather, they dissolve.

In therapy, a problem constitutes the relevant issue for discourse. A problem and the meaning that we attribute to it are no more than socially created reality that is sustained by behavior mutually coordinated in language. It is an entity, a person or a thing, defined in language, that someone is troubled, concerned, complaining, or alarmed about; would like to change; and may have been attempting to change. A *problem definition* is a position that someone takes. It is a meaning that someone attributes, a narrative that someone has developed. I believe each problem is unique to the communicational and language matrix in which it arises.

In contrast to an empirical view of problems, a postmodern language system views problems, including diagnostic terminologies and categories, as not objectifiable entities caused by something or someone. Problems no longer exist in such spatially or socially defined units as an individual, a family, a work group, or a community. What seems to be an identifiable objective reality—a problem—is only the product of descriptions, the product of social construction. Problems cannot be separated from an observer's conceptualizations. The features that we attribute to problems, for example, the personality disorder that we see in an individual or the pathological patterns that we observe in individuals and families, are not features of the problem or the system but features that we give them. And, in turn, these features become self-confirming. Further, in this view, problems—the definitions, descriptions, and explanations of those experiencing them—are always in flux: they are not fixed. Like Gergen (1982), I find it useful to remind myself that any action and its description are subject to infinite revision.

A problem has as many definitions as there are members of the system involved with each other around the problem. There are as many observations, descriptions, understandings, and explanations of a problem, including ideas about its cause, location, and imagined solution (as well as the therapist's role vis-à-vis the problem), as there are persons communicating with themselves or with others about it. Each problem is conceived as a unique set of events or experiences that has meaning only in the context of the social exchange in which it happened. Each person involved in a dilemma has his or her own story about how the dilemma evolved, what it is about, whose fault it is, and what should be done. This includes the therapist's account.

Dueling Realities

Problems are linguistic events, or positions, that are often interpreted and described in conflicting ways. Seldom is there consensus about what a problem really is. What often appears as consensus, if looked at closely, will reveal variations. Indeed, what is perceived by one person as a problem may not be perceived by another in the same way or as a problem at all. Enormous amounts of energy can go into each person's efforts to protect and justify his or her view while attempting to convince the other of its correctness. Often by the time people reach a therapist's office these multiple views, these multiple realities are so discrepant that the participants seem to be engaged in what I have called *dueling realities* (Anderson, 1986; Anderson & Goolishian, 1986). All therapists have had dueling reality clients: the adolescent who thinks he does not have a problem but knows his parents do, the husband who thinks that nothing is wrong except that his wife nags too much, the woman who talks about the well-put-together professional person that her colleagues know and the incest survivor that she knows at home. In mandated cases, for example, parents sent to therapy because they have been accused of physically abusing their child who deny it, individuals often do not believe they have the problem for which the court has ordered therapy. And if they do believe they have a problem, it is often not the other-defined problem. If anything, those made to go to therapy against their will may consider participating in therapy the only problem they have. I often wonder how many people are in therapy for something that is a problem for someone else and how often the lack of space for the coexistence of multiple realities is associated with therapeutic impasses (Anderson, 1986; Anderson & Goolishian, 1986).

I have a bias toward thinking and talking about any problem from a perspective of multiple realities rather than conceptualizing a problem as a discrete reality. A therapist cannot learn what the problem *truly is*. Each event or experience that a therapist learns about is only a single account of a story, only one retelling of it, only one of a polychromatic hue of truths. A therapist learns only one account of the problem at one point in time in one distinctive context, not the unalterable truth. The account a person gives, for example, at home with friends, at school with the counselor, or in a session with a therapist may have small or large variations, depending on such variables as the context of the telling, the experiences of the teller, the combinations of participants in the telling and hearing, and the exigencies of the conversation.

Diagnostic Discoveries

In both psychotherapy and the broader culture, a diagnosis implies that the object of inquiry and the method of inquiry are based on stable assumptions like those in the biomedical realm. Diagnosis operates as a professional code with the function of gathering, analyzing, and ordering waiting-to-be-discovered data. As similarities and redundancies are found, problems are then fitted into a deficit-based classification system such as the *DSM-IV*. This reflects the common theoretical assumption that there is *a* problem that exists in some kind of typical pattern associated with particular categories of problems. It is with this "detectivelike" view that clinicians are trained to search for, to recognize, and to diagnose. In a larger sense, this framework is based on the assumption that language is representational and can accurately depict reality—reality that can be observed.

I have abandoned the view that a therapist is an independent "rather passive recipient and integrator of available information"

(Jones, 1986, p. 42) who collects and sorts out data on a diagnostic map. To my way of thinking, a problem does not have a cause that needs to be discovered; it does not need to be diagnosed, labeled, fixed, resolved, or solved. Such approaches are based on a dualistic worldview that suggests there is an objective reality within which a problem with verifiable characteristics exists. These approaches also draw one into a process of *behavioral confirmation,* in which one person's belief about another person acts to influence behavior and create reality (Gergen, 1982; Jones, 1986; Snyder, 1984). As von Foerster's (1984) "Believing is seeing" suggests, we tend to find what we believe in and are looking for. I would add, and for the same reasons, *believing is hearing.* Consequently, our meaning maps—biases, values, theories, experiences—can restrict the parameter of our and our client's thoughts and actions and thus can narrow our sense of agency. For instance, often clients enter therapy with a diagnosis. A man says his employee assistance consultant referred him to individual therapy for his "obsessive–compulsive disorder," adding, "If I don't deal with this, my wife is going to leave me." A woman says she's just been robbed and she wants therapy to find out whether she's "handling it okay or being too codependent." In each instance a client's words can trigger thoughts and preunderstandings, whether theoretical or based on extensive experience, that can influence whether the therapist accepts a client and how the therapist meets and gets to know him or her. These assumptions (always present to some extent) can lead us to see, hear, and approach a client, and a problem, in ways that close us off to other possibilities. For instance, it would be easy to hear both self-diagnoses as *individual therapy* problems.

If a problem is no more than what the people involved in the communicative actions are calling a problem, then the traditional diagnostic processes and categories are of little use. I believe it is a mistake to assume that problems in any category (for instance, psychosis, alcoholism, sexual abuse) are univariate and that these pluralistic syndromes have single explanations. As Harry Goolishian and I wrote (Anderson & Goolishian, 1988b), "It is our belief . . . that, in the end, we arrive only at *our* own descriptions and explanations of the problem. That is, the therapist reaches a diagnosis based on his or her private observations and experiences of the client's behavior" [emphasis added] (p. 389).

I would urge a shift in focus from thinking about human systems and problems in terms of individual, family, and group topologies or nosological categories. Such modernist universalizing obscures the complexity, uniqueness, and richness of the events and the people involved. I am often asked, for instance, "How do you treat child abuse?" or "How do you work with eating disorders?" Implicit in such questions is the assumption that there are across-the-board commonalities among problems. This shift in thinking can be jarring to therapists who believe that the target of treatment is a system defined by social theory (individual, couple, family, group) and that treatment repairs the defect (known pathological feature) in the superordinate system. Once a therapist has been professionally trained and socialized to think in terms of nested systems, to use a psychological microscope to detect defects, and to follow recipes to eradicate pathology—for instance, to *see* adult children of alcoholics, codependency, borderline personalities, or dysfunctional family patterns and to *treat* child abuse, schizophrenia, or undifferentiated ego masses—it is difficult to imagine or see anything else. Diagnostic systems, for instance, give a sense of legitimacy, confidence, and predictability to both the professional and the client (Gergen, Hoffman, & Anderson, 1995): that is, they serve their socially constructed purposes. Once one has acquired a therapist's toolbox complete with the associated instruction guide based on this hierarchy, the uncertainty and the challenge to the familiar that a collaborative approach introduces can be unsettling.

I share Schön's (1983) view of the often overlooked critical role of what he refers to as a *problem setting process*, "the process in which, interactively, we *name* the things to which we will attend and *frame* the context in which we will attend to them" (p. 40). This process guides the way and determines whether we can solve the problem; that is, a problematic situation can be converted into a workable or an unworkable problem, and vice versa. A collaborative approach aims to create a space and to facilitate a process in which unworkable problematic situations or narratives can be transformed into workable ones with possibilities. And, in my experience, once this happens, problems begin to dissolve.

PROBLEM SYSTEMS AND RELATIONAL SYSTEMS

Multiple, Simultaneous, and Overlapping Relational Systems

We live and work in multiple, simultaneous, and overlapping relational systems. I think of these as more horizontal-like systems in which common or crossover membership is determined by the relevant conversations. This is in contrast to thinking of them as hierarchically layered systems such as a smaller system (for example, family or couple) nested within a larger system (for example, children's protective services or women's shelter). Some of these systems may entail similar realities; others may have discrepant accounts; some may be interdependent; others, independent. All of these systems maintain different agendas and often different expectations of us and we of them. As therapists, we find ourselves members of multiple systems, some of which continue over time, others only constitute momentarily. Among these relational systems are the clinical and training arenas, broader professional associations, and our personal lives.

Because I work in settings with people who want to learn how to be therapists or more successful therapists, I am often temporarily, and in different roles, involved in other therapists' therapy and they in mine. Although this role is typically referred to as that of consultant, I now think of myself or others in such a position as *visiting therapists* (Anderson & Swim, 1993, 1995). A visiting therapist is one who visits, one who is a guest in someone else's therapy.

"Some Fresh Ideas" and "Observe"

During a seminar with a family study group, one of the group members asked Harry to do a *consultation interview* with a family the therapist had been seeing at a community mental health clinic. My role was to facilitate the discussion among the seminar participants. I will share information about the interview and the family that seems relevant to the issues of multiple, simultaneous, and overlapping systems and visiting therapists.

I asked the therapist to tell Harry, me, and his colleagues his goal, and, in his opinion, the family's goal for the interview. I then asked him to tell us what he thought we needed to know about the family and his work with them. The therapist said that he had two goals for the interview: he wanted to get "some fresh ideas" about the case and he wanted to "observe" our clinical work. He decided to be in the therapy room with the family and Harry.

The therapist described *the family:* a father, a nineteen-year-old son diagnosed as schizophrenic who was recently discharged from a psychiatric hospital, an eighteen-year-old son, a daughter in her twenties, and her three-year-old daughter. These were the family members living in the father's home. The therapy, he said, was "basically going well." The only problem was that the family, and the sister in particular, "refused to recognize the brother's progress," and the sister was "hostile" and "demanding more" from both the brother and the therapist. She was described as "persistent and strident" in her concerns for her brother and her criticisms of the therapy. She had even complained to the clinic director.

After the therapist told us what he thought was important for us to know about this family and his work with them, I invited the therapist's colleagues (who would be participating in the interview, as I would be, from behind a one-way mirror) to share their reflections. Quite engaged by the clinical information, they had many comments, critiques, and suggestions that they hoped would serve the consulting therapist, Harry, in the interview. Included in the group was the clinic director, who also was the therapist's supervisor.

The therapist invited all of *the family* members to the consultation because he felt they were critical to sustaining and encouraging the brother's progress. The young man, his brother, his sister, and her young daughter arrived for the interview. Behind the mirror we vaguely heard something to the effect that the father was "parking the car." We were not quite sure, however, what we heard since it was about an hour into the consultation before the father actually arrived. Harry did not make a judgment out loud or have a private interpretation of the father's late arrival. He skillfully and smoothly included him in the conversation much as an accomplished cook folds in egg whites without disturbing the integrity of the original mixture or the egg whites.

In the conversation before the father's arrival, the siblings talked about the mother, who had died years earlier, and her often violent behavior and its effect on her daughter. They also talked about another sister, whom they described as having problems similar to the brother's and who had committed suicide two years earlier by jumping in front of a train. Both of these dead relatives were important members of the current problem system. As well, they talked about the three-year-old granddaughter's significant role in the family, which had meanings important to their understanding of the problems.

What were and who were the members of the overlapping and shifting, and sometimes sequential, relational systems that we were encountering and participating in at the time of the consultation? Among others they included the family members who were living together, the family members and the therapist, the therapist and his supervisor/clinic director, the study group colleagues, and of course us and the study group. Each system was addressing multiple problems and agendas relevant to it.

At the end of the day, parts of these intersecting relational systems dissolved. The study group continued its active conversation but did not discuss the family. The therapist and family members continued to talk together in various combinations. Conversations between the therapist and supervisor dissolved because neither felt a need to continue to talk about the family. Afterward, Harry and the therapist corresponded and talked with each other at conferences about the family.

Granted, some may find the issue that I am addressing too simplistic and obvious. It is amazing, however, how often therapists and teachers remember this only when they run into trouble. They then may blame one system or another for interfering in or sabotaging their efforts. Such blaming falls into the onion-theory explanation in which the superordinate system causes the problem: unfortunately, the family has increasingly been designated as one of these problem-causing systems.

Defining the Family: One Kind of Relational System

In my view, there is no such thing as *the* family. There is no one family; the family does not exist in some rarefied social world. As I see it, the family is a reality based on communication. Consequently, there are as many families as there are members of the system, including the therapist defining it. This is not to say that I do not value family. Family in both its narrowest and broadest senses is important to all of us—to our very existence and identity. It is the intimate context in which we live. Rather, I want to emphasize that members have unique experiences with, descriptions for, and explanations of the family, including their role and reason for being in it.

The definition of a particular family, for instance, perceived by the mother is not the same as that by the father and is not the same as that perceived by their therapist. That is not to say that when a therapist walks into a therapy room and sees a family, he or she is not seeing a family. Rather, the family he or she experiences and influences is the family *he or she perceives*, prejudiced by both professional and personal theories and experiences. This notion of multiple family concepts naturally leads to the question of which family a therapist meets with: the mother's, the father's, the referring person's, or the therapist's.

I believe thinking *family* can be just as obscuring and trapping as thinking topologies and categories. It implies a priori who should be seen and why, without regard to the unique situation and the individuals communicating with each other and with the therapists about the problem. *Family therapy*, which has become very popular among mental health professionals, creates and maintains the illusion that there is such a thing as a family to treat with treatment methods peculiar to the family. This popularity has also created battles over ownership—who is best qualified to diagnose and treat families, who is best qualified to train family therapists. I think that these questions of ownership are moot.

Family and *family therapy* have come to indicate a modality for treating a particular social configuration rather than a paradigmatic shift in the conception of human systems and their problems. This concept can obscure the applicability of a relational systems approach to human associations other than families—for example, individuals, work groups, age groups, and larger social systems.

Today it is nearly impossible for *family* to have a singular meaning in a sociocultural sense. Because families include many sizes, shapes, and varieties, including those related by blood and those not (Goolishian & Kivell, 1981), the term requires multiple shifting definitions. Whether in a narrow view in any one family or in a broader cultural view, the family takes many unique forms. Historically, in the mental health field *family* meant the traditional unit of mother, father, and child or children. This was the family system referred to in psychological research and family therapy. Later the disciplines began to identify modified traditional families—single-parent families, stepfamilies, three-generation families—and eventually others whose members were related by characteristics other than blood or marriage—work families, same-gender couples, families of friends—as if all of these variations could be *known* and defined too. The notion of what a family is continues to change dramatically to include a rich and ever-increasing variety of family units. Unfortunately, psychological theories based on social theory of organization, role, and structure have not kept up with or made allowances for these changes. Furthermore, all of these definitions are embedded with myriad stereotypes, myths, biases, stigmas, and values that influence and constrain clients and their therapists who fail to see each family as a collection of individuals who all have their own definitions of the relational system called family.

From a postmodern perspective, whether working with an individual or a group of individuals who call themselves a family, we are always working with *multiple and shifting socially constructed descriptions and explanations.* On the one hand, the therapist is working with all of these families as he or she keeps in mind that the *underlying* concept itself is a social construction. On the other hand, however, in terms of relational language systems, the therapist is working with *multiple relational selves who happen to call themselves a family.* This puts the individual back into the therapy room. The emphasis, however, is not on the individual in the traditional sense but on the *individual in relationship*, who coordinates thoughts and behaviors in and through language. That is, the family is not thought of as a group of self-contained individuals but as a combination of fluid relational, dialogical individuals.

The implications for therapy are significant and controversial as distinctions in therapy based on social structures fade away and distinctions among individual, couple, and family therapies become irrelevant. Differences between modern and postmodern therapies, and among some postmodern therapies, arise. And they are important distinctions in my approach. How, then, are those systems that we encounter in the therapy domain distinguished?

THE PROBLEM DISTINGUISHES THE SYSTEM

Problems live and breathe in language. *Languaging*, or communicating, within the domain of a problem makes a social system: problems create systems.[1] The problem determines the system. At one time Harry Goolishian and I called those clusters of communicating people, those social units, *problem-determined, problem-organizing-"dis-solving" systems*, or *problem systems* (Anderson & Goolishian, 1988a; Anderson, Goolishian, Pulliam, & Winderman, 1986; Goolishian & Anderson, 1987a, 1987b). We thought of the problem system as a system of social action organized around languaging those issues in people's lives that they define as problems. Problem systems, like problems, exist in language. Any system in therapy and its members have coalesced around some problem. Thus, the assemblage of communicating persons who make up the therapy system is determined by a mutual connection, the problem.

In contrast to current social theorists, we did not believe that individuals, couples, families, and larger systems make problems. The membership of the system is not distinguished by social role or organization such as individual, couple, or family. The therapy system may or may not be marked by such boundaries. It may include, for example, an individual member of a family, parts of a family, the whole family, or people outside the family—individuals who know each other intimately or relative strangers. It may include any combination of those who have strong opinions about the problem and who are trying to solve it.

A *problem system is simply one kind of relational system,* which can be thought of as a system in which the actions of oneself or the actions of others threaten what Gergen (1994) refers to as the "delicate interdependence of constructed narratives [self-narratives and narrative accounts]" (p. 209). That is, for any number of reasons the delicate balance has been upset; now the multiplicity of narratives around the particular person or life event do not yield the necessary possibilities or resources.

A relational language systems perspective that rejects the dualism of objective and perceived reality makes a therapist a member of a problem system. Although conventional systems theories usually include a therapist in a therapy system, a therapist in these theoretical perspectives is in a position—one higher and more specialized than that of the client—that presupposes a hierarchy. Implicit in the rejection of dualism, however, is release from the notion of hierarchy. A therapist, like the other members, simply takes a place in the system. A therapist is not an outside expert.

Inclusion in the membership occurs when a therapist communicates with any member of the problem system, through a conversation with the person making the referral or the client who calls to make the appointment. Sometimes a therapist unwittingly becomes part of the system before he or she is actually involved in a conversation; a therapist may not be part of a conversation about the decision about whether to begin therapy or which therapist to see but is affected by the preconceptions of those in the system, who have their own beliefs, ideas, and expectations about therapy and the therapist in relation to the problem.

"Not Her Old Self"

As an example of this involvement, one person—a spouse, a relative, or a friend—may recommend that another see a therapist. One man anxiously talked with his family physician about his concern for his wife, whom he described as "depressed," "distant," and "not her old self." The husband thought his wife should see a therapist, so the family physician called one. The man told his wife about talking with the family physician and about the therapist who was willing to see her. When the wife went to the appointment she told the therapist that she was not enthusiastic about being there and only went to appease her husband. She warned that, regardless of what the husband had said, she was not depressed and did not need therapy. She had quite another story about the new behavior her husband described as depression: she related it to the influence that her involvement in a community action group had had on her. One can imagine that she had expectations about the therapist, who knew her only through the eyes of the husband and the family physician.

In my view, the anecdote illustrates the notion of socially constructed multiple relational selves. Each person represents not a single individual but a complex web of relationships. The different narratives of the woman were narratives of relationships. The therapist would encounter all these narratives, including the woman's narrative about the therapist. This woman, like other clients referred by someone else, might naturally believe that the therapist already had assumptions about her. In this instance, she might conclude that the therapist accepted her husband's and her physician's accounts of her and why she was there. Clients' beliefs about our assumptions can in turn influence the way they present themselves. It is important, therefore, I believe, for a therapist to behave in a manner I characterize as *incongruent with the client's expectations*. The therapist would want to show this woman that he or she is interested in learning about her from her viewpoint, not someone else's.

Membership in the Therapy System

In this collaborative approach the actors in the human drama of therapy (the target of treatment) are not established, in the beginning or at any time during the course of therapy, on the basis of theoretical modalities, social role, or such structures as individual, couple, family, and larger system. Such social roles and structures do not punctuate therapy's communicative network or dialogical exchanges. Nor is the therapy system defined by outside *objective* observers (for example, the therapist or the referring person). *The therapy system is internally defined by those participating in it.* Identification as a member of the relational system that has coalesced around a problem may mean that person will, or will not, be actively involved in the therapy. The following account illustrates how these decisions are participant-led.

"He's Got to Hear This Now!"

A woman called me urgently requesting an appointment for marital therapy "as soon as possible." She anxiously told me, "Maybe it's really divorce therapy because the marriage is over." She said that her husband was "a computer nerd who sits in front of his computer day and night. [He] doesn't even acknowledge that I exist much less have needs." She added that he was unaware of "how bad" the marriage was, and she was concerned that when he found out he would be "extremely upset," "probably suicidal."

I agreed to see the couple but tentatively wondered aloud whether the woman thought it would be useful for her to meet me first. I explained that since the situation seemed so delicate and critical in regard to her husband's possible reactions, perhaps I should first learn more about the situation and her concerns. The woman firmly said "no"; both should meet me together and her husband had already reluctantly agreed to do so: "He's got to hear this now!"

I made an appointment to see both. Given the available information, I initially imagined that the problem–therapy system would comprise me, the wife, and the husband. I did not designate the therapy in terms of social role and structure—for example, marital or couple therapy. I simply considered that I was meeting with two people who were defining something as a problem. And given the beginning definitions of the problems as presented by the wife, most likely the wife and husband would have distinct views of what the problem was, where each posited it, and what if anything had to happen in therapy.

In this example, the membership of the initial meeting was determined by the conversation between the woman and me. I did not hold the opinion that a fixed, a priori procedure determines who is invited to the first session; I respected the wife's opinion that both should meet with the therapist. I did not consider telephoning the husband to get his opinion; I took the wife's word that her husband had to and would come with her.

Friends

I always want to know with whom my clients have been talking. And frequently they have had, and are having, conversations with friends. Friends are often intimately involved in our problems and our attempts to solve them. Friends are our conversational partners: they listen; they care about us; they give us advice; they sometimes understand; they sometimes do not understand. Why do we fail to take advantage of this resource more often? Perhaps because of habits that we have developed in the way we conduct our therapy affairs or because of professional ideas about matters such as confidentiality and boundaries, we often forget or dismiss our clients' friends. To me, however, it only seems natural to include in therapy conversations those people who are significant in our clients' lives, with whom they are in conversation, and who are resources to them and to me.

It is not at all unusual for me to invite my clients' friends to join us in therapy, on a one-time or ongoing basis. The following anecdote illustrates both planned and spontaneous invitations to friends. I include only those parts of the story relevant to this discussion.

"So, What Would You Think About . . . ?"

A young single professional woman in her late twenties, Karen, called me to say that she and her mother, Alice, had "never had a good relationship" and that she had decided she had "to do something about it" because "my anger at my mother and her negativity towards me are destroying me." Karen said that her mother had agreed to enter therapy with her. Important to this discussion is that the *family* consisted of the two of them. Karen was an only child and her father had died a tragic death when Karen was four. Alice had never remarried, and for various reasons they were estranged from both the father's and the mother's family.

I met with Karen and Alice several times. Both were equally frustrated and pained and both desperately wanted a better relationship. Matters were quite entangled. Upset and through tears they talked about the problems from a variety of angles, including current clashes, the history of their relationship, what they thought contributed to it, what they each wanted the relationship to be like, and so on. They accused each other of changing the story so much that it did not remotely resemble the original. Each, of course, had a version of what the problem really was; each thought the other was at fault, did not understand her, and was not trying. Hopeless and frustrated, each soon declared the other the person who "should be in individual therapy" to deal with "her own issues" before anything could possibly change in the relationship. We discussed this idea and I agreed to have a separate meeting with each. I met twice with each.

When Karen came in for our second meeting her roommate, Jackie, was with her. Karen introduced us in the reception room, then Karen and I went into my office. I remembered that in my first meeting with Karen I had learned that she and Jackie talk quite often about Alice and that Alice and Jackie often talk about Karen. I mentioned this to Karen and asked, "So, what would you think about having Jackie join us today?" She jumped at the idea since she thought that her mother "acts like she's normal in here" and "treats me different in front of you." She thought Jackie could really tell me about her mother and how her "tone of voice just confirms the whole story."

In the meantime, when I met with Alice, I learned more about her best friend, Carl, with whom she frequently discussed her concerns about Karen and their relationship. She told me how she thought her friend was helpful because "he really *knows* Karen" and had "witnessed" her behavior. Karen had already told Alice that I met Jackie so it did not seem unusual to her when I asked what she thought about my meeting Carl. Did she think his perspective might be useful? Would she want him to be present? Did she think he would agree to come? Alice thought about it and later called to say that Carl had agreed to participate but was not sure whether he would be helpful.

After the *individual* meetings, Karen, Alice, and I continued our group sessions. Expanding our in-the-room conversations to include their friends had helped transform monologue into dialogue. Through these new conversational configurations space for new understandings, new meanings, and new hope that they could have the relationship they wanted emerged. This example about friends also points to the shifting and fluid nature of therapy conversations and membership.

Shifting and Fluid Membership

Therapy systems and the problem around which they are organized, like other human systems and their issues, are changed and reinterpreted just as often and as rapidly as other narratives around which we organize meaning and social exchange. Therapy systems, like problems, are open, fluid, and shifting; they exist only in the vagaries of discourse and language. The system and its membership are not predetermined, arbitrary, fixed, or static social structures. The system depends on who is a relevant part of communicative action at a given time. The membership changes as the talking changes and people enter and leave the conversation. It changes as the problem definitions change, as the concerns and alarms shift, as the narratives change.

It must be remembered, however, that whoever initially talks with whom, for example, does not determine who will be communicating later. Since the membership is determined conversation by conversation, by those involved in the conversations, it shifts as the conversations shift. The following account demonstrates these membership changes, which are sometimes unexpected and certainly not solely determined by the therapist or the client.

"Would You Be Willing to See Just Me?"

One afternoon a woman called me and said that she had been referred by a therapist who was her daughter's friend. She stated rather matter-of-factly that she had been married for thirty-two years, that her husband was an alcoholic and had been for most of their marriage, and that his drinking had had disastrous effects on their marriage and children. She wanted me to know, however, that her husband vehemently denied that he was an alcoholic but that her children also thought he was. Further, she said that though she thought that she and her husband really needed marital therapy, he didn't believe in therapy and had refused to consult a therapist. She had been attending Al Anon family support groups for three years and felt that that had helped her tremendously but that she needed more. She wanted to do something different with her life but did not know what to do. Given the situation and the fact that she knew that her husband would never agree to participate, she asked, "Would you be willing to see just me?" She also wanted to know whether I thought that I could help.

I told her that I hoped I could help her, but the situation sounded very complicated and I would need to learn more about her concerns. I could make no promises. We made an appointment for her to tell me her story, when we could put our heads together and decide what the next step might be. From this conversation I gathered that members of the problem system might include at least the wife, possibly the husband, the children, the daughter's friend, and, of course, me.

I was not deciding about whether I would be doing marital therapy with the couple or individual therapy with the wife or whether I should see or talk with any other members of the problem system. I had no specific plans for the session. For example, I did not think that perhaps if I saw the wife I could learn more about the husband and somehow entice him to enter couple therapy. I thought only about the first appointment, whose membership had been determined in our conversation.

To my surprise the next morning the husband called and said that he had his wife on the telephone line also. He angrily and loudly told me that he knew that his wife had an appointment with me and that she would come in and tell me what an "awful, son-of-a-bitch husband I am" and that "I'm an alcoholic." He said, "I know you'll believe every damn thing she says."

"In spite of what she might tell you," he continued, "the idea that I'm an alcoholic is totally absurd. I am not, never was, and never will be an alcoholic." He went on to tell me that he had "a very responsible job," "never missed a day's work," and "did not have martinis at lunch." The problem, he said, was that his wife was "going through the change of life." He then said that he wanted to tell me "his side of the story" and wanted me, he emphasized, to "hear and remember both of our views." She said, "Yes, come."

These conversations illustrate how the membership can change even before the first session. I talked briefly with them together and then we agreed I should spend the rest of the time with the husband. After talking with the husband, I invited the wife back in to discuss whether we should meet again, and if so, who should participate. In this particular case, most of the remaining sessions were with the wife and I occasionally touched base with the husband, who would drive her to the appointments and wait in the car. Once when I was curious about a fight they had just had, I asked her whether she would mind if I asked him to come inside. It was okay with her but she doubted that he would because he was "mad as a dog." So, I went out to the car and asked him in. He agreed.

We know that therapy system membership cannot be predicted by the first session's membership. Each session determines who participates in the next. Each therapy conversation is a platform for and influences the next. The participants in the conversation mutually decide who should attend the next session and when it should occur. In this way of working, a therapy system has no predetermined membership (for example, the couple) and does not meet at predetermined times (for example, weekly at 9:00 A.M. on Tuesdays). Perhaps this is a distinguishing feature. The next account further demonstrates how each conversation informs the membership of the next.

"We're Worried"

A mother called me and said that her family had been referred for therapy by her son's juvenile probation officer. She did not think that the family needed therapy: the boy was the focus of the parents' concern. They felt that something was bothering him and that neither they nor the probation officer had been able to get him to talk about it.

"We're worried," she said, "because he spends all of his time alone in his room or in the woods behind our house." The mother continued: "He's basically a good kid. If you could just find out what it is and talk with him about it, I think that he'll be okay." She also told me that several disappointing things had happened to the son lately, including not making the basketball team and being dumped by his girlfriend.

I acknowledged the mother's concern about her son's recent behaviors and said that it certainly appeared that something was bothering him. Given that neither the parents nor the probation officer had been able to get the son to talk with them, I thought it might be best to meet with only the parents first. That way I could learn more about the son and the parents' concerns, not only to try to relate to the son but most important, to prevent doing anything that would close the door further. The mother thought that this sounded reasonable and believed that her husband would agree. If, however, the mother or father had insisted that I see the son, I would have agreed; the appointment with the parents was simply the *first* appointment. That conversation and those involved in it would then determine the membership of the next appointment.

I did not immediately decide that I would be doing family therapy nor that the problem system would include the family members and the probation officer. The mother told me that she was not sure why the probation officer wanted them to have family therapy. I asked the mother to tell me a little about the circumstances of her son's contact with the probation officer. At the end of the conversation, the mother and I decided together that I would talk with the probation officer on the telephone.

In talking with the probation officer, I learned that no charges had been filed and that the referral was "preventive." The parents, the probation officer thought, needed to supervise their son more closely. The officer said that he would not be involved further with the youth or his parents. He, therefore, was leaving the system; had he remained involved in the case, I would have considered him a part of the problem system. Even then, I would not have automatically included the officer in the therapy sessions or might or might not have talked with him in the future by telephone. Decisions about telephone contact and inclusion in sessions of the referring person or other appropriate professionals (as well as family members) are influenced by the members' ideas about who is in relevant and meaningful communication about the problem, and that assessment can change before therapy begins, as in this case, or during the course of therapy.

Problem Systems or Solution Systems

Colleagues and critics often ask why I refer to *problem* systems rather than to *solution* systems. The question alludes in part to the perceived negative connotation of *problem*. The question also alludes to the often perceived fear and heartfelt risk of participation in reifying the problem or drowning in what some people have referred to as problem talk. Unfortunately, *problem* in our therapy culture has a fixed connotation and is conceptualized as something that requires a solution. *Solution* has the connotation of fixing. I believe that a therapist or therapy neither *solves* problems nor fixes anything. In my experience, that does not happen; rather, problem exploration in the therapy process leads to problem dissolution, not problem solution. Problems are not solved but dissolved in language. In my view, the process through which you talk about something, not its content (for instance, problems or solutions), is the significant factor.

This notion of problem dis-solution is similar to Wittgenstein's view of the aim of a philosophy in relation to the problems it poses to address. His view is aptly captured by Shotter (1994):

> The philosopher's treatment of a question is like the treatment of an illness–where the aim of the treatment is, not so much to *solve* problems, as to dissolve them, to make them "*completely* disappear . . . [to give] philosophy peace, so that it is no longer tormented by questions which bring *itself* in question." (Wittgenstein as cited in Shotter, 1994, p. 11)

With the dissolution of the problem comes the dissolution of the therapy system, the problem system. That is, the systems that coalesced around the problem dissipate. A new system, a new structure, emerges. The members of the new system may or may not be the same. If the problem system included the family, that is not to say that the family dissolved but simply that the problem system dissolved. The problem system and the family are not synonymous, even though each may contain the same people. For instance, the family may still comprise the same four members, but the relationships are different, the narratives are different or have different meanings, and therefore the system is different.

There is little talk about problems in the literature on postmodernism; the focus is on the meaning of what is talked about. Shotter (1993a), for instance, proposes that the difference between what may be considered a problematic or nonproblematic situation is a difference in a *way of being*. It is a question of "not what *to do* but what *to be*" (p. 118); that is, "how he or she is trying to 'place,' 'position,' or 'situate' themselves in relation to the others around them" (p. 122). Shotter is indicating how through language we may move to new "positions" in relation to our own storytelling, and thus to new self-narratives or biographies (p. 130). Conceptualizing therapy systems as language systems whose membership is fluid and mutually determined, rather than as social systems with a priori fixed therapist–theory determined membership, moves both client and therapist into less confining spaces. Let us now turn to the process that occurs within those spaces.

CHAPTER 5

A Philosophical Stance: Therapists' Position, Expertise, and Responsibility

You can't help anyone unless you risk yourself.

—CARL ROGERS

MOST THEORIES OF therapy assert a therapist to be an objective, neutral, and technical expert who is knowledgeable about pathology and normalcy and who can read the inner world of a person like a text. Knowledge and expertise inform a therapist's diagnoses, strategies, and goals. The interest and responsibility are to produce change, through influencing and knowing what change should look like. Implicit in such theories is a relationship between an expert and a nonexpert, an assumption that one person can change another, or at least influence him or her to change. Inherent is an inequality between client and therapist. A therapy informed by a postmodern ideology such as a collaborative language systems approach offers profound alternatives to such a therapist position. What are these alternatives? How is a therapist positioned in relation to, and in relationship with, a client? What is a therapist's intention? What are a therapist's role, expertise, and responsibility?

In my approach to therapy, a therapist's main interest and intention are to establish a dialogical occasion—and through dialogue to create the opportunity for self-agency, freedom, and possibilities that are unique to a client and his or her situation, and in which a client has participated in the invention and enhancement. Such transformations in therapy are represented by, and are inherent consequences of, the dialogical creation of new narrative. In other words, as dialogue unfolds, change occurs.[1]

This view of change or transformation influences and requires that we position ourselves with our clients in a different manner. This altered position is what I refer to as a *philosophical stance*—a *way of being* in relationship with our fellow human beings, including how we think about, talk with, act with, and respond to them (Anderson, 1995). It reflects an attitude and tone that serve as the backdrop for my relationships with clients and the therapy process, how I locate myself in a conversation. It is an authentic, natural, spontaneous, and sustained position that is unique to each relationship and to each discourse. It brings the *person* of both client and therapist back into the therapy room. And it shifts away from thinking in terms of our roles and functions as therapists to considering our *relationships* with the people we work with. The philosophical stance distinguishes a therapist's position, expertise, and responsibility in this approach to therapy from others.

I choose to designate a therapist's position as a *philosophical stance* because it represents and encourages a way of looking at and experiencing the world from within my professional and personal lives. The values and biases that we hold—our philosophy of life—influence the way we position ourselves with, or the stance we assume with, other people. It is a metaphorical position in which our social and personal attributes are convened, and it becomes "part of our discursive construction of personal stories that make a person's actions intelligible and relatively determinate as social actions" (Hermans, 1995, p. 376). A therapist becomes a resource for a way of being.

What are the characteristics and practical perspectives of the stance? How does it reveal itself in the therapy domain? How does it enable a therapist to participate in a joint performance? How does it encourage a generative process and promote a therapy that is characterized by connecting, collaborating, and constructing?

CHARACTERISTICS OF A PHILOSOPHICAL STANCE

Conversational Partners: Shared Client and Therapist Expertise or What Client and Therapist Bring

The focus of a collaborative approach is on a relational system and process in which client and therapist become conversational partners in the telling, inquiring, interpreting, and shaping of the narratives. In this approach the expertise of client and therapist combine and merge. But what expertise does each contribute?

A client brings expertise in the area of content: a client is the expert on his or her life experiences and what has brought that client into the therapy relationship. When clients are narrators of their stories, they are able to experience and recognize their own voices, power, and authority. A therapist brings expertise in the area of process: a therapist is the expert in engaging and participating with a client in a dialogical process of first-person storytelling. It is as if the roles of therapist and client were reversed: *The client becomes the teacher.*[2] A therapist takes more of an "I am here to learn about you from you" stance. As one young client said to her student therapist when the therapist stumbled, made mistakes, misunderstood, and did not know, "When you are as famous as Freud, you will have to tell them that I was your teacher."

A Creator and Facilitator of Dialogue Space and Process

In the collaborative process, a therapist is merely one of multiple authors of yet-to-be-told—shifting and emerging—narratives. Participation is more that of a consultant author who is a facilitator—an inquiring other—than of an instrumental, interventionist participant.[3] A facilitative position promotes a process that keeps all voices in motion and contributing. Central to this therapist stance is a therapist's honest and sincere capacity to be receptive to, invite, respect, hear, and be engaged in a client's story. A therapist wants each person in the conversation to feel that his or her version is as important as any other. It is a position of *multipartiality,*[4] one in which a therapist takes all sides simultaneously. This is in contrast to neutrality, in which a therapist strives not to take any one person's side. In my experience, such neutrality usually leads the people we work with to wonder, to suspect, and sometimes to feel assured of whose side we are on and which version we believe.

When this happens people can easily plunge into competing efforts to lure a therapist to their sides.

What a Collaborative Therapist Is Not

I am frequently asked, "At what point does not being 'the expert' become passiveness?" and "Is an 'inquiring other' enough?" Such questions are based on the modernist scientific notion of inquiry and validity in which examining truth and achieving knowledge are fundamental. Such questions point to the importance, from my perspective, of what a therapist is not.

A therapist is not a narrative editor. When a therapist is a content expert—a knower of the human story and how it ought to be told or formed and retold or re-formed—he or she implicitly takes the role of a narrative expert whose function is to edit—to guide or revise a client's story. The usual task is to get a client to tell his or her own story (as if there is a story to be told) with the goal of resolving the dilemma posed by a client's narrative, thereby changing that narrative. A therapist might accomplish this, for example, by modifying, reassembling, and shaping a client's story to be more useful from the therapist's viewpoint. Or a therapist might provide deconstructive insight into the narrative language so that present solutions are reinforced or new ones can emerge. In my view, such attempts at modifying a client's narrative take the form of narrative editing—revising, correcting, or polishing. A therapist's task is not to deconstruct, reproduce, or reconstruct a client's story but to facilitate and participate in its telling and retelling.

Narrative editing is a slippery slope. A narrative editor position requires the technical expertise to edit. This entails certain risks: it implies the assumption that a therapist has more credibility as a master of human stories than a client. It assumes that a therapist can read a client like a text. It makes a therapist an archaeological narrativist who believes there is *a* story, with an imagined significance, that needs to be uncovered or retold. It risks being guided by the notion that there are universal human stories and that there are no new ones to hear. It risks translating the language and metaphor of a client's first-person narrative into professional, technical language and its assumed beliefs about human nature.

Care must be taken. If we believe that we are part of an interactive circle, we must act congruently with that belief. A narrative editor position, and its associated risks, essentially disregards a client as part of the circle of meaning and makes the construction of meaning take place in a universal sphere rather than a local one. It leaves out, for instance, the single black mother whose son pulled a gun on a fellow student. When a therapist takes a narrative editing position, there is no room for this mother; she does not belong; it is not her story. In turn, the mother's assumptions and fears that her situation could not be understood or helped would be validated. And more important, a narrative editor is a dominant role in which a therapist is in a hierarchical and dualistic position in relation to a client. Inherent is the risk of marginalizing the mother's first-person story and favoring the dominant social discourse. Even therapists who purport to fight certain dominant social discourses inadvertently and paradoxically marginalize a client when they assume their counternarrative (for example, social injustice, gender inequality, institutional colonization) is better for a client.

A therapist is not a tabula rasa or blank screen. Like those we are in conversation with, we take our knowledge, prior experiences, and biases—our preunderstandings (Gadamer, 1975, 1988; Heidegger, 1962) into the therapy arena. We should try, however, to carry them without prejudice, for instance, without a preconceived plan about how a client should approach a problem's resolution. Instead, we should trust this to develop through the conversations.

A therapist is not a negotiator or referee of differences.[5] Nor does a therapist seek to confront or point out differences. The aim is not to strive for synthesis or consensus. Instead, a therapist encourages multiple verses.

A therapist is not a detective who discovers the truth, or what is true or truer, false or falser. A therapist does not search for hidden realities, intentions, and meanings. A therapist is not a unilateral and dominant inquirer, an expert problem definer and solver, an authority on pathology and normalcy. A therapist is not a describer, an explainer, or an interpreter of actions. A therapist is a conversational partner.

A therapist is not an intervenor nor is a therapist passive. I want to emphasize that it is not a mechanical, interventionist preknown way of being. Guided by a client, a therapist, as Gadamer suggested, is only "a part of a circular interactive system" (Gadamer, 1975, p. 361), only part of, not a steerer of, a system of mutual influence. A therapist does not control the conversation, for instance, by setting its agenda or moving it in a particular direction of content or outcome, nor is a therapist responsible for the direction of change. The goal is not to take charge or intervene. The goal is to facilitate dialogue, and through dialogue, create optimal opportunity for newness in meanings, narratives, behaviors, feelings, and emotions. A therapist aims to encourage internal dialogue (silent self-conversation with oneself or an imagined other) and external dialogue (out loud conversation with an other). A noninterventionist, nonhierarchical position does not equal passiveness nor innocence. It does not mean that anything goes, that a therapist is adrift, or that a therapist is not influential. In this stance a therapist is active but not directive. A therapist is always influencing a client; likewise, a client is always influencing a therapist.

A "Way of Being" Versus a "System for Doing"

Therapy, in this view, allows for the development and use of a therapist's own personal style. Each therapist will translate this philosophy of therapy and the associated stance to the therapy relationship in his or her own way, one that is natural and unique to the personhood of a therapist and all that each therapist carries with him or her. Each therapist's translation is highly individual and is unique to every therapy situation—the individuals involved, the conversation's relevance, and the conversation's context. In other words, a therapist's talk and behavior will be different from client to client and from session to session; it will be distinctive to the therapist and situation. This "doing-what-the-occasion-calls-for" requires resiliency. It entails the ability, flexibility, and willingness to allow shifts in thinking and behavior to flow with what the situation demands. Lynn Hoffman (personal communication, October 1994) once referred to the adaptability and changeability associated with the philosophical stance as being "poised for action."

The uncertainty that results when a therapist's talk, action, and thought are informed on a moment-by-moment basis, and therefore not known ahead of time, is often unsettling because in the Western world we are accustomed to the certainty of recipelike informed behaviors. We are used to identifying and seeing a therapist's forestructure in action. When we do not see what we expect to see, it is difficult to imagine what a therapist is or will be doing. This is partially why at times when others observe a therapist working from the collaborative approach they may not be able to see anything different than what they expected to see. I do not suggest, however, that it is impossible to observe a therapist or several therapists over time and find similarities and patterns. As research demonstrates, we tend to observe what we believe in and find what we are looking for (Jones, 1986; Rosenhan, 1973; Scarr, 1985). This also applies to the research itself.

Toward illuminating the philosophical stance concept for my students and visiting colleagues, I often have them spend time with several therapists whose practices are informed by a collaborative stance. I want them to experience that although the same assumptions inform each therapist's practice, there are differences among us and from circumstance to circumstance. I want them to appreciate the particular resources that each situation requires, to understand that they can express their personality and style in their work (that need not and should not emulate mine or anyone else's) and can be their most imaginative and creative selves. We shrink the parameters in which we can think or act, and thus limit our—and consequently others'—creativity and options when we try to duplicate another's style.

A Guest

I consider myself a guest, albeit a temporary one, who visits clients for a brief moment, who participates with them in a small slice of their life, and who floats in and out of the continuous and changing conversations they are having with others. I want to be a tolerable guest. The psychiatrist Sue Chance (1987) similarly compares her relationship with her patients to that of a dinner guest as she talks about saying "good-byes."

> My comings and goings aren't meant to be the centerpiece of my patients' lives. I am a dinner guest. I'm there because I was invited. There is an etiquette. Perhaps I teach them manners. Perhaps I share some recipes. Perhaps I bring a dish they've never tried. However, I don't live in their homes. They do.
>
> The same goes for my friends. It behooves me to be gracious. When I say good-bye, I hope I do it thoughtfully. I hope they know how much I appreciated the invitation, how much I enjoyed their company. I hope I leave something of me. I know I take something of them. (p. 21)

As she continues she talks about the kinds of conversations that make a difference, those that stay with her, those that clients take out of the therapy room.

> I've had my own dinner guests. And, I know which ones were insincere. And, I know which ones were rude. Eventually, I forget they were ever there. The companionable ones stay in my mem-

ory. I recall the conversation. I recall the pleasure of sharing my table with them. Sometimes I look at the chair where they sat and I can almost see them. I can certainly feel their presence. I remember wistfully watching them go and knowing it was in the inherences of things that they should. (p. 21)

I have heard clients say similar things. Lars, a client reflecting on his conversation with Harry Goolishian, said, "I see him every so often in front me saying that." Another client, Alice, who years after therapy in high school and college happened to meet her therapist, Harry Goolishian, described her experience of him and their conversations like this:

When I was in high school I needed to talk to you every week. I was so fearful of going off to college, that I couldn't make it. I couldn't imagine what I would do if I could only see you once a month when I came home. You know what I did. I carried you around with me in my head. When I needed to I would ask myself, "What would Dr. Goolishian say?" or "What question would Dr. Goolishian ask me?" and you would tell me. Then when I graduated from college and moved east, you went with me. One day I realized that I didn't need to carry you around with me because I really didn't need to talk to you anymore. I could talk to myself. But every now and then when I would need you, I would invite you into my head like you invite an old friend over to dinner.

Therapist Change: A Risky "Learner" Position

A therapist who assumes this kind of philosophical stance and is involved in this kind of dialogical process also risks changing. In a mutually influential therapy process in which change is a natural consequence of dialogue, a therapist, like a client, will be subject to that change. It seems illogical to presume otherwise, to think that we could be involved in a transformative process and not be transformed ourselves. As one student said, "I've got it. If I can't possibly change my thoughts about something, how can I expect my client to." This means that we may change an idea or opinion about a problem, a person, or a situation. This means that we may change a behavior. A more sobering thought, however, is that this means that our ethics of practice, deeply held morals, and cherished values will surface, be exposed to challenge, and also change. I believe that this is partially what unleashes our creativity and propels us on a journey of lifelong learning and personal growth. We can be proactive in this journey if we think about and operationalize the notion of research-and-learning-as-part-of-everyday-practice.

Research and Learning as Part of Everyday Practice

Postmodernism as an ideology critique, and thus a philosophical stance, requires and enables me continually to be aware of, leave open to question, and reflect on what I know or think I know. This awareness, openness, and reflection combine to become a research-and-learning-as-part-of-everyday-practice process through which I am being transformed as a professional and a private person. How and what I learn is a fluid, interactive, and socially constructed process. It involves multiple, mutual reflecting conversations with myself, clients, colleagues, students, and others. These reflections become part of a generative learning process that is broader than simply learning a client's story and broader than the therapy experience itself. Being, defining oneself as, and developing as a therapist is a process. Interestingly, this brings us back full-circle to the "self-as-process."

Schön (1983) offers an invaluable perspective on professional knowledge and research as part of everyday practice in *The Reflective Practitioner: How Professionals Think in Action*. He challenges professionals who do not reflect on their practice—who do not reflect on their thoughts and actions.

> Many practitioners, locked into a view of themselves as technical experts, find nothing in the world of practice to occasion reflection. They have become too skillful at techniques of selective inattention, junk categories, and situational control, techniques which they use to preserve the constancy of their knowledge-in-practice. For them, uncertainty is a threat; its admission is a sign of weakness. (p. 69)

In this circumstance, technique takes precedence over person.

I agree with Schön that institutional and professional bureaucracy mandates and reinforces technical expertise and knowledge, and the assumption that a professional is autonomous and isolated (pp. 326–338). Opportunities for innovation, collaboration, and adaptation to changing environments are lost. Schön urges that professionals instead recognize that their expertise is embedded within a context of meanings, and that their actions may have different meanings for different people (p. 295). To circumvent technique takeover and isolated practice, or what I think of as "automatic pilot" expertise, he argues for "knowing-in-action" (p. 49) or "reflection-in-action" (p. 126)—we should not only reflect in action, but reflect on our reflecting-in-action. Reflection and reflections about reflections in action are about connecting, collaborating, and constructing, and in my view, signify a postmodern form of knowing. It is a continuing self-education experience in which the practice of therapy itself is, in Schön's (1983) words, a "source of renewal" (p. 299) for a therapist as well. This source (along with a not-knowing posture) is, I believe, a critical distinction between those professionals, in this case therapists, who get bored or burned out by their work and those who do not.

It is important here to mention Tom Andersen's (1995a, 1996) expansion of his reflecting team practice to the evaluation of clinical work, which beautifully exemplifies the notion of research as part of everyday practice. With Andersen's encouragement and consultation, several therapy teams and clinicians have invited their clients and community colleagues to not only help them evaluate their practices but also to take part as coresearchers. Clients and community colleagues participate in designing the evaluation, including the questions to be asked. They ask, for example, "What questions do you (the client or colleague) think we should be asking you?" and "What kind of information would be helpful to you?" (Kjellberg, Edwardsson, Niemela, & Oberg, 1995; Kjellberg et al., 1996).

They have found that this collaborative and inclusive approach to research has enhanced professional–professional and client–professional relationships. Most significant and with far-reaching implications, this collaborative approach brings the practitioners to the forefront of research and challenges the convention of research performed by "outsiders" in the academy. Evaluation and research performed by "insiders" become a learning opportunity for practitioners and useful in their future practice. It is a prospective dialogical process that, in Gergen's words, "presses the dialogue forward" and a collaborative one that, in Shotter's words, creates a "conversation in which people feel they belong."

Being Public

Related to reflecting (and to sharing one's work in general) is the notion of being public—more readily revealing, more readily sharing out loud my private inner dialogues and monologues: my thoughts, prejudices, wonderings, speculations, questions, opinions, and fears. And, in doing so, opening myself to feedback, evaluation, and critique. Consequently, I expose myself more as a person to all those with whom I work. I choose to use the word *public* rather than *transparent,* a word sometimes associated with a feminist critique, because I do not think that another person can see through us or we through him or her. Rather, we can see only what we each choose to show the other.

This public stance contrasts with the more usual private or secret aspect of a professional's role. The professional who is "ordinarily expected to play the role of expert," according to Schön (1983), is

> now expected from time to time to reveal his uncertainties. Whereas he is ordinarily expected to keep his expertise private and mysterious, he is now expected to reflect publicly on his knowledge-in-practice, and about himself . . . and open his special knowledge to public inquiry. (pp. 297–299)

Reflecting can encourage and assure the emergence of a therapist's multiple voices or perspectives. A therapist, like a client, can have many thoughts, some compatible, some opposing. The Dutch psychologist Hermans (1995), who has an interest in the dialogical nature of the self, likens this to the polyphonic voices in Fyodor Dostoyevsky novels.[6] In his books, Dostoyevsky is only one of many characters: "Instead of being 'obedient slaves' in the service of Dostoyevsky's intentions, the different characters are capable of standing beside their creator, disagreeing with the author, even rebelling against him" (p. 377).

Reflecting and showing myself to the other permit me and the other to have more flexibility in dealing with the only natural, multiple, and sometimes conflicting opinions about the complex predicaments clients present. They allow me to have or assert a strong opinion and to participate in controversial situations without polarizing or freezing positions. Everything said is provisional grist for the mill.

From a postmodern perspective, a professional is

> advocating and acting on their [e.g., a therapist's] own views of reality while at the same time subjecting them to reflection, of taking an adversarial stance toward their opponents' [e.g., a client's] view while at the same time striving to understand them. (Schön, 1983, p. 350)

Being public is not limited to professional information but includes the personal. Here I am not talking about what might be called self-disclosing or violating boundaries in the sense of sharing personal secrecies or intimacies, although I am not as hesitant about or opposed to letting others know about me as some therapists may be. Our clients are naturally curious about us; why shouldn't they be? Remember Sabrina's "I don't know anything about you"? And how later she said she wondered [referring to her therapist], "Is she married? What kind of relationship does she have?" Then at the end of the session she asked.

Another client that I interviewed about her experiences with three different therapists said, "Isn't it funny that you're supposed to trust your therapist but you really don't know anything about them. It's like you stand there always naked in front of someone who's always fully clothed. It would just be nice to know a little about who the therapist is."

In this vein, at the end of a session I give a client, and any others present, the opportunity to ask me questions. In a typical instance I told a client, "I have been asking you a lot of questions, so I'm wondering if you have any questions you would like to ask me?"

"I'm a bit curious about what you do in Texas," he replied.

I told him some about what I do and my interest in learning more about people like him and the kinds of struggles they have, ending with "Okay?"

He said, "That's very interesting."

"Anything else you want to know?" I asked.

He simply replied, "I think that's okay. I see this as a possibility to learn more about myself and to see what's happening around me."

To position oneself more openly and reflectively with clients requires, in Schön's (1983) words, that "in order to broaden and deepen their capacity for reflection-in-action, professional practitioners must discover and restructure the interpersonal theories of action which they bring to their professional lives" (p. 353). I would add, "And which they bring to their personal lives." Some theories do not allow for reflecting of this nature; it would be an inherent contradiction. Open, public reflections, for instance, might be considered nonempirical, might be thought to violate principles of confidentiality, to cross boundaries, to be unethical, or might be considered too relativistic. More important, they might threaten the comfort and certainty of knowing and expertise and thus the very existence of the theory itself.

Shared Responsibility and Accountability

Responsibility and accountability are cultural ideals and values. We want people to take responsibility and be accountable to and for themselves and others. We sometimes, however, do not create contexts and relationships that allow or encourage it. To the contrary, we create ones that take it away. We are trained to participate in *unequal* conversations. We are trained to take responsibility away from the client. We are trained to be experts, for instance, in how other people ought to live their lives, what a good narrative is, or what change would be most effective.

In my experience, when a therapist invites and allows a client to collaborate, responsibility becomes shared. Often people mistake therapists who work collaboratively as naively abdicating therapist responsibility; this is not the case. When a therapist takes this reflective philosophical stance, the dualism and hierarchy between a client and a therapist collapse and responsibility and accountability are shared. In fact, I find that in shared responsibility and accountability a therapist becomes even more responsible and accountable to a client.

Some social constructionists confront the issue of moral responsibility. Shotter (1974, 1975, 1990, 1995a) argues and pleads for increased and shared responsibility and accountability. He wants "to reconstruct psychology as a moral science of action (and agency) rather than a natural science of behavior (and mechanism)" (1995a, p. 385).[7] Shotter's (1995a) bottom line is that "claims to one's own unique, special 'inner experiences' [what we think we know] cut no ice in the world at large unless one can render them in some way accountable to others" (p. 386). Similarly, the analytic philosopher Alasdair MacIntyre points to social constructionism's moral responsibility as taking people's lives away from the control of experts, and placing

> responsibility for their own forms of life back into the hands of the people in relation to each other—where the task now is to identify those moments and situations in which people might confront each other as ethical beings. (Cited in Shotter, 1995a, p. 387)

Others make the same challenge. The psychologist Mark Freeman (1995) asserts, "There aren't many psychologists for whom the freedom and responsibility issue is even salient; generally speaking, the presumptions of the discipline won't allow for it" (p. 357). He differentiates between moral responsibility as "responsibility

for our own actions" (p. 358) and "responsibility *to* others, especially to those whose rights have been eclipsed or who suffer need-
lessly" (p. 358). Some feminist philosophers and psychologists and
women's studies theorists (Code, 1988; M. Gergen, 1995; Hughes,
1988) who hold the self as relational also highlight the notion of
responsibility: Mary Gergen (1995) warns, "This move to relational
selves does not eradicate the language of moral choice and action
. . . [but] suggests the need for revisioning what constitutes moral
action through the lens of pluralism" (p. 366). Lorraine Code (1988)
calls for responsible knowledge; Judith Jordan (1991) argues for
mutuality of responsibility.

Kenneth Gergen and the communications researcher Sheila
McNamee (1994) suggest that the goal of exploring relational
responsibility is neither to change one or another defective person
nor to resolve conflict. Rather, it is to expand the range of relevant
voices ("relational realities") admitted into the conversation. Being
more responsible and accountable is part of what enables a therapist to be more public, open, and forthcoming.

"But, You're the Expert"

Therapists often fear that clients expect certainty, pay an expert for
answers, and will not accept a therapist who takes this philosophical stance and invites collaboration. In my experience, this need
not be a concern; I find that it is not difficult for clients to join in
this kind of collaborative culture. As Shotter's "sense of belonging"
suggests, clients welcome it and want it. As the words of the
Swedish mother of the two anorectic daughters doggedly suggest,
clients often plead for it: "But we know our daughters more than
any other person. We know their reactions and their feelings . . . we
know when they can be trusted better than any [prejudiced] nurse
or doctor."

It is unfortunate when therapy reaches the point where clients
such as the members of this family experience experts as thinking
they know them better than they know themselves and each other
and when the experts' knowing yields suspicious descriptions and
pejorative treatments. Professionals then participate in creating
what they see. That is, if a person, for instance, is heard and treated
with suspicion, most likely all his or her subsequent behavior will
be viewed this way, or he or she may actually start to act in ways
that warrant suspicion. There can be considerable difference, for
instance, between the way a therapist who believes a father

molested his daughter and seeks to verify it treats him and the way a therapist who wants to be in dialogue with the father treats him.

Skepticism about a client's willingness and ability to participate collaboratively has more to do with our own expectations and our own uneasiness with uncertainty than with a client. This does not mean that I ignore that clients sometimes say, "Tell me what to do." Of course, some do. When this occurs, I respect their wishes and take them seriously. I do not assume, however, that I know what they what; nor do I ignore their request and expect them blindly to trust me. I respond to each request, and each response depends on the conversational context of the request.

On Purpose

Keep in mind that the philosophical stance is part of an overall way of being that shows itself, and that a client experiences, from the first point of client–therapist contact. The stage for collaboration is set in the initial contact and must be attended to throughout the relationship. The stance is not a technique or a theory. It is not manipulative, strategic, nor contrived, as thinking about it cognitively might suggest. It is not deliberate in the sense of being acted; however, it is intentional.[8] I purposely want to be open, genuine, appreciative, respectful, inviting, and curious—all important characteristics of being in a therapy relationship that is mutual, collaborative, cooperative, and egalitarian. I purposefully choose to be this way because I value it.

Assuming such a philosophical stance enables me to join a client in a collaborative relationship and dialogical process. Because it is a way of being, it frees me to work in a variety of settings (teaching, organization consultation) without regard to persons involved (graduate students, executives), agenda (learning, team building), or type of dilemma (stuck case, supervisor–supervisee conflict).

How does the philosophical stance look in action? How does this conceptualization serve to inform and form a collaborative therapy process and system? What does a therapist do as the process expert? First, I address these practicalities by looking at the therapy process; then I turn to the voices and words of clients and fictional characters for illustration and advice.

CHAPTER 6

Therapy as
Dialogical Conversation

*Dialogue . . . is precisely that which liberates us from the author-
itarian claims of those-who-are-in-the-know.*
—G. B. MADISON

*The dialogic mind may collapse when attempting a dialogic
dance with monologic reason.*
—STEIN BRATEN

THE TRANSFORMATIVE NATURE
OF DIALOGICAL CONVERSATION

I HAVE A LONG-TIME interest in understanding and creating a backdrop on which to capture the nature and essence of the therapy
conversations and conversations about therapy in which I find
myself involved. I believe that conversation is the most important
vehicle for the construction of meaning; however, I have experienced that new meaning does not emerge from all conversations. I

have wondered, What is peculiar about a conversation that has the potential to allow new meaning to develop? I challenge my students to think of the times in their lives when talking with someone helped them see a situation in a different light, seeded a new idea, or gave them a sense of freedom or hope; how did they differ from other times that were not helpful?

All human behavior, from a postmodern view, is intentional and situated in a sociohistorical reality that is produced, reproduced, and changed by the language through which we are able to know it. We are not simple passive recipients of internal demands of psychic or biological structure, nor are we simple results of external constraints of context or feedback. Human systems, singularly or plurally, are not reified mechanical structures. We are intentional agents who create ourselves and our environments in continuous communicative interaction with others. This continuous evolution of meaning and reality is based in dialogue and symbolic interaction. All social action can be conceived as the result of a system of acting individuals who coordinate—fit and link—behavior to themselves and to one another through interpretative processes and narrative constructions. We live storied lives with one another.

Conversation in this postmodern interpretative and narrative perspective is a linguistic phenomenon: a meaning-generating process. Its transformational nature[1] rests in the dialogical nature of the conversation and its capacity to re-relate the events of our lives in the context of new and different meaning. Through conversation meaning that is unique and appropriate to the situation and the people involved in it develops. That is, change emerges in and through the redescriptions that result from the telling and retelling of familiar stories. In the telling and retelling not only do new stories emerge, but a person changes in relationship to them: the narrating self changes.

Therapy is characterized by conversation/dialogue between (out loud) and within (silent) a client and a therapist. I refer to the process of therapy as a *dialogical conversation*; dialogical conversation is a generative process in which new meanings—different ways of understanding, making sense of, or punctuating one's lived experiences—emerge and are mutually constructed. In turn, the therapy conversation (connected with and informed by conversations outside the therapy room, and vice versa) and the newness that results from it lead to self-agency and problem dissolution.

Therapy Conversations and Change

Therapy relies on finding new ways to dialogue about those parts of clients' stories, that is, their lives, that concern or alarm them. The aim is not to discover knowledge or information, but to create new meaning and understanding mutually. Successful therapy for me is the unfolding of constructed history and autobiography through the coexploration of familiar, told stories and the cocreation of new, yet-to-be-told stories (Anderson & Goolishian, 1988b, 1990a; Goolishian & Anderson, 1987a). These evolving and cocreated personal narratives of identity allow new direction in meaning, new history, new dialogue, and therefore a new future. Toward this end, a conversation must permit a *transformation of the narrating self* of the client. In Shotter's (1994) words,

> therapy consists in us gaining access to a language within which we can account to ourselves for ourselves. . . . "Therapy" of this kind is never over; there are always further "connections" between elements of our past that future projects will reveal as unknown to us. But it is how people recollect their past as a result of their need to act "into" an interest in the future, thus to "reshape" what has been—not how they must act "out of" a fixed past—that is crucial, not just in personal psychotherapy, but in us curing what Wittgenstein saw as a sickness of our time. Where, as he saw it, an aspect of that sickness lies in our incapacity for wonder, . . . our incapacity to recognize that the strange, the unique, the novel, the unknown and the extraordinary lies hidden within our everyday mundane activity. (pp. 11–12)

In such a therapy conversation, in such an interpretive process whose natural, spontaneous consequence is change, both client and therapist risk change. Both client and therapist risk a transformation of self. In other words, it would be impossible for a therapist not to change. As Lorriane Code (1988) proposed, "In genuine dialogue, as contrasted both with polite conversation and with adversarial confrontation, both of the participants are changed" (p. 188).

What exactly then is a dialogical conversation? What is its transformative essence? How does this kind of therapy conversation differ from one in which no newness evolves? How does a person, a narrating self, change in relation to a story? What does having a dialogical conversation with another person or with oneself look like or feel like? What is the difference, if any, between a conversation with a friend and one with a therapist? What was it about Sabrina's conversations with Jane that was so helpful? First, let's turn to the notion of conversation in general: What is a conversation?

CONVERSATION

Conversation is more than simply talking. In its fullest sense it can be thought of as the very essence of our existence. For Rom Harré, "The primary human reality is person in conversation" (1983, p. 58). Similarly, for Shotter (1993a),

> Life by its very nature is dialogic. To live means to participate in dialogue: to ask questions, to heed, to respond, to agree, and so forth. . . . Those denied this possibility can, to say the least, be expected to feel humiliated and angered. (p. 62)

A single definition of conversation is impossible because a conversation does not exist as a thing itself (Searle, 1992). Each conversation occurs and is formed on a moment-by-moment basis and is peculiar to its context, participants, and circumstances. I do, however, identify characteristics basic to all conversations:

1. All participants enter a conversation with a framework that includes what they bring from their everyday lives, for instance, self-identity.
2. Each conversation occurs within a context, for instance, local (more immediate interpersonal) or universal (cultural, social, historical).
3. Each conversation is embedded within and will become a part of, will be influenced by and will influence, myriad other past and future conversations—no conversation is a single event.
4. Each conversation has a purpose, expectations, and intentions that all participants contribute.
5. Each outer, spoken conversation between participants involves inner, silent conversations within the participants.

Although these characteristics apply to several kinds of conversations, to understand the transformative potential of conversation in general and therapy conversation in particular, I find it useful to distinguish between only two kinds of conversations: those in which new meaning emerges and those in which it does not. I refer to these as dialogical and monological conversations. First, what do I mean by dialogical conversation? What is its essence?

DIALOGICAL CONVERSATION: SHARED INQUIRY

Dialogical conversation—in therapy and other contexts—is distinguished by *shared inquiry:* the coordinated action of continually responding to and interacting with; of exchanging and discussing ideas, opinions, biases, memories, observations, feelings, emotions, and so forth. Shared inquiry is a process in which the participants are in a fluid mode characterized by an *in-there-together*, two-way, give-and-take exchange (Anderson & Goolishian, 1988b; Goolishian & Anderson, 1987a). It is characteristic of a conversation in which people are talking *with* each other, rather than *to* each other. In this conversational arrangement participants do not assume they know what the other person is saying, means, or wants; rather, each is committed to learning about and trying to understand the other by negotiating meanings through the use of language. Language comes alive as participants engage in a genuine exchange of viewpoints in order to understand the issues at hand and to achieve some purpose with others and with themselves (Gadamer, 1975). Seeking understanding and generating meaning through shared inquiry are the essence of the dialogical process and, likewise, of a collaborative language systems approach. Shared inquiry has several features: dialogical space, mutual exploration and development, understanding from within the conversation, internal dialogue, expanding and saying the unsaid, conversational background, belonging to the conversation, and shared intentionality.

Dialogical Space

The opportunity for shared inquiry involves a *dialogical space*—a metaphorical space between and within the conversation participants (Anderson & Goolishian, 1988b; Goolishian & Anderson, 1987a). Dialogical space refers to room in one's thoughts to entertain multiple ideas, beliefs, and opinions; in contrast, in *monological space* (see Braten, 1987, 1988) an idea or an aggregate of ideas is static and excludes other ideas. Dialogical space or conversational context is critical to the development of a generative process that promotes fluid, shifting ideas and actions. It can be likened to the Irish family therapists McCarthy and Byrne's (1988) use of Irish mythology's Fifth Province: an imaginary place where members of the four provinces "caught in webs of conflict and competition from which there appeared no exit" would meet to "dis-position" (McCarthy & Byrne, 1988, p. 189).[2] Here *disposition* refers to dialogue or conversation. Searle (1992), in a less poetic yet still metaphorical way, also highlights the relevance of space in the structure of conversations: "Each speech act creates a *'space of possibilities'* [my emphasis] for appropriate *response* speech acts" (p. 8). Dialogical conversation/therapy allows a space/context that a client's everyday space/context may not allow. This requires of a therapist the ability to create and maintain a dialogical space in which the other is, in Shotter's (1995b) words, "free to roam over a whole range of possibilities" (p. 68). Without dialogical space a familiar story cannot be narrated in a way that provides an opportunity for transformation in the narrating story and the self.

Mutual Exploration and Development

A therapy conversation is a mutual search to understand and to develop shared meanings to address the purpose that has brought a client and therapist together and that preoccupies a client. It is the mechanism through which a client and therapist participate in *shared inquiry: the mutual puzzling* that involves exploring the familiar (for example, what a client is attempting to make clear to a therapist—a client's story, view of the problem, ideas about solutions) and developing the new (for example, meanings, realities, and narratives).

Therapist learning leads to shared inquiry. A shared inquiry process begins and is guided by the relevance of a conversation as a therapist learns about the other person's storied experience in a genuine, thoughtful, and open manner. What begins as a therapist's learning about a client begins to arouse the client's curiosity as well, inviting that client to join the therapist in a shared inquiry into the issues at hand. As a therapist begins to learn about and understand a client's story—his or her view, experience, desires—this therapist learning mode, initially an asking–telling–listening sequence, shades into a conversational process characterized by shared inquiry. As shared inquiry develops, fixed, frozen, or monological constructions begin to change. In this exploratory and creative process, client and therapist form a *conversational partnership*, a mutual relationship, in the telling, inquiring, interpreting, and shaping of the narrative. Therapy becomes collaborative; as in Shotter's (1994) description of the process, a client belongs *to* and participates *in* the conversation as he or she struggles with the therapist to understand and with the process of interpretation.

Shared inquiry is necessary to develop understanding that reflects and is informed by the personal, first-person narrative understanding of clients. Their narrative accounts rather than my theoretical descriptions and explanations lead. What emerges from the therapy conversation must originate within it and be shaped and determined by all involved, rather than by external theories. This is collaboration. My role as a therapist is to participate with a client in a first-person linguistic account of his or her relevant life events and experiences. Shotter (1993a) describes this form of conversation, which Harry Goolishian and I (Anderson, 1990; Anderson & Goolishian, 1988b, 1992) wrote about, as follows:

> They want to open up a "space" for a form of conversation within which the first-person voice of clients can be heard, a space within which it is possible for clients to express "who" they *are*, a space in which they can communicate in some way what it is like *to be* them and how they experience their uniquely troubled world. (Shotter, 1993a, p. 118)

Braten (1984) similarly describes a dialogue in which all participants can make room for one another's creativity and consciousness as intersubjective.[3] A therapist is only "a part of a circular interactive system" (Gadamer, 1975, p. 361), only part of the "circle of meaning" (Gadamer, 1988), the dialogical process through which interpretation begins with a therapist's preconceptions or preunderstandings (Heidegger, 1962).[4] That is, the meaning that emerges is influenced by what a therapist and client bring into conversation and their interactions with each other about it. The issue of new meaning relies on the novelty (not-knowing) of what a therapist is about to hear and the ability of that therapist to attend simultaneously to both inner and outer conversation. Gadamer (1988) has stated:

> A person trying to understand a text is prepared for it to tell him something. That is why a hermeneutically trained mind must be, from the start, sensitive to the text's quality of newness. But this kind of sensitivity involves neither "neutrality" in the matter of the object nor the extinction of one's self, but the conscious assimilation of one's own bias, so that the text may present itself in all its newness and thus be able to assert its own truth against one's foremeanings. (p. 238)[5]

Understanding from Within the Conversation

Understanding in any conversation is always circumscribed by the context of the conversation and is necessarily always unique to its context (Garfinkel, 1967; Shotter, 1993a). It must be known within the development of the conversation itself, and can only be known by those involved in it (Garfinkel, 1967), not by an observer. Likewise, as David Hoy (1986), referring to hermeneutic understanding, suggests, "there is no privileged standpoint for understanding" (p. 399). For instance, therapists (or supervisors or consultants or team members) often talk of a "metaposition," referring to a privileged position above or outside an event (for example, behind a one-way mirror). We cannot be meta to an event or to a therapy conversation. We simply participate in it; that is, observe it, hear it, or converse in it from different positions, from different angles, from different preunderstandings. Each position is one of many possible ones. Each person in a conversation participates from a unique perspective and experience; for various reasons, these may be quite different from those of other participants. This is part of the reason that the experiences of a therapist in a therapy room and the observers behind the one-way mirror often differ. It is one explanation of why a child welfare worker's, a parent's, and a therapist's experience of the same interview can be so different or a mother's report of dinner with her daughter's boyfriend can vary so from the daughter's or the boyfriend's recollection.

We are interpretive beings, though not in the traditional psychotherapy sense. Rather, understanding is an *interpretative process*, a narrative whose aim is that denoted by the German word *deutung:* grasping the deeper sense or significance. In the process of interpreting, of grasping deeper sense or significance, meaning is added to the other person's story. Shotter (1984, 1993a) describes the dialogic nature of conversation as "joint actions" in which "people coordinate their activity in with the activities of others and 'respond' to them in what they do, what they as individuals desire and what actually results" (Shotter, 1993a, p. 39). One implication of joint action is that

> the influences that shape the saying of words do not all originate in the speaker him- or herself. The very act of saying a word in a practical circumstance is a joint action: it is open to the influences of both past and present others at the very moment of its performance, and their influences may be present in it too. (Shotter, 1995b, pp. 66–67)

It is possible to get close to another person's experience, but we can never fully understand what it means to him or her. We can only approximate an understanding through what we think he or she is saying. Understanding does not mean full, unabridged agreement. One person (for example, a client) can only agree that he or she believes that the other person (for example, a therapist) to some extent understands. When approximating understanding does not occur, it is partly because we may not ask the *right* questions, make the *right* responses, or have the *right* background to draw from for that local dialogical exchange. *Right*, however, does not refer to correct but to fit or coherence. Complete understanding is never possible, primarily because through the interactive process of telling and retelling the experience, the teller's story (for example, a client's story), including teller's experiences and teller's understandings, changes, as does the listener's story (for example, a therapist's story). In the process of trying to understand, something different is produced.

The ethnographer Harold Garfinkel (1967) strongly believes that in any conversation participants will refuse to understand what is being said except in terms of the meaning that has been negotiated in the local context of the immediate dialogical exchange itself. Understanding and meaning are, according to Garfinkel, always a matter of difficult negotiation. What is being talked about in any conversation must always remain unclear until the participants take advantage of the many mutual opportunities suggested to one another during the exchange to create a shared and locally contextualized understanding. From this perspective, understanding is always developing and always depends on the dialogical event itself. The changing understanding is the development of new meaning.

Brice Wachterhauser, professor of philosophy (1986a), states that according to Gadamer,

> in the course of a *real, open* conversation, that is, a conversation where the participants actually devote themselves to understanding the issue and not simply to "scoring points" or "defending" a position, that, for example, insights, metaphors, and frameworks can emerge that may suggest new ways of seeing the subject matter, or new conceptual vocabularies can be hammered out that will help move a discussion onto new ground. [Emphasis added] (p. 33)

Because meaning is generated as we go along in conversation, we cannot predict its outcome. We may speculate about where we might end up, but we cannot guarantee it. "In a genuine dialogue the meanings that emerge in the dialogue propel each participant toward understandings that were not foreseen or intended" (Wachterhauser, 1986b, p. 227). The *logic* of the dialogue often contains possibilities of meaning that emerge only in its context. This is the wonderment of dialogue.

Internal Dialogue

Conversation occurs in language. As we converse we are simultaneously actively preparing and forming our responses. We are putting our thoughts into words. The Russian psychologist Lev Vygotsky[6] (1986), in his *Thought and Language*, talks about this thoughts-into-words process in terms of the interactive nature of thought and language. This making sense of, giving meaning to, and saying thoughts out loud is not a linear process but one of dialogically putting pieces into relationship with each other. Vygotsky calls this social construction of mind process "inner speech":

> The relation of thought to word is not a thing but a process, a continual movement backward and forth from thought to word and from word to thought. In that process, the relation of thought to word undergoes changes that themselves may be regarded as developmental in the functional sense. Thought is not merely expressed in words; it comes into existence through them. Every thought tends to connect something with something else, to establish a relation between things. Every thought moves, grows and develops, fulfills a function, solves a problem. (p. 218)

Vygotsky continues, "The connection between thought and word, however, is neither preformed or constant. It emerges in the course of development, and itself evolves" (p. 255).

Thus the newness does not simply result from shuffling narrative pieces around and putting them together differently to create, for instance, a different understanding of the past, although this could occur. The new narratives that emerge in our exchanges with our clients are not the result of the ingenious improvisation of new narrative introduced by a therapist (for example, from theory or other normative concepts). As Vygotsky suggests, the newness evolves.

Expanding and Saying the Unsaid

As therapists we often think of life events as things. We are lured by our theories into believing there is *the* story about the event, *the* part that we can discover, know, and understand. When we believe that we know the point of the story, so to speak, we cut off and close access to the unsaid. In "Dissolving Tidal Waves" you will meet Lee Ann, who thought she knew Carol and consequently closed off both her and Carol's possibilities. This closing off is dramatically illustrated by Shotter's quote from Umberto Eco's (1984) *The Name of the Rose:* "There was no plot, and I discovered it by mistake" (Shotter, 1993a, p. 135).

The philosopher Hans Lipps believed that any linguistic account contains a "circle of the unexpressed" (as cited in Wachterhauser, 1986a, p. 34); Gadamer (1975) called this the "infinity of the unsaid" (pp. 424–425). No communicative account—no word, no phrase, no sentence—is complete, clear, and univocal. All communications carry unspoken meanings and possible new interpretations. All communicative actions are an infinite resource for new expression and meaning. The subject and content, therefore, of all discourse, and in this case therapy, are open to evolutionary change in meaning.

In therapy the resource of the *unsaid* and the *yet-to-be-said*—the circle of the unexpressed—refers to a client's internal private thoughts and conversations. Like Vygotsky's (1986) notions of inner speech and the process of putting thoughts into words, these include both thoughts that are not clearly formed and those that have not been spoken. It is a resource that resides totally in the inventive and creative aspects of language and narrative, not in the psychic structure (for example, the unconscious), the biological structure (for example, the brain), nor the social structure (for example, a family). Rather, this capacity for change lies in people's ability to be in language with one another and, through the linguistic process, create and develop the realities that have meaning for them and through which they continually reorganize their mutual living and develop self-descriptions that provide "new and empowering accounts of ourselves instead of disabling ones" (Shotter, 1991a).

From this view, psychotherapy (as shared inquiry) is a process of forming, saying, and expanding the unsaid and the yet-to-be-said—the development, through dialogue, of new meanings, themes, narratives, and histories—from which new self-descriptions may arise. However, in saying the unsaid and the not-yet-said, in telling and retelling, there are still infinite possibilities that are not apparent. Shotter (1993a) warns,

Stories may tell us what in certain circumstances we *should* do to fit our actions into a particular order, but their danger is, that by revealing in their telling only a selection of the possibilities open to us, they can so easily conceal from us what that range of possibilities is. (p. 147)

Conversational Background

I believe that Shotter's concepts of conversational background and sense of belonging provide one way of thinking about generative or dialogic conversations and distinguishing them from restrictive or monologic ones. These concepts are influenced by Bakhtin's (1986, 1990) concepts of human beings as *dialogically and responsively linked* together and with an *invisible third party:* "Each dialogue takes place as if against the background of the responsive understanding of an invisibly present third party who stands above all the participants in the dialogue" (Bakhtin, 1986, p. 126).

Shotter (1995b) offers his notion of the *social* "conversational background" (p. 52), suggesting that people in conversation understand each other "not in terms of inner mental representations but *reactively* or *responsively*" (p. 49). That is, we are "*dialogically* or *responsively* linked in some way, both to previous, already executed actions and to anticipated, next possible actions" (p. 53). Any utterance, according to Bakhtin (1986), "always has an addressee" (p. 126) (who may be one's self or another), but each utterance also addresses the anticipated responses of a special, invisibly present, third person Other or Otherness. It is as if "another voice, created by the dialogue or conversation itself, emerges from within the background between the dialogue partners" (Shotter, 1995b, p. 50). These three "form-shaping agencies" (p. 54) constitute the social conversational background that "allows or permits" our actions (p. 53). Shotter is suggesting that the "influences structuring our actions cannot be wholly located within ourselves; *nor* in any of the other individuals in the situation either; *nor* simply in the context itself apart from any of the individuals within it" (p. 53).

Again, as Searle (1992) suggests, "in a local dialogue or conversation, each speech act creates a *space of possibilities* [my emphasis] for appropriate *response* speech acts"(p. 8). What emerges in this space does so on a moment-to-moment basis (Shotter, 1995b) and cannot be predicted. Meaning, for instance, according to Garfinkel

(1967), is "tendentious" and cannot be stipulated in advance. *You* and *I* find out, and, Garfinkel emphasizes, can *only* find out, what it means as we go along.

The essence of the *as we go along* dialogical exchange is what Shotter (1995b) calls *responsive listening:* "instead of us acting out of an inner plan, we act responsively 'into' a situation, doing what it 'calls' from us" (p. 62). He is referring to an active rather than a passive attempt to understand, to bridge the "gaps [and] boundaries [in conversations that occur when] what one person says or does must be accounted for, made sense of, or responded to in some way, by an other (or by the person themselves)" (Shotter, 1993a, p. 33). It is through that struggle with each other to see and make connections, which neither person can do alone, that newness arises (pp. 61–62). Gergen (1994), in a similar vein, conceptualizes the essence of the dialogic process as *supplementation* (pp. 264–271).[7]

Belonging to the Conversation

Like Shotter (1993a), I believe *being responded to* creates a sense of belonging and being connected that is critical to dialogue:

> For individual members of a people can have a *sense* of "belonging" in that people's "reality," only if the others around them are prepared to respond to what they do and say *seriously;* that is if they are treated as a proper participant in that people's "authoring" of their reality, and not excluded from it in some way. For only then will they feel that the reality in which they live is as much theirs as anyone else's. (p. 39)

Theresa's words refer, I believe, to this sense of belonging as she reflects on her previous therapy experiences and on expectations she had of her current therapy. She talks about her newfound realization that there are many ways to address a problem and to call upon her and her therapist's wisdom. In a therapy evaluation interview in response to the question, "Did you ever feel that we were imposing our vision on you?" she said

> No, the contrary, you would share with me your experiences but never implying how things should be. In the more traditional therapies [referring to her other therapy experiences] I felt that way, the therapist telling me that I was wrong and I had to realize it. Here I felt like moving forward and building something new.
> In the traditional therapies this is not allowed, you go where

the therapist tells you. There is only one way chosen by the therapist. Here you choose it together. . . . With you is the challenge, the energy, "we are a team" and "we are in this together" [as if you said let *us* do it] . . . [she continues referring to her newfound sense of agency] I thought that after five years where I was totally absorbed [in my problem] that I didn't have this capacity anymore. And I realize that it is there, it has been there all along. I can reconquer this space of self-affirmation and I can nurture and reconcile with myself.

Thomas, a client whom you will meet again in chapter 7, was telling me about his experiences of therapists and doctors who did not understand him, saying how he felt, sadness, and loneliness. In contrast and relief he had found his current therapy team human and helpful, a process and relationship in which I think he felt he belonged. In his words,

I felt that maybe for the first time except for a few personal friends that these people believed me. I felt no bad vibrations, no signs in their body language or facial expression that "this is not true." They let me say what I wanted to say and they listened. This process took a long time.

Students also comment on a sense of belonging and not belonging:

The atmosphere beckoned to me, "Take a chance. Get out there."

I didn't know it would be possible to ask and have my questions answered.

I came to this workshop expecting to listen, to be "a fly on the wall," taking in what others already knew. I found that *just* listening here is impossible . . . I never talk in class . . . but here I feel invited in . . . I wanted to talk.

Being in this kind of conversation, as Shotter warns, and I believe, "does not mean that we will unthinkingly feel a sense of total harmony with those around us" (1993a, p. 39). Being in dialogical conversation does not presuppose agreement. Rather, dialogue requires that there be room for familiar views, confusing ambiguities, and vigorous attitudes to exist side by side. And, it requires that there be room for alternate inventions and opinions to emerge. Toward this end, "We *must* offer each other opportunities to contribute to the making of agreed meanings" (Shotter, 1993a, p. 27). When this opportunity is present we can have a sense of belonging without agreement.

Shared Intentionality: Having a Conversation on Purpose

I believe that all human behavior in its broadest sense involves intentionality, including conversation. We are intentional agents; we cannot act without intention. All behaviors are "directed toward or are about something other than themselves" (Shotter, 1995b, p. 51): "I mean to," "I have a reason for," or "My purpose is." Our intentions, however, do not stand alone. From a social construction standpoint, purpose and intention, like meaning and reason, are not neutral; they are relational. They are socially constructed and cannot be separated from their context. In this vein, some advance the notion of shared intentionality (Harré, 1983; Searle, 1992; Shotter, 1993a). Searle (1992) speaks of all utterances in terms of intentionality.

> One of the things we need to recognize about conversations is that they involve shared intentionality. Conversations are a paradigm of collective behavior. . . . The phenomenon of shared collective behavior is a genuine social phenomenon and underlies much social behavior. We are blinded to this fact by the traditional analytic devices that treat all intentionality as strictly a matter of the individual person. (pp. 21–22)

Shotter (1993a) suggests that joint action has "an *intentional* quality to it" (p. 39). He talks about this quality as a move from individual intentionality, usually associated with and involving inner mental activities, to shared intentionality, responding to or acting into rather than acting out of, which he calls "practical intentionality" (Shotter, 1995b, p. 60).

What, then, is the purpose or intention of a therapy conversation? How can shared intentionality develop? For therapists who want to participate in a dialogue, there is a need to find the point of, the intention of, any of a client's actions, thoughts, or statements and to jointly interpret its intended meaning through the conversational process rather than to assume we know a priori the intent of any action, thought, or statement. It is important, however, that a therapist's intention be compatible with, relevant to, the intention, the purpose of the conversation. That purpose, however, is not determined ahead of time but on a continuous and mutually negotiated basis. The importance of ensuring continuous and mutually negotiated intentionality—shared intentionality—is one of the distinguishing features of therapy dialogue as I understand it.

FROM DIALOGUE TO MONOLOGUE AND BACK AGAIN

In monologue, the participants do not offer each other the opportunity to *be* in conversation. There is no openness to the other. "One perspective reigns and reality becomes closed" (Goolishian & Anderson, 1987a, p. 532). In contrast to dialogue, the space for shared inquiry is absent; room exists in the relationship only for single perspectives; no newness is possible (Anderson, 1986). Elsewhere I talked about monologue as *breakdowns in conversation* and the conditions under which (for instance, why and when) dialogue collapses into monologue (Anderson, 1986).

In making this distinction, I draw primarily on the Norwegian sociologist Stein Braten's distinction between monologue and dialogue (1987):[8]

Thinking and communication that are monological, and which may involve control through the monopoly of a single perspective in terms of which a domain is defined, are distinguished from thinking and communication that are dialogical, and hence allow for creativity and consciousness through the complementary autonomy of participant perspectives. (p. 10)

As Braten (1988) suggests, this partly results from "our tendencies towards psychological consistency, reduction and closure" (p. 3). He further suggests that socialization makes us susceptible to submitting to the "one who has defined the domain and on whose premises the knowledge has been developed and, hence, is acknowledged as the source of valid replies about the domain in question" (Braten, 1988, p. 4). Dominance prevails, but with no assurance of equity through expertise defined by that dominance.

Similarly, influenced by Bakhtin's notions of monologue, Shotter (1993a) refers to "monologism," which "at its extremes, denies the existence outside itself of another consciousness with equal rights and equal responsibilities, another *I* with equal rights (thou)" (p. 62).[9] Quoting Bakhtin, he continues, "Monologue is finalized and deaf to the other's response, does not expect it and does not acknowledge in it any *decisive* force" (p. 62).

My intent in distinguishing between monologue and dialogue is not to pathologize one (monologue) and normalize the other (dialogue). I do not suggest, for instance, that disagreement is pathological. I do not suggest that a soliloquy is necessarily monological. I use these terms simply to distinguish between different kinds of conversations in general and different kinds of therapy conversations in particular—those in which the possibilities for internal and external monologues are lessened and those in which the possibilities for internal and external dialogues are enhanced.[10]

Breakdowns

One way of conceptualizing conversational breakdowns in a family, for example, is that when its members are facing *a* problem it is not unusual for them to have multiple, discrepant realities about *the* problem and its remedy and to operate from "realist" language. For many reasons unique to the circumstances of *the* problem and the family members and their relationships, when their views are out of harmony and they cannot negotiate those disharmonious views, their differences begin to collide in subtle and not so subtle ways. When this happens, there is no longer a common effort and an unresolvable situation can develop.

Differing realities develop, continue, and often escalate to *dueling realities* (Anderson, 1986; Anderson & Goolishian, 1986) as members' attentions and energies focus on protecting their views, convincing others of the correctness of those views, and experiencing others' views as unfounded or even crazy. Such competing actions can become more divergent and ensconced over time. Give-and-take discussions cease, ideas are no longer exchanged, biases are no longer mediated, views become entrenched, conversations become repetitious, understandings between people cease to exist, and room for familiar and distinct views to exist simultaneously side by side without controversy or prejudice shrinks. Furthermore, this collision of dissimilar views can become a greater problem than the original concern or issue.

Under these circumstances and with these barriers, conversational space constricts and dialogue collapses into monologue. It is *as if* a brick wall has been erected. "There is no longer a cross-fertilization of ideas or a crossing of perspectives" (Anderson, 1986, p. 9), nothing shifts, no new meanings are generated. Each person talks only to himself or herself and repeats the same conversation. The result is parallel internal and external monologic conversations in which no one feels respected, heard, or taken seriously. The exchange becomes a conversation in which no one belongs or is connected.

Similarly, conversational breakdown can occur in therapy. Clients and therapists have their own prejudices, ideas, and opinions. A client's ideas and opinions may be, and often are, incompatible with a therapist's. When this happens, the differences have the potential to become sources of friction, thinking ruts, or boredom that threaten or shut down conversation. A therapist, however, does not strive to have a client in agreement with or consensus. This is not the aim. This does not mean that I devalue consensus or synthesis; rather, I believe that seeking consensus or synthesis closes us off to the richness of the other and the unknown. If a therapist is willing, differences can be taken advantage of; they can become springboards for curiosity, learning, and openness to the other.

As therapists we are prone to think of a breakdown in a therapy conversation as an impasse or as *resistance*. Often this is punctuated with a client and attributed to an inherent characteristic of an individual or a group of individuals. A family, for instance, is blamed for being in denial, or an individual is blamed for sabotaging change. I want to emphasize that conversational breakdown is a dynamic phenomenon of an interdependent/interactional process that exists *between* individuals, that exists *in* a relationship.

Although any breakdown in conversation is an interactional/relational process, I have previously (Anderson, 1986) punctuated impasses and resistance in terms of a therapist's:

> (a) failure to have an awareness, understanding, and appreciation for the multiple realities operative in a given situation (including their own) and (b) failure to work within these realities in a manner that opens the flow of communication rather than narrows it and in a manner that maximizes the opportunity for ideas to be fluid rather than static. (Anderson, 1986, p. 13)

My intent is not to emphasize or locate causality in a therapist, but to suggest that he or she is in the position to and responsible to recognize and act *in* the impasse. Or, as Harry Goolishian often said, "The only person a therapist can change is him- or herself."

STRUCTURE AND COMPONENTS
OF A THERAPY CONVERSATION

How do we achieve this kind of dialogue, one that is generative, one that is collaborative and egalitarian, one in which a client is the expert? How do we create a dialogical space? How do we find new ways to talk about a client's concerns? How do we shift from a realist language to an interpretive language that leads to other ways to view the problem? How do we access and expand on the unsaid? If I observe several therapists practicing from this philosophical stance and look for similarities, what will those similarities be? What kinds of things should I keep in mind if I try to work this way?

The Conversation's Structure

The structure of the therapy conversation is spontaneous, determined by moment-to-moment exchanges that zigzag and crisscross. It does not follow a predetermined script such as a structured question guideline or sequenced actions. I cannot know my questions ahead of time; I cannot choose words to produce a specified outcome. I want to participate in the kind of process I am describing naturally, not artificially. For I am inside, not outside, the process I am trying to create. Hence, the conversation may appear disorganized to an outside observer or one who has a preconception of what the conversation should look like. It may appear that a therapist does not have control of the interview because indeed he or she does not. A therapist does not control the interview by moving the conversation in a particular direction of content or outcome, nor is he or she responsible for the direction of change. The newness, for example, rather than being developed or introduced by a therapist from outside the conversation, emerges within the dialogue. The outcome of such a conversation cannot be predetermined or predicted. It cannot be "traced back" (Shotter, 1993a) to any one person. It is jointly constructed through the evolving conversation. It is important that both client and therapist be comfortable with the outcome.

A therapist talks with one person at a time. This does not mean that the conversation is staid or that a person cannot speak when he or she wishes. Rather, the process allows the therapist to give full attention to each telling of the story, though, of course, being aware of the others in the room. I have been told that I tend to lean toward the person I am talking with as I am often deeply immersed in what he or she is saying.

As we talk, others present assume a reflective listening position in which inner dialogue becomes possible. They listen and hear undefensively because the story being created between a therapist and the person is different, and they have a sense that the therapist also considers what they have to say important, they will also be heard, and they want to add to and expand the story rather than correct or interrupt it. Often someone remarks, "Oh, I didn't know that" or "I haven't heard you say that before." It is not that secrets or unseen details are revealed. The content is usually not new; somehow the pieces are arranged differently, similarly to Shotter's notion of "moving things around" and Gadamer's of moving the "discussion onto a new ground."

From behind a one-way mirror a therapist listening to me talk with a mother and daughter she was working with captured the essence of this reflective listening experience as she shared her inner dialogue.[11] Her tone displayed an "Aha" quality.

> I leaned forward and it had come to me. It's almost like watching and listening to the family; order comes to mind watching and observing the family. It's like maybe starting in the middle of the book [referring to what she had done before, thereby missing understanding]. Things [are] being said in a sequence. There are things being said that aren't different. I've heard [this] before but watching and listening this way is very different. . . . It's not so much about who they are; I felt like I had that . . . but the pieces are fitting together more in a way that makes sense . . . listening back there was very different—being out but in—you don't hear it the same way.

She now had a "better grasp" of this family and felt she understood the mother's and daughter's differences "in a new way." There seemed to be "hope where previously there was none, like a burden's been lifted off my shoulders." She was beginning to have a new sense of agency.

In another instance a wife wondered about the differences between the conversations she and her husband had at home and in therapy. "I don't know what it is. We talk about the same things in here that we talk about at home but somehow in here it's different. Here we talk about things differently."

Both instances are similar to what Tom Andersen (1991, May) refers to as one of his aims in therapy: "I want to talk with people in a way that they have not talked with themselves or with each other before." Part of talking differently involves listening differently.[12]

Interrelated Components

A dialogical process entails six interrelated simultaneous, overlapping, and sequential components, all subject to the philosophical stance (Anderson, 1986):

1. *A therapist engages in and maintains an internal dialogical space with himself or herself.* First and foremost, a therapist must enter the therapy relationship with and maintain an internal dialogical space. This means that a therapist makes room for the other by not entering with formed ideas and plans about a client and the problem or its solution.

2. *A therapist initiates and maintains an external dialogue with a client.* A therapist creates space for, invites, and facilitates an external (oral) dialogical process.

3. *A client engages in an internal dialogue with himself or herself.* The external dialogic process enhances a client's ability to engage in internal dialogue rather than monologue. For instance, after hearing a fragment of a story, a client or a therapist may pose a question in a novel way or offer a curious comment, which acts to kindle internal thoughts and musings. The voiced shared inquiry process generates a similar internal process.

4. *Clients engage in external dialogue with each other.* As an individual begins to talk with a therapist and with the self differently, he or she starts to talk with others differently. All people present spontaneously join in the telling of the story, adding to and expanding on it rather than correcting the other's version.

5. *A client engages in internal and external dialogue outside the therapy room.* One conversation leads to another. Internal and external dialogue within the therapy room allow people to talk with themselves and others differently outside the therapy room as well. This is part of the transformational capacity of dialogue and narrative. It is not static, contained by walls or by time: rather, it is a fluid ongoing process in which each conversation becomes and is influenced by other conversations.

6. *A therapist engages in internal and external dialogue outside the therapy room.* He or she, like a client, takes the in-the-room conversation and thoughts-in-motion with him or her. These will influence and blend into other conversations, which, in turn, will do the same.

PRACTICALITIES OF A THERAPY CONVERSATION

A system and a professional's practice entail pragmatic and social aspects that can enhance and impede the opportunity for dialogue. These considerations are not the essence, but simply tools that reflect a stance, a way of thinking about people, oneself, and the task at hand. These tools include, for instance, space arrangements, note taking, appointment making, and system factors.

Space Arrangements

Something as simple as a room's arrangement can enhance or hinder two-way dialogue in therapy, education, and consultation. The opportunity for dialogical conversation is diminished when people are lined up side-by-side on sofas, students are seated in rows of chairs with a teacher standing in front, a therapist is seated in a chair separated from the other seating, or a consultant stands behind a podium. In each instance, it is likely that the person at the front of the room or the one with the best chair may act or be perceived hierarchically. Opportunities for conversation and collaboration are enhanced when people are seated so that they can see each other and the arrangement of the chairs suggests impartiality. Whether the context is therapy, teaching, or consultation, I favor a room with similar chairs placed in a circlelike arrangement. In teaching and consultation, I frequently ask permission to rearrange rooms and also like to walk around the room and be close to the people I am talking with.

Note Taking

Since I want to be immersed in the conversation, I do not take notes in sessions (with the exception of the recording process described in the consultation discussed in chapter 11, which I consider critical to dialogue). In my experience as a therapist, it is difficult to convey interest, easy to miss what is being said, and likely to promote self-consciousness when I am absorbed in note taking during a session. Paying careful attention to a client's story as he or she chooses to tell it instead of how I want to hear it has helped me develop a good memory for people and their stories.

Appointments

Because I believe that therapy or consultation begins with the first contact between a professional and a client, I make my own appointments. This procedure eliminates the tendency to inherit the meanings developed in the interactions that have taken place between an intake person, a secretary, a business manager, or any other go-between person who may talk with a client before I do.

Amenities

It is easy to forget how much a system's ambience influences our relationships with our clients and thus our therapy, our teaching, and our consultation. I favor a client-friendly atmosphere and informal setting over one that is formal and puts distance between me and the other person. I want support staff who talk with clients or students by phone and receive them in the office to have a friendly, courteous, and helpful demeanor.

These and other pragmatics and social practices of our profession reflect attitudes about ourselves and the people we work and live with. They can help build bridges between client and professional, colleague and colleague, friend and friend. They can offer invitations for collaborative relationships, transformative conversations, possibilities, and, ultimately, client, professional, and personal successes. In the spirit of a postmodern therapy they can help us be welcomed guests in other people's lives.

A Lingering Question

How can a dialogical therapy conversation of the kind I describe make any difference at all to the myriad diverse clients we meet? What is its relevance, for instance, to the angry, exasperated, single black mother, whose son was mandated to therapy by the juvenile courts because he pulled a gun on another student in school; a woman who does not have the status or expertise (which a therapist may have) to negotiate with the court and the school in behalf of her son; and who does not have the advantage that a therapist may have of living in a better neighborhood? These are her forceful ideas as she told me of the conversations she had with herself as she struggled about whether to go to the therapy appointment, in anticipation of what she thought a therapist would want to hear and what she thought a therapist would know.

> When I was told to come here today, I was afraid that I wouldn't say the right thing, that I should say what you wanted to hear, and that if I didn't, *you* would tell them, yes, take my son away. I wanted to say the right thing—for my son. . . . I tried to give him a good home, to teach him right, but what can I do with this stuff

around me—drugs, pimps, shootings, gangs. Rich white kids go to hospitals. My black son goes to jail! You can't understand that. You can't help me with that!

Or how, for instance, can these kinds of conversations make any difference to a five-member, two-generation Bosnian refugee family who exist in a small kitchenless room in a refugee camp in Croatia? Having lost all their personal belongings, their home, and their country, and knowing her husband does not have enough education or the right job skills to immigrate—having lost the context of their lives—the wife says, "You can't imagine what it's like not to be able to cook your own food day after day, month after month. My husband can't work; there's no money. We have no future."

What is common to these statements is a sense of not being understood, of not belonging, of hopelessness, and feeling that understanding, belonging, and hopefulness are not even possible. Can we attempt to understand these people and their situations through dialogue? Can dialogue be of any help to them? Can hope and pragmatics commence in dialogue? To continue to address these questions, I now turn to the voices of the experts: the clients.

CHAPTER 7

Client Voices:
Practical Advice from the Experts on How to Create Dialogical Conversations and Collaborative Relationships

In order to arrive at what you do not know
you must go by the way which is the way of ignorance.
—T. S. ELIOT

Nobody sees a flower, really—it is so small—we haven't time,
and to see takes time, like to have a friend takes time.
—GEORGIA O'KEEFFE

THE CLIENT'S VOICE has been paramount in the evolution of my collaborative approach to therapy (Anderson, 1991b, 1995, 1996a, 1996b; Anderson & Goolishian, 1988b, 1992; Anderson, Goolishian, & Winderman, 1986b; Goolishian & Anderson, 1990). This prominence has been influenced by my long-standing curiosity about and fascination with clients' described experiences of therapy and therapists and by my belief that a consumer's input into the development of a product, and its continuous redevelopment, is essential. I do not want to imply that I set out to develop a client-informed or -designed therapy. Along the way I realized how much I had learned from clients and how much my thoughts about and actions in therapy were influenced by their voices. This realization reflects my commitment to research as part of my everyday clinical practice. Whenever I have had the opportunity, I have systematically interviewed clients in my practice and clients referred for consultation about their experiences of both successful and unsuccessful treatment, including their experiences with the professional who was treating them.

The more attention I paid to what clients were saying, the more I understood that they knew more than I did or ever would about their lives, and the more I realized how my *knowing* interfered with the telling of their stories and the accessing of their resources. As a consequence, I have elevated the client's voice to center stage; again—much like flipping the usual roles of therapists (knowers) and clients (not-knowers)—therapists learn and clients teach.[1]

Here I present and discuss what I have learned from clients' first-person voices—their reflections about therapy and their relationships with their therapists.[2] Included are the voices of my clients, other therapists' clients with whom I talked on a one-time basis, and clients whom I interviewed specifically about their therapy experiences. Drawing upon this *advice from the experts,* I continue an examination of and provide a framework for creating what I call *dialogical conversations* and *collaborative narrative relationships*—a process and a relationship characterized by *connecting, collaborating, and constructing.*

A cornerstone of the conversation and the relationship is the concept of *not-knowing* (Anderson, 1990; Anderson & Goolishian, 1988b, 1992; Goolishian & Anderson, 1987a, 1990). Not-knowing is the key feature that distinguishes my collaborative approach from other therapies and that makes a pivotal difference in a therapist's intent, direction, and style. What is not-knowing? What does a therapist do with what he or she already knows?

"NOT-KNOWING"

"They are not respectful. They say what is [in] the text [what they learned from books]. They describe the problem in their terms."

Knowing—the delusion of understanding or the security of methodology—decreases the possibility of seeing and increases our deafness to the unexpected, the unsaid, and the not-yet-said (Anderson & Goolishian, 1988b). If we always see and hear things as we are accustomed to, then we will miss, neither see nor hear, that which is different and unique. A not-knowing position reflects the challenge of subject–object or knower–known dualism advanced by postmodern endeavors such as contemporary hermeneutics and social constructionism (Gergen, 1982; Shapiro & Sica, 1984; Shotter & Gergen, 1989; Wachterhauser, 1986a). Not-knowing is critical to the embedded assumption that the dialogical creation of meaning is always an intersubjective process. It allows possibilities that knowing does not. *One of those possibilities is dialogue.*

Not-knowing refers to a therapist's position—an attitude and belief—that a therapist does not have access to privileged information, can never fully understand another person, always needs to be in a state of *being informed* by the other, and always needs to learn more about what has been said or may not have been said. In *not-knowing* a therapist adopts an interpretive stance that relies on the continuing analysis of experience as it occurs in context and as it is related and narrated by a client. Interpretation is always a dialogue between therapist and client and not the result of predetermined theoretical narratives essential to a therapist's meaning, expertise, experience, or therapy model. Several aspects of not-knowing enable a therapist to be continually informed by his or her client and to have forever developing understanding.

Uncertainty

Being willing to doubt. To be uncertain requires that we leave our dominant professional and personal discourses—what we know or think we know—suspended, hanging in front of us; that we be continually aware of, reflect on, and be open to examination by ourselves and others. This requires being able not to understand too quickly, to let go of early assumptions and stereotyping thoughts, to avoid premature understanding, to doubt what we think we know, and to prevent valuing our knowledge over a client's.

Instead, we must be able to have an open mind, open to challenge and change, open to the unexpected. This is part of what allows us to have the room in our heads for the other, the space for possibilities that is such a critical aspect of dialogue.

Being willing to risk. In my therapy room a therapist is not *safe*; is not safely ensconced in *knowing*. Being in a not-knowing position makes therapists vulnerable: they risk change, too. This risk includes letting clients be center stage, allowing them to lead with their stories as they want to tell them, not being guided by what a therapist thinks is important and preselects to hear. This risk challenges across-the-board assumptions, categorizations, and generalities. *Generality* here refers to what is produced in the reshaping of a particular prior text to a new context (Becker, 1984, p. 435). In this vein, I think it is unfortunate that early-arrived-at diagnostic impressions, interpretations, treatment strategies, and goals are so tempting and valued (Gergen, Hoffman, & Anderson, 1995). Such premature evaluations can lead a therapist to ask questions whose purpose is to verify therapist realities more than learning about client realities. And, whether couched as a *DSM-IV* diagnosis, a clinical assumption, or a research hypothesis, knowing has the potential to guide a therapist or researcher to act in such a way as to confirm his or her knowing (Jones, 1986; Scarr, 1985). When we selectively listen and respond to a client's story from a knowing manner, we seek, intentionally or unintentionally, to confirm our beliefs, biases, expectations, and learned truths. A therapist's selective listening and responding can hinder dialogical exchange by prematurely fixing or narrowing the range of discourse, and by leading to early closure of a client's story, consequently impoverishing options for both client and therapist. More important than whether a therapist has preconceived ideas is what he or she *does* with these ideas. Equally important, when we look for the familiar we become blind to and thus lose the specialness of each client and the uniqueness of his or her situation. Gergen (1988b) warns, "Once one has fixed on a given interpretation, increasing the number of events lends no additional strength to the interpretation. It merely demonstrates the conceptual agility of the observer in generating a veneer of consistency among interpretations" (p. 36).

A turn to not-knowing makes therapy, and the questions in therapy, different from traditional diagnostic exploration. If we truly do not know, then we must learn. If we attempt to learn, then we attempt to understand what the client is telling us. Knowing and understanding in this mode are always *on the way*. A therapist must risk being a learner again with each client—a very humbling and freeing experience.

Humility

Not-knowing means humility about what one knows. In effect, a therapist is more interested in learning what a client has to say than in pursuing, telling, validating, or promoting his or her knowledge or preoccupations. For example, I would not think of a mother who is afraid for her eleven-year-old son to walk to school by himself or to spend the night with a friend as overprotective. I would not try to lead her, for instance, to the way I believe she should parent, feel, or think. Rather, I would talk with her in a way that allowed us mutually to explore and develop options for addressing actions, feelings, and thoughts that are unique to her concerns, her beliefs, and her life circumstances, not mine. Toward this end I might want to learn more about her fears; what is her worst fear; what influences her ideas about parenting. Have other people given her advice, and if so, what advice? Were these issues in her family when she was growing up, and if so, how were they handled? The intent of the questions would be to learn more, to participate in her narrative as it is, and as it might be. I would not want these or other questions to give her the impression that I was searching for a particular answer or that there was a right answer. Neither would I presume my child–parent experiences, opinions, and theories would fit hers. If I offered any of them, however, I would do so in a humble manner. Humble here does not mean meek, unsure, or timid; I want to have an unassuming manner.

A not-knowing position prevents the artificial and premature closure that often results from a preplanned outcome. Operating from a position of *knowing* independently predetermines the possibilities and destroys the codevelopment of new meaning through the stories and narratives generated in therapy. This implies, for example, that therapist-goal-oriented therapies— whether a therapist's goal is to interrupt dysfunctional patterns, drive toward a solution, search for an exception, or create a replacement narrative—that are directed by preexisting knowledge, theory, or experience limit the options available to the therapy discourse by emphasizing and seeking out only what is already known.

What Not-Knowing Demands

A therapist's expertise in not establishing understandings, explanations, and interpretations based on prior experiences, formed truths, and knowledge is required. With this aim, a therapist joins a client in the natural unfolding of the client's story, talking with, learning about, and trying to understand his or her concerns, views, expectations. A therapist genuinely wants to learn how a client makes sense of things: to grasp the current story, not determine its cause; to learn what, for a client, gives it shape. A therapist does not know a priori the intent of any talk or action, but must rely on a client's explanation, learning the significance of what a client is saying from him or her.[3] A therapist must learn how, what may seem like nonsense makes sense to a client.

What Not-Knowing Does Not Mean: Prelearned Professional Knowledge

Not-knowing, as Jacques Derrida (1978) says, "does not mean that we know nothing but that we are beyond absolute knowledge . . . approaching that on the basis of which its closure is announced and decided." Not-knowing does not mean withholding, pretending dumbness, being deceitful, or maintaining neutrality.

I do not challenge that therapists have prelearned knowledge—theoretical and experiential, professional and personal. Great amounts of time, money, and energy advance knowledge of how to diagnose, predict, and treat. I do not suggest that this learning should or can be erased. A therapist cannot be a blank screen, void of ideas, opinions, and prejudices. A therapist cannot be neutral. All are impossible. To the contrary, we each take who we are, and all that that entails—personal and professional life experiences, values, biases, and convictions—with us into the therapy room. We must be able to have, share, and advance our opinions, ideas, and feelings.

I concern myself with what we take in. We must be able to be challenged and to challenge ourselves. We must be able to commit to a dialogical interplay that encourages an egalitarian and mutual search for understanding. In such a collaborative process, we are less likely, wittingly or unwittingly, to exploit perceived social power in a therapist–client relationship in the interest of preserving our own knowledge base or that of our cultural institutions and discourses.

The following illustrates a not-knowing position.

"He Believed Me"

A competent and creative, yet frustrated psychiatrist colleague requested a consultation with Harry Goolishian for him and a troublesome client he thought had an intractable problem and with whom he felt at an impasse.[4] His client, Lars, a Norwegian merchant seaman, believed he had a chronic disease and was infecting others, even killing them. Although Lars had talked some of difficulties in his marriage and his current inability to work, his attention was riveted on the disease. He was distraught and frightened.

During the interview, Harry asked Lars, "How long have you *had* this disease?" Looking astonished, and after a long pause, Lars told how it all began, including numerous attempts by doctors and psychiatrists to relieve his growing fear and conviction about his contagious disease. When he was a young merchant seaman in the Far East, he had had sex with a prostitute. Afterward, remembering the lectures on sexually transmitted diseases given to the crewmen on his ship, he feared that he had exposed himself to a horrible sexual disease. Panicked, he went to a local clinic, where the nurse ordered him out of the waiting room. He said that the nurse didn't believe him, and told him rather bluntly that they did not "treat sexual perverts"—that he "needed confession and God, not medicine." After he returned home from sea, still frightened that he was infecting others, he saw several doctors. "No one believed me," he said. On several occasions he was referred for psychiatric consultation. All failed to relieve his growing fear and conviction about his contagious disease. Over time he became uncompromisingly convinced that no one understood the seriousness of his contamination.

As Harry showed interest in Lars's dilemma and let him tell his story the way he wanted to, Lars began visibly to relax, even to become somewhat animated, and he began to share in Harry's curiosity. Harry's intent was not to challenge Lars's reality or story, or to talk or manipulate him out of his delusion. Harry wanted to learn about it, be sensitive to it, to maintain coherence with it.

Colleagues observing the interview were critical of Harry's question "How long have you *had* this disease?" They feared that the question reinforced the man's "hypochondriacal delusion." A safer, more neutral question, they suggested, would have been "How long have you *thought* you've had this disease?" The not-knowing position, however, precluded the stance that Lars's story was delusional. Lars said he was sick. Thus, Harry wanted to learn more about his sickness. To do this required not-knowing questions.

Trying to understand Lars and what could appear as his "nonsense" or "psychosis" was an essential step in a continuous process of establishing and continuing a dialogue. It meant moving *with* the narrative truth of Lars's storied experience rather than challenging it and assigning meaning to it such as *delusional*. Moving with his narrative involved a mutual process and was, therefore, not the same as reifying a delusion. By not-knowing, Harry made room for the story to be retold in a way that allowed for new meaning and new narrative to emerge, and it provided a starting point for dialogue and open conversation.

Asking a safer question like "How long have you thought you've had this disease?" would have imposed a predetermined, knowing view that the disease was a figment of the client's imagination, a distortion that required correction. In response to such a question, the suspicious client would have been left out of the story and left to act according to his own preconceived ideas and expectations of the consultant. Harry would then have been the latest in a line of professionals who did not believe Lars, who knew better, and who asked knowing questions. Once again, Lars would have felt misunderstood and alienated. In the hallway after the interview, Lars's psychiatrist asked how talking with Harry had been for him. Lars said, "You know, that son-of-a-bitch believed me!"

I do not believe or want to suggest that a not-knowing question can produce a miracle cure or that any one knowing question can beget a therapy impasse. No question can by itself influence a dialogical or nondialogical occasion. The question itself does not cause someone to shift meaning, to give up an idea, or to have a new idea. Rather, conversational questions, like each comment, each utterance, and each gesture, are elements of an overall process and exemplify an honest, continuous therapist posture of not understanding too quickly, not determining the frame for the dialogue, and not-knowing. Each question is an element of the overall conversational process and represents a general therapist posture.

Six months later the psychiatrist eagerly shared the continuing effect of the interview on him and Lars. He said, "I felt freed from having to prove that his fear was an irrational delusion." Therapy sessions now seemed less difficult. Lars's life situation was much better, and whether or not he was infected was no longer an issue. Lars was now working steadily, was dealing with his marriage, and had a new daughter.

Two years later I received a letter from the psychiatrist:

I saw Lars today and that is why I got the impulse to write you a few words. I told him that Harry died last fall, and he reacted very strongly, saying "He was a wonderful man." I asked Lars what impressed him the most, and he said: "He believed me, but you know he said something that made all the difference. You know after telling him about my struggle and what I did, Harry said 'As a man you did what a man had to do.' That sentence just made the difference. I see him every so often in front of me saying that."

Harry's not-knowing created a starting point for a dialogic exchange: Lars's internal conversation, the psychiatrist's internal conversation, and their conversations with each other and others. Lars's conversations with the therapist led him to have new conversations with himself and to compose a new self-narrative through which he was no longer the prisoner of a chronic disease but the hero of his life.

In my conversation with clients, like Harry's conversation with Lars, I do not want to deconstruct or instruct the marginal voice to make it what I know or think it should be. Instead, I want to create room for and learn about it. I want to immerse myself and be led into a client's world with an attitude and action that demonstrate sincere interest and respect, and that promote a client's feeling heard and confirmed. This creating room for the other is the first step to being able to talk *with*, toward dialogue, toward change.

Next I take the words and experiences of clients to identify six intertwined features related to not-knowing that characterize therapists who engage in dialogical conversations and collaborative relationships, to serve as guidelines to help you learn how to create them. These guidelines include: (1) trust and believe, (2) ask conversational questions, (3) listen and respond, (4) maintain coherence, (5) stay in sync, and (6) honor a client's story.

TRUST AND BELIEVE

"He believed me."
  "These people believed me."
  "I didn't have psychological trust."

Clients say they want to be trusted and believed. A story can never be historically accurate. Each person's account, telling, and retelling will be unique. Each listener will hear and respond to the story differently. And each account may vary over time, from context to context and circumstance to circumstance. Therapists are trained to *know*, with radar set to catch perceived inconsistencies in a client's story or parts where the story does not fit with what they think it ought to be. Frustrated by clients whose stories are inconsistent, I believe as therapists we often respond—out of our own need for clarification—by confronting the inconsistencies, trying to find or verify the perceived *accurate* version, or in some instances simply not believing the client.

The not-knowing position—similar to Bruner's (1990) "narrative posture" suggests a different kind of therapist posture or expertise, an expertise that is limited to the process of therapy rather than to the content (diagnosis) and change (treatment) of pathological structure. Thus a therapist would not be driven by a search for the truth, but by a need to understand. In the examples that follow clients talk about trusting and believing.

"Listen to Me and Believe in What I Say"

All members of the Swedish family spoke at one time or another about not being allowed to talk, not being listened to, and not being believed. In the following brief excerpt, I am talking with the youngest daughter about how the therapists and doctors in the family sessions did not talk with her. I asked her, "So, help me. When you said that you agreed with your mother that the doctors should also talk with you, would they talk about you like you weren't there?"

"Yes. But I don't think they thought it was like that."

In the next instance the oldest daughter talks about the nurses on the hospital ward acting as intermediary between her and the doctor.

"I'm very occupied by your wish to talk more. If you had that opportunity, what would you really wish to talk about? What would you want the doctors to hear?"

"I want them to listen to me and to believe in what I say. And that I'm not trying to manipulate all the time. Well, it's sort of like you're two persons, and one is trying to get well, and they should listen to that part and try to encourage it. I'm the one who knows myself best and what would be best for me."

I imagine that the therapists and the doctors have their own equally valid versions.

"After They Saw Her, They **Believed Me"**

I consulted with a couple and their hospital therapy team who were in a conflict about whether the wife should be discharged from the hospital and referred to outpatient therapy. She had been hospitalized for three weeks with severe depression. The husband was very reluctant to agree to his wife's leaving the hospital unless he had some reassurance that if she became this depressed again, she would be readmitted. Wondering about his reluctance, I asked. Swelling with emotion, he talked about the worry and difficulty of finding a hospital that would admit his wife. He said that for days she had refused to get out of bed or eat and had threatened to kill herself. He had stayed home from work because he feared for her life. He called several places seeking help for his wife. Unable to convince anyone of the severity of her situation, he vividly described how he picked her limp body up out of bed, put her in their car, and carried her in his arms into the hospital emergency room. "After they saw her, they *believed* me," he said.

"These People Are Really Trusting Me"

I had the privilege of talking with Thomas and his current therapist Hugo about Thomas's five-year ordeal of going from therapist to therapist and doctor to doctor in his search for help. Briefly, Thomas, diagnosed as paranoid schizophrenic, had been placed on medical leave of absence from his job because of difficulties with his fellow workers and boss. The situation had become quite complicated for several reasons. Thomas's particular job-related difficulties were viewed as a rather sensitive political issue; he desperately wanted to continue his career but the disability insurance representative had strongly recommended permanent retirement, which he refused. Several other tragic events had occurred in his life over the past ten years. He pursued his cause passionately, and because of his intensity people in authority often refused to talk with him and his boss felt threatened by and afraid of him. During his search for help Thomas not only felt that no one had understood him or had helped him but that no one trusted or believed him. He spoke of his resulting lack of "psychological trust" in the doctors, and his observation that the therapists' body language indicated that "they didn't *believe* me." Remembering that he had said that he had been helped by his current therapy team, I commented, "You said you had lots of confidence in them." He replied:

> I said to myself, these people are really trusting me. They really have confidence in me. . . . I felt that maybe for the first time except for a few personal friends that these people *believed* me. I felt no bad vibrations. I saw no signs in their body language or facial expressions that said "This is not true."

"I Would Hope So!"

The therapist Susan Levin (1992) has discussed her interviews with women who have been battered; her comments illustrate the risk of not believing clients. One woman, Nan, gave an account of going to seven therapists who either blamed her for her husband's violence, took his side, or told her to leave him. After six years, Nan finally found a therapist who she felt listened to her and heard her. Levin remarks,

> Nan's repeated dissatisfaction with her previous therapists is something that I may have attributed to a problem (or pathology) if I had been listening defensively, or prone to analyze or distrust her perception of reality. (p. 72)

Nan's words supported Levin's caution about indicating distrust or frustration.

> The nine months before I left him [referring to her husband] and three months after that, any sense that I would get, by that point, of someone disapproving of me or thinking that someone with my brains and background should be able to walk away, any sense of that would send me fleeing. (p. 73)

Levin gave several examples of facts a therapist might question or psychological defects that could be attributed to Nan's dissatisfaction. She discusses what could have happened had she pursued any of these with Nan.

> I would have looked for questions that I could have asked to help Nan clarify exactly how she found these therapists, what they specifically said, what had happened first, and so forth. Pushing, and pressuring her, through questions about "facts" to get her to recognize that she was distorting the truth, or at least to convince myself of the facts. This is possibly the type of thing that happened to Nan, over and over again, in therapy. . . . Had I indicated a distrust, or frustration with her story, the interaction would have taken on a very different style and feel. I would have become the inquisitor and the expert, defining what was important for her to talk about, and placing me in a position where I knew better than she did about what her "real" experience [the true one] in therapy probably was. She might have fled the interview. I would hope so! (p. 73)

Levin recounted her confusion after conversations with Jean, whose descriptions of her relationship with her husband and their marriage were not consistent during the initial and follow-up interviews. Nor did they match the referring therapist's follow-up report. As with Nan's story, Levin could have drawn several conclusions from those inconsistencies and asked never-ending questions as she searched for the correct version. She did neither; she accepted all versions. Levin reflected on her own confusion and reminded us of how easy it is to forget that "people have lives and minds that change, often outside of our involvement, and are not stagnant receptacles of information like facts that we can 'gather'" (p. 84). Drawing on the work of the Netherlands psychologist Sybe J. S. Terwee (1988), Levin reminds us that "looking at multiple descriptions of the 'same' event can lead to never ending interpretations, if one is trying to figure out what *really* happened" (p. 84).

Many considerations influence the ways a story is told and is heard, described, and interpreted, including the teller, the listener, the context, and the circumstances. Norman Denzin (1989) cautions, "A story that is told is never the same story that is heard. Each teller speaks from a biographical position that is unique and, in a sense, unshareable" (p. 72). Similarly Gergen (1982) provides a fascinating example: "If I see my good friends Ross and Laura approach each other at a social gathering, and Ross reaches out and momentarily touches Laura's hair, precisely what have I observed?" (p. 60). He illustrates the multiple possibilities for identifying behaviors, and hence, the multiple versions of a story that can be created about any one behavior. Each time a story is told about Ross and Laura, the version varies, depending on the narrator and numerous other variables. Given these, any account or revision of the story is as true as any other.

ASK CONVERSATIONAL QUESTIONS

"You ask hard, complicated questions, but you ask them in a nice way."
"She asks good questions."

Clients say that one of the most helpful aspects of successful therapy experiences is the therapist's questions. Questions are the core of any interview or therapy conversation. They can facilitate or hinder the story a client wants to tell. As clients commented on questions that therapists asked, it was particularly striking how often they felt that therapists asked questions that, in their words, "did not seem relevant," suggested that the therapist "did not hear a thing I said," "made me feel unimportant," "insulted my integrity," or made them "felt blamed"—or questions that simply did not allow them to tell their stories.

Answers Before Questions

From a postmodern perspective because emphasis is on openness to new narrative and because the therapy narrative can never be known outside the dialogue of the moment, questions are always asked from the position of not-knowing. In other words, because a not-knowing position enables a therapist to express interest and curiosity in a client, questions from this position are more likely to come from inside rather than outside the local conversation. Questions from this position help a client tell, clarify, and expand on a story; open up new avenues and explore what is known or not-known; they help a therapist learn about and avoid misconceptions of the *said* and the *not-yet-said*. In turn, each question leads to an elaboration of descriptions and explanations; each question leads to another question—a process of continuing questioning that provides springboards for a dialogical process.

I call such questions *conversational questions* (Anderson & Goolishian, 1988b; Goolishian, 1989; Goolishian & Anderson, 1990). They invite a client to talk *with* the therapist; they invite a client into a shared inquiry. In my experience questions based on a not-knowing stance help me enter the client's subjectivity.[5] Ivar Hartviksen (personal communication, 1990), a Norwegian psychiatrist, captures this point in the statement "The question is the only tool I have in my work. It is the only way that I have of *wondering*, of *participating* in the patient's life."

To some extent, however, our questions are always influenced from outside the immediate context of the conversation. When outside knowing or discourse takes precedence, it can create tunnel vision, limiting what we are interested in and ask about. It allows questions that demand and configure a client's stories to match what we already know on the basis of our previous experiences of clients. It also inspires questions that limit the meaning and understanding that can be generated through the more local conversation. The more questions are based on preknowing, searching for answers, or verifying a therapist's assumptions, the more a therapist loses contact with his or her clients' experiences as well as their own. This is what I believe these clients are referring to in their comments.

This concept of conversational questions moves away from the traditional static practice of asking questions based on a methodology, or generated by techniques or preset questions for information gathering or validating hypotheses to which we think we know the answer before asking the question. This makes therapy a more dynamic process in which a client's developing narrative brings a therapist's own horizons of understanding into question.

A therapist's task is always to find the question, the tool, through which to learn more about the immediate recounting of experience. This means that what we have just been told, the coposition narrative, is the answer to which a therapist must find the next question; it gives the therapist the next question. That is, questions result from the immediate dialogical event, the developing narrative informs the next question, and the narrative is constituted differently by the questions directed at it. In this local and continuing process of question and answer, of recounting and redescribing, possibilities for understanding, meaning, and change are open and infinite.[6]

Bruner (1990) similarly distinguished between questions in interviews that make sense out of what is said from a paradigm of understanding external to the narrative and those specific to a local exchange. Bruner's first category is similar to what I think of as "answers before questions": rhetorical or pedagogical questions. Rhetorical questions give their own answers; pedagogical questions imply the direction of the answer. Questions in traditional therapy are often of this nature; that is, they imply direction (for example, correct reality), yet leave the client some distance in order to reach the answer.

"You Have to Ask the Right Question"

At a workshop in northern Norway I was chatting with a participant sitting across from me at lunch. She was friendly, smiling, and seemingly self-assured. She must have realized that I did not recognize her so she introduced herself:[7] "I know you don't remember me but I'm Anna. You interviewed me one time and the first thing I told you was, 'You have to ask the right questions.'" She was partly right. I did not recognize her at first, but hearing this I remembered her instantly although she looked markedly different from the woman I had met several years ago in a consultation interview. Anna was a nurse whose therapist was worried about her chronic suicidal tendencies and thought another perspective might be helpful.

Anna proceeded to tell me about her experience of the interview and of the dramatic changes in her life since that time. She told me that when we first met she did not want to talk with me. I remembered how lifeless she seemed when we were introduced. I remembered I shared her therapist's hope that our talking would be helpful to her and to their work together, but that I was not sure I would ask the right questions; I said something like "Would you mind if I started with something like telling me a little bit about yourself, perhaps where you live, and how you and Dr. X met?" She touched upon her work, her divorce, and her daughter. I remembered being curious about her daughter and her distress that she had moved away. Could they each be responsible for their own lives? she worried. I remembered her sense of despair, her belief that she had nothing to live for; I remembered that she did not care about eating or grooming. I puzzled with her over her distress, her worries, and her questions. I remembered wondering, "How come?" "What if?" and "What if I met your daughter?" I thanked Anna for introducing herself and sharing her experiences with me. I told her that I would like to hear more if she ever wanted to tell me.

Some months after our chance meeting I received a letter from Anna in which she said our recent conversation had "awakened more thoughts." As she looked back she was "glad to be alive." The words that follow are from her letter. English is not Anna's first language; I think that accounts for what I consider the poetry of her letter.

> I was like a person without a mimic and body language—in a deep sadness. I did not want to be alive. But I tried to make it possible to have a new life—to be independent. To eat and walk for my own. To see colors and flowers. Sun and summer. But inside it was dark. For years and months I longed for death. I sat like a clown with a smile outside and inside it was dark. I wanted death.
>
> You had to ask the right questions because I had a secret to hide. I could not talk with you about all the problems. I had to hide. You asked and I told you about my independence and my new life without my daughter. I was worried about her and we talked a lot about that part of the problem.
>
> When you interviewed me I became sure to be in life and try struggling against death. You let me find out that I had to eat for my own sake, go for a walk.

Referring to her continuing work with her therapist, she wrote, "Most significant was the talking. He helped me out of sadness by talking and talking and he gave me responsibility for my own life."

She also commented on the way I talked with her, the profound impact our talking had on her own professional work with patients:

I have seen backwards and am glad to be in life, and now I can see all my meetings with people [her patients] are ruled by the responsibility everyone has for his or her own life. The respect for people's meanings and feelings! I can say how I feel, to be glad, sorry, or angry. Now today I can stand in my feelings and I try to be a hero of them. But the strong feelings—they have ruled me. Try to be honest! Stand in the situation without running to death. Ask questions, of yourself, of others. I do not know about the future but I feel good in the present. I am painting a little, and try to make some clothes with the knitting machine.

She ended her letter, "Ask questions!"

Anna's story illustrates the transformative power of narrative. Our conversation was part of many intertwined ongoing conversations: those she and her therapist were having, those she was having with herself and others, and those her therapist was having with himself and others. Our conversation led Anna to have new conversations with herself and with her therapist. Anna composed a new self-narrative through which she became free of her suicidal prison and became the heroine of her own story—not one written, edited, or guided by me or by her therapist. Her heroic feelings yielded a sense of possibilities (for life and future), a sense of self-agency she had not felt before. She was able to realize the hope and freedom that many clients talk about.

Two years later, out of the blue, I received a brief note from Anna written on a napkin.[8] "I am out of all problems now. . . . Nobody knows what the problems have been, but now I can live my life . . . I have learned a lot of [from] my problems." She continued with news of her daughter, her two grandchildren, how well everyone was doing.

What was the right question? you may be wondering. I do not know; Anna never said. The right question cannot be known ahead of time; it is not a product of being smart, clever, or wise. There is no question template. Each question results from an attempt to understand the just-said and the unsaid; each is an element of the overall conversational process. Right questions are the ones that arise from being immersed in a client's world. My guess is, or to be more honest, I would like to think, that what Anna referred to as the right question was not the question at all. Rather, I think she meant careful attention to, and interest in, learning more of what distressed and worried her, rather than a pursuit of preconceived ideas about depression, suicide, abandonment issues, or stuck therapy. I would like to think that she was referring to my learning in a way that gave her a sense of being invited into and belonging to the conversation.

"A Lot of People Are Predictable"

Anna's challenge, "You have to ask the right question," reminds me again of Thomas, who searched for five years for the right doctor, the right therapist. Referring to his search, I tentatively conjectured, "If this is something you've been struggling with for five years, you must be a little bit tired of it all or very frustrated or annoyed. I'm not sure what the right word would be."

He poignantly responded, "A lot of people are predictable when you talk about this."

"Predictable? In what sense?"

"I know what they're going to ask me."

"Oh, really—"

"And what kinds of answers they want. That is kind of boring. It makes you feel kind of hurt. It makes you feel very heavy inside. It's kind of sad that people don't have more kinds of fantasy and don't think more critically what's happening. . . . They think they know what the problem is and they stick to it."

As he told his story, Thomas identified two kinds of people who were not interested in his story as he wanted to tell it but in the version they either already knew or wanted to hear. Not wanting, if possible, to make the same mistakes that others had made I proposed, "So, why don't we start there? What do you think are the most important things for me to know about you and what do you think people miss or are not paying enough attention to?"

Moments later he spoke of the two kinds of therapists and doctors he encountered when he tried to tell his story—those who used it "as a kind of entertainment" and those who wanted to "hear all the details." Neither "heard" his story, and therefore both missed what was important to him.

I questioned, "What is it that people miss or that even *I* could miss? What is it that you wish people wouldn't miss?"

"What it means to be alone in a situation, because alone is what you really are."

He talked about the impossibility of doctors' knowing what his problem really was, what it was like for him. He suggested that that is why a doctor should not summarize his situation for another professional but let him tell it instead. Doctors, he said, "often make wrong diagnoses when they rely on other people's accounts, especially when those people know you only through someone else's report." And he talked about the tension that developed when the patient disagreed with the doctor. Thomas said that doctors did not share their opinions with him and were "not collegial," to which I asked, "Meaning partners on the same level?"

"I think you understand," he replied.

"I think I do, but I may not."

He continued his story, which aptly illustrates the potential pitfalls awaiting a therapist who already "knows" a client's story and asks questions only to elicit that story, or when a therapist is only interested in the details of the story he or she wants to hear and never really hears the client's story.

"You Shape the Explanation by the Questions You Ask"

Our questions communicate something about us and what we think; they participate in the construction of their own answers. I want to ask questions that allow a client to construct the answer. The following striking interchange from Anne Rice's (1990) *The Witching Hour* characterizes how the questions we choose to ask, as Thomas indicated, sometimes not only prevent us from hearing what a client would like us to hear, but can also influence the selection and construction of the person we meet in therapy and the story he or she tells.[9]

> "But there are many possible explanations [of who I am]. You shape the explanation by the questions you ask. I can talk to you of my own volition, but what I tell you will have been shaped by what I have been taught through the questions of others over the centuries. It is a construct. If you want a new construct, ask. . . . "
>
> "If you prod me to speak to you in complete and sophisticated sentences, and to allow for your persistent misconceptions, mistakes, or crude distinction, I can do it. But what I say may not be as near to truth as you might like."
>
> "But how will you do it?"
>
> "Through what I've learned of human thinking from other humans, of course. What I am saying is, choose—begin at the beginning with me if you want pure truth. You will receive enigmatic and cryptic answers. And they may be useless. But they will be true. Or begin in the middle and you will receive educated and sophisticated answers. Either way, you will know of me what I learn of myself from you." (pp. 926–927)

Any question can be asked, any comment can be made, anything can be talked about. What is important, however, is the stance from which it comes—the manner, the tone, and the timing. Any question, like any comment, private inner thought, or opinion, is best offered in a tentative manner. Tentativeness does not equal vagueness but being open to the other person and leaving room for his or her participation. I believe questions asked in this manner afford a client license to respond to them, to reconstruct them, or to ignore them.

"Conditional Questions"

I am reminded of the words of a revolving-door-treatment failure, Bill, a thirty-year-old man who had been hospitalized several times for psychosis and unable to work for years.[10] During his present therapy he had improved and had been able to resume his career as a computer programmer. He said that he now felt more capable of managing his life (self-agency). He also said that his current therapist was different from his previous therapists. This conversational context influenced his therapist's question, "What, if anything, could your previous therapists have done differently that would have been more useful to you?" Perhaps Bill's response refers to not-knowing.

> That is an interesting and complicated question. If a person like you had found a way to talk with me when I was first going crazy . . . at all the times of my delusion that I was a grand military figure . . . I knew that this was a way that I was trying to tell myself that I could overcome my panic and fear. . . . Rather than talk with me about this, my doctors would always ask me what I call "conditional questions."

The therapist asked, "What are conditional questions?"

> You [the professionals] were always checking me out . . . checking me out to see if I knew what you knew rather than find a way to talk with me. You would ask "Is this an ashtray?" to see if I knew or not. It was as if you knew and wanted to see if I could. . . . That only made me more frightened. If you could have talked with the me that knew how scared I was . . . we could have handled that crazy general.

Shotter (1994) perceived Bill as being involved in a conversation that "touches" him, a conversation that is "continuous with his being" (p. 6). He calls it a "form of talk" in which Bill was involved, in contrast to previous forms of talk in which Bill was external to the "means-ends, problem solving talk of professionals intent upon applying their '*theories*', and, on the basis of their '*observations*', of coming to an accurate *'picture'* of Bill's supposed *'inner mental state'* [my emphasis]" (p. 9). A not-knowing position reduces the opportunity for what Bill called conditional questions and permits a therapist to ask conversational questions.

LISTEN AND RESPOND

"You listened to me."
  "You heard exactly what I said."
  "All I really wanted was for someone to hear me."

Clients say they want to be listened to and heard. In the majority of my conversations with clients about their experience of therapy and whether it was helpful, the factor most common to unsuccessful therapy was not being listened to or heard. But what is listening? What is hearing?

Listening is a taken-for-granted aspect of psychotherapy, so much so that writing about listening may seem naive. Introduced by Freud, listening was little talked about until the 1950s, when its association with empathy was recognized (Jackson, 1992, pp. 1626–1627). The primary role of listening in psychotherapy, second only to observation, has been attaining a form of knowing, gaining clinical information. Listening for the most part has been a passive position or process. The active part, so to speak, occurs in a listener's head as what is heard is silently sorted out and made sense of. The belief has been that if a therapist could be a good listener—an empathetic listener, an attentive listener—or, as Reik (1951) suggested, could have a "third ear," such listening would lead to uncovering and accessing the feelings, thoughts, and meanings that were beyond or below (for instance, that the client was unaware of or withholding) the client's actual words. This knowing through a special kind of listening with a therapist's ear guides interventions. It is almost as if the *talking cure* and *healing listening* are separate, step-ordered processes.

In contrast, I think of listening and hearing as interrelated, active, mutual processes. I define *listening* as attending to, interacting with, responding to, and trying to learn about a client's story and its perceived importance. The storytelling process, even though it involves both a teller and a listener, is far more complex than one person's telling a story and another person's listening. It involves *hearing*, which Levin (1992) defines as "a process involving a negotiating of understandings" (p. 48), "an interactive struggle for shared meaning that occurs when two people (or more) attempt to come to a mutual understanding of something" (p. 50). Listening and hearing go hand-in-hand and cannot be separated.

Responsive–Active Listening–Hearing

In my experience, negotiation of understanding that involves dialogue (one part of which is listening) is done in a distinct way that includes special therapist attitudes and actions that I call *responsive–active listening–hearing*. Responsive–active listening–hearing invites clients to tell us what it is like for them, what are their inner concerns. Shotter (1995b) suggested of this kind of listening and responding that we do not act out of an inner plan, we act responsively "into" a situation, doing what 'it' calls for" (p. 62).

Each client has an ideological base (including preconceptions, prejudices, experiences, and anticipations) that is unique and that influences the construction of his or her view of the problem and the story about it. To help a story be sharable a therapist must plunge into a client's world and show an interest in that client's view of the problem, its cause, its location, and its solution. Equally important, a therapist should learn a client's expectations of therapy and therapist.

This kind of listening and hearing requires that a therapist enter the therapy domain with a genuine posture and manner characterized by an openness to another person's ideological base—his or her reality, beliefs, and experiences. This listening posture and manner involve showing respect for, having humility toward, and believing that what a client has to say is worth hearing. It involves attending considerately, showing that we value a client's knowledge about his or her pain, misery, or dilemma. And, it entails indicating that we want to know more about what a client has just said or may not yet have said—best accomplished by actively interacting with and responding to what a client says by asking questions, making comments, extending ideas, wondering, and sharing private thoughts aloud. Being interested in this way helps a therapist to clarify and prevent misunderstanding of the *said* and learn more about the *unsaid*. Linguistics scholar Deborah Tannen (1990) suggests, "We all want, above all, to be heard—but not merely to be heard. We want to be understood—heard for what we think we are saying for what *we* [my emphasis] know *we* meant" (p. 48).

To prevent assuming understanding or filling in the blanks too quickly, and to assure hearing what the client means, a therapist might ask, "So that I am not misunderstanding, are you saying . . . ?" "Is that similar to . . . ?" "Does that mean . . . ?" or "A moment ago you said . . . did you mean that?" Such comments and questions that seek not to misunderstand must be offered in a tentative, curious manner that conveys genuine interest in getting it right.

Responsive–active listening–hearing does not mean just sitting back and doing nothing. It does not mean that a therapist cannot say anything, offer an idea, or express an opinion. Nor does it mean that it is just a technique. Responsive–active listening–hearing is a natural therapist manner and attitude that communicates and demonstrates sincere interest, respect, and curiosity. The therapist gives as much room and time for a client's story as necessary, and, yes, at times, without interrupting. That is, it does not bother me nor do I draw an inference if a client chooses to talk for a long time.

How does this kind of listening–hearing promote dialogue? How does it promote relationships? Let's turn again to the voices of contemporary fictional characters who talk about listening, hearing, and dialogue.

Fictional Voices

I find that characters in fiction sometimes capture the essence of listening that invites the speaker into dialogue. Listen to the protagonist in Anne Rice's (1976) *Interview with a Vampire*.

> I was at a loss suddenly; but conscious all the while of how Armand listened; that he listened in the way that we dream of others listening, his face seeming to reflect on everything I said. He did not start forward to seize on my slightest pause, to assert an understanding of something before the thought was finished, or to argue with a swift, irresistible impulse—the things which often make dialogue impossible. (pp. 283–284)

Smilla, the Greenlander in Peter Høeg's (1993) *Smilla's Sense of Snow* who has a *sense of snow* like her sense of her own skin, expressed this essence of listening as she considered the detective who was questioning her and her own reflections on the experience of being questioned.

> I say nothing. I let the silence work on the investigator a little. It has no visible effect. His sand-colored eyes rest on me without flinching and without embarrassment. He will stand here as long as it takes. This alone makes him an unusual man. (pp. 43–44)

She continues,

> Very few people know how to listen. Their haste pulls them out of the conversation, or they try internally to improve the situation, or they're preparing what their entrance will be when you shut up and it's their turn to step on stage.
>
> It's different with the man standing in front of me. When I talk, he listens without distraction to what I say, and only to what I say. (p. 44)

As Smilla tries to describe, through words and gestures, tracks in the snow and how they are made, she constantly anticipates the detective's judgment and looks for signs that he doesn't find her reliable.

> Even I can hear how unconvincing it must sound. I wait for a scornful remark. It doesn't come.
>
> He looks out across the roof. He has no nervous tics, no habit of touching his hat or lighting his pipe or shifting his weight from one foot to another. He has no notebook that he pulls out. He is simply a very small man who listens and thinks things over carefully. (pp. 44–45)

One More Person to Flee

When a therapist fails to listen actively and hear responsively, he or she risks being all too quick to ask questions, offer comments, make assumptions, and extend suggestions that can leave the client feeling unheard, frustrated, and criticized. Such actions block dialogue and inhibit mutuality. The more emotionally, value, and culturally laden the story is, for example, family violence, the more difficult it is for a therapist to listen and hear. Nan, a woman Sue Levin (1992) interviewed, compellingly illustrates this as Levin portrays the failed therapies and situations in which Nan felt unheard.

> "You mentioned having reached out to a number of people: family, friends, previous therapists, church; did you ever feel like that anybody understood?"
> "Never really did," Nan replied.
> "Never did."
> "Never ran into another person who had been through it. Therapists were the worst because I would, um, each time we would select a new one I would get hopeful. And we would go in there and things would get worse usually. Things would usually get much worse because my husband was not capable of dealing with issues. He just

couldn't, I mean the man was very sick. So, we would go to therapists who would be working on some kind of model. You know,
where you're supposed to take whatever it is that caused the fight,
and work it out. And the fact is the fight was there before whatever
caused it was there. The fact is, that I understand now, is that when
the tension started building up in him, then he started looking for
whatever it was that he would select as the reason for the fight. And
the dynamics, um, didn't come out of causes you could write on
paper, or work out in a therapy room. ... Most of our therapists
were men and most of them blamed me." (pp. 71–72)

Sue could have questioned Nan's facts and perceptions of these
therapists; she could have challenged Nan to recognize that she
was distorting the *truth*. If Sue had taken this tack, she most likely
would have ended up being just one more person to distrust Nan,
one more person to be frustrated by her story, and one more person to flee.

MAINTAIN COHERENCE

"Oh, just one last thing before I leave."

Clients say they want a chance to tell their stories. Toward this end,
a therapist must create and safeguard room for a client's first-
person narrative. A therapist's authentic commitment to being
open to the other person's story, being curious about what the
other person wants to talk about is critical to creating and safe-
guarding room. This involves working within a client's reality—his
or her language, vocabulary, and metaphor—about the problem
and its imagined solutions. This making room for, this immersing
in, and this being led by a client's story are what I think of as maintaining coherence. In other words, when you do not know and try
to learn, you maintain coherence.

Such honoring of a client's reality is often confused with wittingly or unwittingly, overtly or covertly, reifying the problem,
drowning within a client's story, or being led around by the nose.
Talking within the spouse abuser's or substance abuser's story, for
example, is not the same as participating in denial, condoning culturally defined inhumanity, or abdicating social and ethical responsibility. Nor does it perpetuate the problem. Quite the opposite: in
my experience, maintaining coherence is an important step toward
transcending fixed positions, thus enhancing dialogue. People will

talk about what they want and need to if we give them the opportunity. If we think, for example, that an abuser needs to confess and we act in any way to elicit that confession, we impede the story. Hence we inadvertently participate in creating parallel monologues between client and therapist. Maintaining coherence allows room for the other person's familiar experiences and descriptions; according to Bateson, "In order to entertain new and novel ideas, there has to be room for the familiar."[11] Thus, it allows a client room for movement, and energy is not taken up with promoting, protecting, or convincing a therapist of a client's view.

Maintaining coherence helps lessen the chance that a therapist's voice might dominate and shape the story to be told and thus preclude a client's version and the development of future versions with helpful nuances. Our client Thomas reflects this point in his account of his unsuccessful attempts to get help for his problem from therapists who knew the story ahead of time and tried to shape its telling to match the version they knew. Thomas was, in Shotter's (1994) words, left out of the "conversational realm" (p. 9). Shotter referred to three clients who felt that their therapists understood:

> Being brought back into the conversational arena within which they had their being in the first place, they all experience the kind of language used as continuous with their being . . . and in which now, new possibilities for its formulation, new ways in which it can be talked about, can be formulated. (p. 9)

When the client is not included in the conversational arena, he or she may talk or act in ways that we sometimes experience and label as uncooperative, resistant, in denial, or even paranoid. Or, when a listener misses or precludes a client from saying what is important to him or her, at the end of a session that client might drop a bombshell like "Oh, just one last thing before I leave" or open a new area of conversation for which there is no time: "What I really want to talk with you about is. . . . "

In a collaborative approach, a therapist does not control the interview by moving the conversation in a particular direction of content or outcome, nor is a therapist responsible for the direction of change. Braten (1984) describes the process as intersubjective, a dialogue in which all participants can make room for one another's creativity and consciousness. Thus the *newness* emerges and is cocreated within the therapist and client's dialogue, rather than being developed, introduced, or offered by the therapist.

The therapist simply becomes only "a part of a circular interactive system" (Gadamer, 1975, p. 361), only part of the "circle of meaning" (Gadamer, 1988), the dialogical process through which interpretation begins with the therapist's preconceptions. That is, therapist and client always enter the therapy arena with expectations about what will be discussed based on their prior experiences. The meaning that emerges is understood from the interaction of that which they each bring and that which emerges. The issue of new meaning relies on the novelty (not-knowing) of what it is that the therapist is about to hear and the therapist's capacity to attend simultaneously to the inner and outer conversations of each member of the system.

I want to stress that maintaining coherence is not idle, superficial, goalless chitchat that leads nowhere or further solidifies preconceptions held by either client or therapist. It is part of a purposeful conversation intended to restore dialogue. This aspect of maintaining coherence and the emphasis on local meaning and local language merit attention.

Local Meaning and Language

The stories generated in therapy must be adequately specific, local accounts of first-person experiences to permit understanding, albeit transient understanding, around the nature of the struggle and ultimately culminating in new narrative. Local meaning and local language are important because of the range of experiences and multitude of ways of knowing these experiences, which differ from *knower* to *knower* and from therapy to therapy. Maintaining coherence with a client's, another therapist's, or a student's language allows us to come close to the development of a locally (dialogically) shared understanding and a local (dialogic) vocabulary, one that is developed between persons in dialogue, rather than from (although influenced by) broadly held cultural sensibilities. Engagement in a dialogue in the language that clients use in their everyday problem descriptions and interpretations is critical to shared local understanding. This engagement requires that the discourse of therapy avoid placing itself in the culture or language of external descriptors and metaphors such as psychological theory or family models (such as psychodynamic or structural) (Gergen, 1988a; Smedslund, 1988). Such professional language is our conceptual lens, which makes sense to us but often not to a client. It tends to be a hierarchical language, which can dominate, constrain what can be expressed, and, consequently, inadvertently silence. Our professional language can easily lead us to understandings reduced to stereotypical theoretical concepts and thus lose touch with a client's experience. It can also lose touch with a therapist's experience. Our professional language sometimes does not invite collaboration.

Consequently, I try to use cooperative and collective language: words, phrases, and sentences that tend to invite the other into conversation and that tend to include/refer to all involved, including, for instance, me and any others who may be present such as colleagues, students, and workshop participants. This signals a talking *with* rather than *to* or *about*.

For instance, when meeting with a therapist and a client I might ask, "What have the *two of you* been talking about?" or if the therapy system has four members, "What have the *four of you* been talking about?" I might ask, "How long have the *two of you* been meeting?" If there are observers of our conversation I might ask, "What do *you* think *we* need to know?" When a consultee presents a case in a consultation group, I might ask, "How do *you* hope *we* can be of help to you?" As a further example, Harry said to Lars, "How long have you *had* this disease?" I find that such language does several things: It includes everyone in the conversational system as more equal and sets a collaborative tone, not placing myself or the therapist apart in a hierarchical or dualistic position. It does not refer to therapy or problem, giving me a chance to learn the client's language and not to impart a professional language. This is not to imply that if a client, however, uses words such as *therapy* or *problem*, I would ignore or refuse to use those words.

Content and Process

Therapists often ask, "But how do you choose what to really listen to?" "How do you know what to respond to?" And, "What if the client is not talking about what they really need to/should be talking about?" These questions focus on content. Using a narrative analogy, stories involve both content and process—the facts of, the telling of, the listening to, and the interacting with. Although both content and process are critical, the importance of content, influenced by cultural expectations and the professional socialization of therapists, often unfortunately outweighs the relational process through which the content meaningful to a client is developed.

The wife who earlier reflected on why therapy had been helpful further remarked, "I don't know what happened. We talked in here about the same things we talk about at home over and over again. But somehow talking about it in here was different. After we talked about it in here, things changed."

What I want to emphasize is not the content or subject area but the *way* a therapist inquires. There is a difference between talking about things as shared inquiry and keeping score on or being a detective concerning who said or did what. I do not want to seek any particular kind of information; rather, I aim to stay close to the understanding of the moment, work within and slowly outside that parameter, and make only small shifts in the conversation. Using a dialogical process affords more movement and potential than focusing on and getting mired in content. Students often want to know the difference between a content question and a process one. The difference is in the question's intention: A content question seeks data and information. A process question facilitates dialogue.

Elevating the importance of content elevates the importance of skills and techniques and the mechanistic, objective aspect of some therapies. When this happens, the difference between a therapist's objective experience of a client and a client's subjective experience of himself or herself can be lost (Toombs, 1990, p. 237). That is, what is everyday practice for a therapist is not everyday for a client. A heightened content significantly risks staying close to a therapist's understanding and missing a client's, and in turn hinders a dialogical process.

STAY IN SYNC

"It takes time."
  "You didn't rush me."

Clients talk about how therapists often seem to lack patience. They have spoken of therapists who expected too much of them and those who expressed disapproval when they failed to comply with their requests such as homework assignments or advice. In my opinion, all are partially associated with timing. We sometimes make the mistake of going along at our own pace and ignoring the client's, and in doing so, we do not stay in sync with or match his or her rhythm. My bias is that *knowing* is often the culprit that speeds us up or steers us in a direction that may be too different from our clients'.

I am reminded of Sabrina's comment "Like running side-by-side with your client, rather than saying 'come on you can do it' [gesturing a 'come to me' with her hands] or 'go ahead' [gesturing a pushing motion]." Thomas likewise talked about why therapists need to take time in talking with them: "If you do it [interview] in a hurry it would be easy to jump to [wrong] conclusions." Another client felt that her therapist was "on a walk with me, right by my side."

In my experience, like the tortoise, I get there faster by going slower.[12] And, I get where *we* choose to go rather than where I choose to lead or force a client to follow—faster by walking side by side with the client rather than pushing from behind or pulling from in front.

Observers of my work often comment on my patience. One colleague, referring to a client with a complicated and detailed story, said, "What patience you have to sit there and listen to all of that." Or, as an observing cybernetician once said, "That woman is a boredom-making machine." Such comments represent ideas about how a conversation should be. I do not equate staying in sync or matching a client's rhythm with patience. Patience usually means being tolerant, waiting until the other person has finished so that we can then say what we really want to say or believe is true. I do not experience what appears to be patience this way. Flowing with clients, letting them tell the story at their pace, is not boring. If a therapist is genuinely immersed in and participating in what another person deems important, he or she will naturally stay in sync with a client's rhythm. I resonate with Tom Andersen's (1995a, 1995b) philosophy "Life is not something you can force, it has to come."

HONOR A CLIENT'S STORY

"Take me seriously."
　"Validate me."

Clients say they want to be taken seriously and validated. I am reminded of Hans, a forty-three-year-old man, and the elderly aunt and uncle who had raised him.[13] They were referred to consultation by the halfway house that in their words was "forced to discharge Hans prematurely." The aunt and uncle were not worried about where Hans would currently live, but they were desperately anxious about his future after they died, if these crises recurred as they had for over twenty years. Hans, formally diagnosed as a chronic schizophrenic, self-diagnosed himself as "I'm confused about who

I am" and the problem as "They kicked me out because they got mad at me because I overslept and didn't get to work on time."

In talking about this recent incident Hans said, "They don't understand me," to which the therapist replied, "Does anyone understand you?" "My aunt," said Hans. Turning to the aunt the therapist asked, "What do you do to make him feel you understand?" "I take what he says seriously," she said, and Hans nodded in agreement. Shotter (1995a) emphasizes "the importance of people being able to voice their own 'position' in relation to others around them and to have what they say, as Hans's aunt so powerfully indicates, *taken seriously* [my emphasis] by being actively responded to" (p. 387).

The Perils of Professional-Led Stories

Assigning a professional's story precedence over a client's understanding is not new. Extensive behavioral confirmation process research on the influence of the observer's preconceptions of what he or she expects to see, and does see, indicates that the observer often not only sees but actually participates in creating what he or she expects (Jones, 1986, 1993; Rosenhan, 1973; Snyder, 1984). For instance, if we think in terms of and look for family patterns, we will see them. If we think in terms of diagnoses, we will diagnose; if a client extends a weak handshake and we believe that a weak handshake is a sign of passiveness, we will most likely see more signs of passiveness. If we think that a comment like Sabrina's,

> You don't know a whole lot about me. You're sitting here listening. What's going on in your head? How do you work? Are you listening to the words I'm saying? What are you picking up on? What do you want? Where are you trying to take this session? . . . What are you trying to master? What are you trying to demonstrate to all of them?

is an attempt to control, we will see control. Snyder and Thomsen (1988) offered a comprehensive review of studies that indicate the rapidity with which therapists "know" a client's problem whether the knowing is in the form of a hypothesis or a formal diagnosis. Significant among these are findings that therapists frequently form their initial clinical judgment in the first three minutes of contact with the client, often influenced by the referral information or the client's records, and those judgments, in turn, influence the treatment of choice and its outcome (Gauron & Dickinson, 1969; Sandifer, Hordern, & Green, 1970).

Van der Merwe and his colleague (1995) quote Wittgenstein's reference to this believing is seeing or perceiving is seeing phenomenon: "'Seeing as' is a remarkable feature of perceiving . . . 'see' means both seeing something 'as' in accord with some vision one *really* has, and seeing something out there in the visual field" (p. 43).

Other Professional-Led Stories

Professional-led rather than client-led stories are not unique to the therapy profession. Beckman and Frankel (1984) reported thought-provoking results of a discourse analysis of patient–doctor interactions as doctors solicited chief complaints. Their study overwhelmingly concluded that physicians participate in inhibiting the collection of relevant information by, among other things, interrupting, making premature hypotheses, not showing interest in or giving opportunity to elaborate complaints, and doing most of the talking. Their data specifically showed that

> after a brief period of time (mean, 18 seconds), and most often after the expression of a single stated concern the physicians in our study took control of the visit by asking increasingly specific, closed-ended questions that effectively halted the spontaneous flow of information from the patient. (p. 694)

To compare this with another profession, the legal scholar Peggy Davis (1992) described law as an "interactive, culturally embedded process," and studied the processes of promoting or discouraging hierarchical professional roles (p. 186). Analyzing language in simulated client–lawyer interactions, she found that in general

> people in the role of lawyers assumed a decidedly dominant role in interactions with their clients. They controlled the flow of topics and, after the initial telling of the client's story, talked more than their clients. People in the role of clients behaved consistently with the assumption of lawyer-dominance. They spoke more haltingly, used more hedges, and made more frequent use of other linguistic forms associated with tentativeness. (p. 187)

Davis identified "interactive patterns that distinguished relatively controlled and relatively open interviewing styles which began in the opening moments of the interview" (p. 187). In the controlling or lawyer-centered style, the lawyers asked many questions, made many requests, and dominated the choice of and flow of topics. Clients were hesitant and uncertain, used imprecise terms, and tended to conceive the problem in the lawyer's language. In contrast, the open or client-centered style was character-ized by a shared selection of topics, mutual control of the interview, less client uncertainty, and less lawyer interference with the client's conceptualization of the problem.

Similarly, the law professor Richard Sherwin (1993), interested in professional–client interactions from the perspective of power, described how people in positions of power guide or tell another's story—controlling the flow of topics and setting the pace, thus reflecting more of their sense of reality than the client's. Both Davis and Sherwin advocate a client–professional relationship in which there is room for a client's expertise to be combined with a professional's.

Connecting, Collaborating, and Constructing

This practical advice from the experts suggests ways to invite clients into *dialogical conversations* and *collaborative narrative relationships* that are illustrated in the following excerpt from a conversation between a therapist, Sylvia, and her client, Theresa, as they talk about Theresa's struggle with a chronic gastrointestinal problem, insomnia, and her associated anxiety.[14] Theresa's words capture the essence of the relationship and process in which therapists and clients, doctors and patients, or lawyers and clients engage each other to become conversational partners in the telling, inquiring, interpreting, and shaping of narratives. I am struck by the similarity in her and Anna's earlier words concerning how talking permitted them to be open and not to hide. Theresa speaks to the kind of conversational interactions between client and therapist that are similar to what Kathy Weingarten (1991) calls *intimacy* and Judith Jordan (1991) calls *mutuality*.

> THERESA: When I first came I was physically ill and that was limiting and scary. The fear limited my capacity to look at my self and made me weak and fragile. The first step was to recover my health.
> SYLVIA: How did *we* [my emphasis] do it? Where did we build the diving board to jump from?
> THERESA: I felt so deprived of myself, on the floor. I had nothing to lose. This [metaphorical therapy] provided me a place of trust. A place to start the dialogue. The possibility not to hide anything and the sense of working towards problem resolutions.

The nuances, richness, and moments of this kind of relational process are difficult to convey. Toward this end I have tried to let the client's voice have a place of prominence and to represent the client's meanings as best I understand them. These client narratives, which were once alive, breathing dialogue—shared storied experiences that the client, I, and others participated in—are now merely memories of our experiences and my interpretations on paper. All client voices speak to a process and relationship characterized by connecting, collaborating, and constructing (Anderson, 1992).[15]

In the next chapter I continue to focus on this process and relationship as I share an annotated partial transcript of a consultation interview.

CHAPTER 8

A Glimpse of a Good
Mother–Bad Mother Story

*Everywhere I encountered messages about the criteria for being a
good mother and the criteria for being a bad one.*
—KATHY WEINGARTEN

CONTEXT OF THE CONVERSATION

I HAD AN OPPORTUNITY to be a *visiting therapist* with my colleague Sue
Levin and her client, whom I will call Natalie.* The following is a partial transcript of a conversation that we had. I believe that it illustrates
the *essence* of my approach to therapy: its process, its philosophical
stance, and the change that is the natural consequence of the process.

The idea for my visit developed in a discussion Sue and I had
just minutes before Natalie's appointment. When Natalie arrived,
Sue asked her whether I might join their session. She told her that

---

* I thank Master'sWork Productions for producing this interview as a
videotape. I thank Britta Lödgö and Gunilla Ström for their helpful reflections on this interview.

I wanted to videotape our talk and hoped that together the three of us might have some fresh ideas about Natalie's life situation. Natalie agreed, provided that she would have the option of requesting that the videotape be erased.

I do not think of myself as a master consultant or therapist who participates from a metaposition, has privileged knowledge, or has better ideas. I see myself as a guest who drops in on an ongoing conversation. I emphasize that I want only to join the conversation, not to interrupt it or change its course.

I knew nothing about Natalie, or about her and Sue's work together, before we met except that her name was Natalie and she had to return to work in an hour. I wanted to learn about her in her presence and, most important, from her. If Sue had wanted to tell me about Natalie before I actually met her, I would have listened. Then, when I met Natalie I would have shared what I had learned with her. In this situation, Sue said that she preferred that Natalie and I talk and that she would feel free to join in at any time.

Our conversation began with Sue's introducing Natalie to me. Natalie spontaneously joined in and began to tell her story. Although you will learn about Natalie along with me as her story unfolds, I will give a preview of the interview. Natalie was struggling with the effects of divorce on her relationship with her daughter and her daughter's decision to move to her father's house. Natalie and Sue had had five previous sessions. Natalie consulted Sue about her daughter, age fourteen. The cast of characters consists of Natalie, her second husband, their ten-year-old son, their fourteen-year-old daughter, and their fifteen-year-old son, who currently lives with his father, Natalie's ex-husband. Also mentioned in the interview are Natalie's mother, the daughter and older son's stepmother, and aunts. Our conversation lasts forty-seven minutes.

Here I share transcripts, four excerpts in chronological order from this conversation, one excerpt from a later conversation between Natalie and Sue, and a six-month follow-up telephone conversation. I note the times of each excerpt to give you a sense of the pace of our talks.

But first, I would like to leave some questions hanging in the air as you read the transcript: What preconceived ideas and what theoretical lenses do you bring to this interview about therapy and about Natalie? Which of those ideas, if any, might inadvertently close you off to Natalie's story and lead her to tell the story you would like to hear or think she ought to be telling?

From the Beginning: A Sensitive Dilemma

Sue, Natalie, and I are sitting in a semicircle with Natalie in the middle. Natalie is dressed in a business suit, is very attractive, and has a beautiful smile. She sits up straight in her chair with hands clasped, ankles crossed, and head slightly tilted. She appears to be quite attentive, yet a bit tense or nervous. She listens carefully, provides good eye contact, and speaks quickly, often responding as if she already knows what I'm about to ask. She occasionally uses hand gestures but is not overly animated. We talk through tears and laughter. After reminding me of the time boundaries, Sue begins.

> SUE: It was in relationship to a current struggle with her daughter, and concerns around her daughter and how to mother her and how to continue to mother her, I think, are maybe the current issues that Natalie and I have been talking about. She has two children from a previous marriage and one from her current marriage, and the younger two are with her, and it's the middle child which is the daughter that [laughs], I'm confusing you [laughs], that we're talking about.
>
> HARLENE: Okay. And her name is . . .
>
> NATALIE: Alicia.
>
> HARLENE: Alicia, and she's how old?
>
> NATALIE: Fourteen.
>
> HARLENE: Fourteen.
>
> NATALIE: She has always lived with me and I remarried when she was two, and she now wants to go and live with her dad. But it's . . . things that are so upsetting is my relationship with her and the way I'm feeling. I feel like she's an enemy in my house, that she decides that what we do is wrong and it's not a good house and it's not a good place to live and goes around telling other people that. I think that's what it is that's, that's more my ego of . . . I've always been a pleaser and want to look good to other people [laughs], and deep down I feel like, "Well, there must be something wrong with a young girl who wants to leave her mother."
>
> HARLENE: So, not only is she maybe ruining your reputation in the community, but you're really, really concerned about "Am I doing something wrong?"
>
> NATALIE: Well, I'm really concerned about how I feel about myself and how I feel about her, and her behavior sometimes gets, I mean, the horrible things she says to me, and I've always

tried to make everything perfect for her, you know. We moved here, she didn't like the school, put her in a private school. Go around . . . she can't adjust, so I go around trying to fix everything and I really, it feels, unappreciated [laughs], but now we've decided that she must, she's probably just going to have to go. You know, she's going to have to get her way, and . . .

HARLENE: So it's gotten really, really bad.

NATALIE: [agrees, indicating here and elsewhere an affirmative nod]

HARLENE: Now, and when you said she goes around saying that "we are doing things wrong," she means you and . . . ?

NATALIE: . . . my husband.

HARLENE: . . . and your husband.

NATALIE: She and my husband don't have a good relationship now. And why that . . . I feel . . . I feel really resentful toward him also for some of it, and I really feel like right now I'd just like to knock all of 'em off a cliff [laughs].

HARLENE: So you're really upset and angry at all of them.

Comment: Here I am not trying to reflect what she just said or to point out her anger but to check with her to make sure that I am not misunderstanding.

NATALIE: I am, I'm upset and I'm angry, and I'm . . . it's interfering with functioning in my life, and I'm tired of internalizing it that I'm just this bad person, and I know intellectually I'm not. In fact, I'm the *other* way. I try to make everything *too* right.

HARLENE: So how've the two of you been talking about this? You said this is kind of the current concern, and is this what you initially came in about, or . . . ?

Comment: Here is an example of how I use what I call collective and cooperative language: referring to the *two of them* (Natalie and Sue) *meeting* and referring to *current concerns*.

NATALIE: Initially I brought Alicia to see Sue.

HARLENE: Brought Alicia to see Sue, so . . .

NATALIE: And she *does* see her sometimes, you know, without me.

HARLENE [agrees]: So the two of you have been meeting for how long? Are there different combinations?

SUE: Yeah, different combinations.

NATALIE: Yeah.

SUE: Overall it's been maybe . . . six months?

NATALIE: I'd say six months. It was first Alicia maybe every two weeks and then I just recently started coming. Sometimes I'd, you know, meet with Alicia. But her dad is not trustworthy and he'd tell . . . what she wanted to do this last summer, and so I called him, we agreed that he was going to say that she couldn't, she needed to be with me and she . . . he was going to back me up and have her stay. But then he tells her things, you know, lets her believe that he will come there, which he will, now, he *will*, and he's . . . I feel like he goes behind my back. He didn't do what we agreed upon, and so we were telling her two different things.

HARLENE: And this is something that's happened over and over again? Is that what you're referring to or . . . ?

NATALIE: Recent . . . well, he's always been like . . . I have a very hard time dealing with him, and so, I mean, I think Alicia just has a lot of problems and she gets reality mixed up and she . . . but now I'm really concerned about my*self* and how I'm going to make . . . you know . . . I was concerned how I was going to live with her for another four years, now I'm concerned about how I'm going to be when she's gone.

HARLENE: Just how you're going to make it, yeah.

NATALIE: [agrees]

HARLENE: So in terms of continuing to talk today, you want to talk more about yourself in terms of when she's gone? It sounds like you think she really *is* going?

Comment: Here I check with Natalie to make sure I have a sense of her agenda.

NATALIE: Yes, I do.

HARLENE: Okay.

NATALIE: I don't know what's *normal*. I don't know what's . . . you know, everybody talks about teenage girls being . . . maybe I just, I'm too sensitive. I don't know what's *normal* for me to feel. I know I go overboard . . . I . . . though my history is to be . . . to go overboard and to be . . . you know, everything's just the end of the world, you know, but it's starting to affect me on how I treat her and how I am in the family and, because I'm so *angry*.

HARLENE: So you don't know whether you're . . .

NATALIE: I just feel like she's an enemy, I blame my husband, I just . . . I don't *know*. I'm a mess [laughs].

HARLENE: Wow. She's fourteen and the older . . . ?

NATALIE: My son is fifteen.

HARLENE: Fifteen.

NATALIE: He lives with his dad. He left when he was about twelve.

HARLENE: When he was about twelve.

NATALIE: [agrees]

HARLENE: And then the youngest child of . . . ?

NATALIE: . . . is my husband and mine together and he's ten.

HARLENE: He's ten. So she's the girl and the middle one. Okay. So do you think that you're worrying about your daughter or reacting more strongly than most moms in your situation would be?

NATALIE: I don't know. I don't know, but I see other children her age and if they come over, and they don't act . . . I mean she's just very *intense* and she just, from that frame of reference . . . they don't cause terror and chaos in the home all the time. I don't think that has to be. But my son that's *ten* starts to talk like that too, now, you know. It seems to be the going thing. So . . .

HARLENE: I mean, do you think he's learning from *her* or it's just . . . ?

NATALIE: Yes, I do.

HARLENE: Okay. It's not just that that's the way kids are these days.

NATALIE: And then Alicia tells it that we fight, that she can't live here because we fight too much. She's mainly the re . . . when she's not there, it's peaceful [laughs].

HARLENE: Wow.

NATALIE: So, not all together . . . I know that's not *all* her, but . . . I would just like to sail off into the [laughs] . . .

HARLENE: . . . be a runaway mother and wife, it sounds like.

NATALIE: . . . you know, I'm just really, really angry. I just want her to leave *right now* if she's going to leave, because she's going to have to stay . . . what we've decided until the end of the *year*, and for school. And, I don't know. I hate answering to her father.

SUE: One other complicating thing, I guess, just that I've been thinking about while I'm listening to you talk, is that, as Natalie said, Alicia's really intense and Natalie has always done her best to try and understand Alicia's distress and a lot of it doesn't make sense a lot of times, because from Alicia's perspective, as Natalie was saying, you know, the family's just *terrible* and they're always fighting and nothing ever goes well and so Natalie really struggles with that. And, I guess there's now another part of it, which is that you found yourself not wanting to try and understand or be as sympathetic as you've been in the past with Alicia and how hard that is for *you*. I guess I'm thinking I'm hearing you say you've got another couple of months *with* her, and I guess maybe the question may be, "How can I continue to work with her or, you know, love her and care about her and be a good mother in the next couple of months?"

NATALIE: Yeah, I see myself like my mother as very controlling and very "couldn't let go" even as adults . . . "Well, poor me, look what you're doing to me," and all that. Well, that's kind of how I feel I'm doing to her. You know, like, "You're *leaving* me."

HARLENE: [agrees]

NATALIE: If she *really* wants to live with her dad . . . she's never lived with him, you know, if *that's* what she's saying *now*, that's what the reason is, not that she wants to leave *me*, but that she just wants, you know . . .

HARLENE: That's what she's actually telling you now?

NATALIE: Yeah.

HARLENE: Okay?

NATALIE: Well, then . . . why can't I just say "Okay"? It's just that I don't know if it's that I . . . part of it's that I'll miss her, but part of it's that I don't want to look bad, and . . .

HARLENE: Okay. Or feel like a failure? That you've failed?

NATALIE: Like a failure, yes.

HARLENE: Okay, and then you said that you're very sensitive to your ex-husband in terms of . . . ?

Comment: I continue to try to learn more about what concerns her, what is most important for her now.

NATALIE: It's very hard . . . I mean he just says two things out of both sides of his mouth. He just, you know, and then *I* end up looking like the nut [laughs]. I mean, you know, just . . . it . . . and I don't, you know . . . it's been a *long* history of court battles and things, so, you know, I'd just as soon not deal . . . we . . . she wants to go to a priv[ate] . . . I mean, I'd just as soon not deal with him. He wants to go to . . . she wants to go to a private school when she goes there, and I've traditionally been the one that's paid for things. *Now* nobody's paying child support to anybody because he's taking care of the son and I'm taking care of the daughter. Well, I'll *pay* if she goes there, but what I've decided to keep from being in on the decisions and on the fights and in on what's going to happen *is*, I'll just pay a certain *amount*, and it's between she and her dad which school she goes to and what she does with the money, to take myself out of that.

HARLENE [agrees]: So we've got *two* things. We've got you're concerned about what to do and how you're going to be over the next couple of months, and then what's going to happen and how you're going to be once she leaves.

Comment: I listen respectfully, actively, and responsively as I try to learn about what Natalie wants me to know and try to hear what she wants me to hear. My manner is tentative as I ask questions, make comments, share thoughts out loud, pose checking-out statements, and offer imagined ideas that are often left hanging, unfinished. I often summarize as a way of making sure that I have heard, as best I can, what she said, what she wanted me to hear. For instance, is this what she's concerned about and wants to talk about? My utterances are not made, for instance, as questions to answer, comments to lead Natalie in a particular direction, ideas to seed, or truth summaries. Instead, they are the tools I use to learn more about Natalie's story, to give her a chance to correct any of my misunderstandings, to clarify or expand on what she has just said. My aim is to facilitate a process.

I scan, often return to things Natalie has said earlier. Scanning helps keep all directions, paths, and possibilities open. It lessens the chance that I might dominate the story to be told, for instance, by choosing to pursue a direction that will close off one important to Natalie. I believe that when we relentlessly pursue one line of thought we inadvertently, or sometimes purposefully, signal to a client that this is what is important.

Let me return to my last comment: "So we've got *two* things. We've got you're concerned about what to do and how you're going to be over the next couple of months, and then what's going to happen and how you're going to be once she leaves."

NATALIE: Yes.

HARLENE: Now what . . . you said something about the end of school. Is that . . . what's the two-month punctuation, that she'd leave in two months?

NATALIE: Well it's going to be like till the end of school, till the end of May, when she'll be in school, and then she'll *go*.

SUE: It's three months.

HARLENE: Oh. Okay, okay. So the end of this semester and then she'll go and spend the summer and start school there.

NATALIE: [agrees]

HARLENE: Okay. And so you're going to miss *her*, you're going to think people are going to think *badly* of you? You're going to also feel like a bad *mother*?

NATALIE: [agrees]

HARLENE: Which of those or any others we would want to add to the list bothers you the *most*, do you think, or *will* bother you the most?

NATALIE: . . . I don't know. I have so many feelings I don't even know what . . . [laughs].

HARLENE: Where to begin?

NATALIE: Yeah . . . I feel like I need some support, you know, of . . . I just don't even want to tell people I work with that my daughter left. You know, I just don't want anybody to *know* . . . 'cause I told them about how I'd look for the school, you know, and they, you know . . .

HARLENE: So again it was not only being a *public* failure, but somehow in your own heart, your own gut, sort of verify to you that you really are *failing* her? Is that what we're really talking about? Feeling like a failure as a mother or, I guess, as a person?

NATALIE: Yeah, that's my mother's role model . . . was that was all that was important. You know, if you were a good parent, your children turned out perfectly, and she had all passive children [laughs], you know, that just did that, you know, and so that's what my idea of being *worthwhile* is.

HARLENE: And so you blame yourself a lot, and have . . .

[Another example of a *hanging* comment]

NATALIE: Yeah, *even* in my job. I've gone back to school, I've got my CPA license, now I'm working at a financial planning firm, which is *so* interesting, and I still keep thinking, "Well, maybe if I was just *home*," you know, and that's the only thing I have that gives me any *good* feeling.

HARLENE: Oh, that that would make everything okay . . .

NATALIE: If I quit *working*.

HARLENE: . . . and that she . . .

NATALIE: And that's the only thing I have that's worthwhile in my life [laughs]. So I don't know why I even *think* that.

HARLENE [agrees]: So you keep searching for, "what I've done or not done that's made this awful problem with my daughter"? What have people told you in terms of their evaluation of this, of the situation, or what they think's going on? What . . . I mean, has Sue told you anything in terms of what she thinks is going on with your daughter, or does she think you've done anything wrong . . .

SUE: Have I said . . . ?

HARLENE: . . . or friends, or family, or . . . ?

NATALIE: That I've done anything wrong? No. No, you haven't. I don't know. I don't have an understanding of Alicia or, you know, reactions to her . . . I *feel* like I'm doing like my mother, "Oh, you've hurt *me*," you know, instead of just saying . . . because I have heard of people saying, "Well, if you want to go live with your dad, whatever makes you happy, let's just *do* it." I have heard people *say* that. Why is it *killing* me so?

HARLENE: So that's a big question . . .

NATALIE: It's a *failure* like my husband, my ex-husband, who *wouldn't* work, *wouldn't* pay child support, would *tear* the kids apart . . . take them out and tell them stuff that she still throws back to me until we had to get an injunction against him almost not to see the children and then we went to court, we had joint custody, we got so . . . the judge gave *me* custody because he was such a nut.

HARLENE: Because it had gotten so bad.

NATALIE: Yeah. And now he's *winning*. He's looking like the perfect *home*. Because they never fight *there*, and that's just the perfect home. And look what all I've done. You know, blood, sweat, and tears and he's coming out looking like . . . smelling like a *rose* [laughs]. I guess that's what bothers me.

HARLENE: So that's a big piece. You've mentioned two or three times being like your mom.

Comment: I comment on something that she said earlier.

NATALIE: Yeah.

HARLENE: Say more about that . . . or that you think you're like your mom or your fear is that you are.

NATALIE: Yeah. I don't want to be like that, controlling, in that, "You are *doing* this to me." You know, I want to take care of my*self*. But why should I not let Alicia know that I'll *miss* . . . that I don't want her to go? You know, I don't know. I . . . you know, but I told her, you know, it would be okay because

I *did* have to lean to the left last time, that killed me *too,* and I was very depressed for about two years.

HARLENE: Okay, now I'm not connecting on something. So you're saying, "Why should I not be able to tell her that I'm missing her?" And that's . . . you think you *shouldn't* do that or . . . ?

NATALIE: I feel like maybe, like if she saw me crying, you know, that night, a few nights ago, you know . . . I don't know. I don't want to make her feel guilty. I don't *know.* I just really don't have . . . sometimes I feel like I hate her.

Comment: Natalie's tears are visible as she searches for words for her feelings. It's like the Latin word, *alexthymi*: not having words for feeling or connections between feelings and mind.

HARLENE: [agrees]

NATALIE: . . . that she's my enemy. You know, I just want her away from me.

HARLENE: So you just find yourself sort of spinning all the time. Gosh.

NATALIE [agrees]: And I'm having a hard time with me living there with all this, you know, going on.

HARLENE: What about your husband? What's his take on all of this?

NATALIE [laughs]: Well . . .

HARLENE: What's his theory as to what this is all about in terms of with your daughter and with you and the two of you?

Comment: Natalie had mentioned her husband (Alicia's stepfather) in the beginning of the interview. So, curious, I return to him. Some readers might have been interested in learning more about their relationship when she first mentioned him. I saw no need earlier to pursue her relationship with her husband; instead, I chose to catalogue her comment and return to it if and when it came up later. This was a choice that I made as I was keeping in my thoughts the reason for our talking and it seemed to be only a very temporary part of what we were talking about. Perhaps I could have asked at the time whether that was something that she and Sue were talking about.

Natalie tells us that her husband, who has been in Alicia's life since she was eleven months old, blames Alicia's father. She first talks a little about Alicia's father and then shares her theory that Alicia has always been her husband's favorite. And, she believes, the way he shows his favoritism may be part of the problem. As she puts this part of her story on pause, I comment, "That's another big question mark."

NATALIE: Oh, you know, he wants to blame my ex-husband for telling . . . you know, telling her she can come, and he's *always* done . . . my ex-husband has always told them that . . . you know, tried to stir things up. But he [Alicia's stepfather] won't take responsibility for some of the . . . he's been a good step-parent, I mean, he has provided and he has been there, and he has gone and taken, you know, just like they're his child, you know, children, both of them. Went to all the school things, took them to all their ball games, you know, just did every-thing just like a regular father. But he has this one problem with Alicia that he's always chosen to needle her and tease her and annoy her.

HARLENE: Your husband now?

NATALIE: Yes.

Comment: I will briefly summarize what Natalie tells me. She is upset with her husband, Alicia's stepfather, because he "teases" and "picks on" Alicia so much and neither she nor Alicia likes it. As a matter of fact, Natalie says it makes her very angry. They have talked about this in therapy but "he doesn't seem to be able to *help* it." I learn that he teases Alicia because she is his favorite and in his family that is how they "show you care about somebody." I won-der why the stepfather does not "get" what she and Alicia have tried to tell him. Natalie does not know; I comment, "That's another big question mark."

As we return to the transcript, Natalie has just talked about how confused she is and how many issues there are. (This is eighteen minutes into the conversation.)

From Something Wrong to Question Marks

NATALIE: Yeah, some, I mean I think . . . well, I don't know. I'm just really confused.

HARLENE: Yeah, sounds like it. I mean it sounds like there's just so many . . .

NATALIE: So many issues.

HARLENE: So many issues and so many pieces. It's like which . . . how do you even pursue one of 'em because they're all so interrelated. Let's go on the theory that you *have* done something wrong. What have you done wrong? Let's say you've caused all of this. What have you done? What have you caused?

Comment: As we continue, Natalie returns to her thoughts that she has done something wrong to cause the problem with her daughter. I suggest, "Let's go on the theory that you have done something wrong." This comment is not meant to be paradoxical or provocative but to be in keeping with Natalie's fear of having done something wrong.

> NATALIE: Well, first thing that comes to my mind is I was divorced.
> HARLENE: Okay, you divorced her dad.
> NATALIE: I'd tell her that I didn't have any choice, but I *did*. I knew when I *married* him. I guess, that's my biggest sin.
> HARLENE: So, okay, so you think . . .
> NATALIE: [laughs]
> HARLENE [agrees]: . . . that you divorced her dad and that's part of it.
> NATALIE: [agrees]
> HARLENE: Okay, what else?
> NATALIE: Well, that's what the . . . that's what the long . . . it's a very legalistic, religious background, my family, and Alicia's picked that up. We've talked about that, how she really is more like the daughter of my mother other than me.
> HARLENE: Oh, she holds more of their . . .
> NATALIE: [agrees]
> HARLENE: . . . sort of beliefs than yours . . .
> NATALIE: Than my brother. They're all in church music and all, and so that's what she likes. She's very hypocritical. And then she comes home and tells me to go to hell [laughs], you know, but she sings in the choir [laughs], you know, it's like, but . . . so . . .
> HARLENE: Okay. So, one of the things you did wrong is you divorced him, but that's something *you* believe? Or you're saying that's something more that your family believes?
> NATALIE: Well, see, I don't *know* if . . . deep down what I believe. It's just intellectually I know I had no choice and that it was a mistake and people make mistakes in marrying.
> HARLENE: Okay.
> NATALIE: But I *feel* that *she* is trying to punish me because she . . . that's what she's mad about.
> HARLENE: She's mad about the *divorce*?

NATALIE: Right. Because she has a picture of me in my twenties on this little stand-up frame on her dress . . . on her desk with her dad on the other side of it. And that's what it all goes back to. You know, "Well you just don't understand," and "You just shouldn't have gotten divorced."

HARLENE: Okay. So *she* blames you.

NATALIE: Yes.

HARLENE: Okay.

NATALIE: And that's where *all* the problems started. She can't go on with her life because "She's had just a *horrible* life because her parents were divorced."

HARLENE: Okay, so let's see, so far you've done two things wrong. You married her dad and you . . .

NATALIE: Divorced him.

HARLENE: Divorced him. Okay, what else? What else have you done wrong to create this nightmare?

NATALIE: Then I married the stepfather [laughs].

HARLENE: Married the stepfather, okay, okay. What else?

NATALIE: Then I had another child who . . . this is the big thing . . . his . . . my husband's mother lives in Houston, here, with us. I mean, she doesn't live with us, but in this . . . and this is the first time we've lived in the same city with her.

HARLENE: Okay.

NATALIE: And this is her grandchild, my son. Well she makes a real big point of . . . you know, she acts on the outside like she's treating Alicia like she's part of the family, *too*, but she'll, like, go buy Alicia . . . and she'd take some chocolate or something. She'll buy Alicia one little thing and she'll buy Joey six or seven things. You know, she makes a . . . you can really *tell*.

HARLENE: So even though she tries not to be partial, you think she's obvious . . .

NATALIE: Well, I don't . . . I think she knows *exactly* what she's doing and that that's just how she *is*.

HARLENE: Oh. Okay. Okay, so she's obviously partial to her own . . .

NATALIE: Right, and that really hurts Alicia . . .

HARLENE: . . . biological grandson and that hurts Alicia.

NATALIE: Yeah, that's what she says. "I don't feel like I'm part of this family," and that's *one* thing she brings up.

HARLENE: Okay.

NATALIE: And it's not that she wants some things, it's just, it's so obvious.

HARLENE: [agrees]

NATALIE: And so that's one mistake. Another mistake . . .

HARLENE: So that's another mistake. You had another child . . .

NATALIE: [laughs]

HARLENE: . . . and you happen to, I guess . . .

NATALIE: He's being favored . . . he's being treated as part of the family and she's not.

HARLENE: Okay, and you moved back to Houston, where she is, okay, so we've got about six of them now. What else [laughs]?

SUE: Right, moving to Houston, although, may not seem like as big of a thing, but compared to like, for example, moving back to Baton Rouge . . .

NATALIE: Oh, yeah, that would be . . .

SUE: . . . that would be a big mistake, the choice of where you moved. Uh huh.

NATALIE: Instead of Baton Rouge, we moved to Houston.

HARLENE: Oh, so you think we'd add that on the list.

NATALIE: Yeah, *she* says, "If you just would've moved to Baton Rouge . . . that you know, now I'll keep living with *you* and then I could see my dad and whenever I wanted to." But we *had* to leave there because it was just . . . dealing with her dad was awful.

HARLENE: What else have you done wrong?

NATALIE: Oh, let me see. I went to *work* [laughs].

HARLENE: Okay.

NATALIE: Left my children, went to work. I only went to work about three or four years ago.

HARLENE: She was about eleven or so, okay.

NATALIE: [agrees]

HARLENE: Okay. What else have you done wrong?

NATALIE: Sometimes I say things that are awful to her when I get, you know . . .

Comment: As we continue to talk, Natalie's narrative begins to shift away from what she did wrong and her failure as a mother, to the failure in the relationship with her daughter. Something is not the way that she would like it to be.

Remember, in the very beginning of the interview, when Natalie said, "Things are upsetting in my relationship with her and the way I'm feeling"? Earlier she had focused on having *caused* the problem; here she's still talking about the same events. The events haven't changed, but she's beginning to understand them differently and attribute other meanings to them.

She shifts from what might be thought of as an unsolvable problem to a solvable one. That is, there's more possibility to create, to have the kind of relationship she wants with her daughter, *than* to correct her past failure as a mother. This shift was not my intent; it evolved through the dialogue.

> HARLENE: It sounds like you just feel like pulling your hair out at times and get really frustrated when things aren't going well, and particularly, I guess, as I'm imagining as hard as you try . . .
>
> NATALIE: [agrees]
>
> HARLENE: . . . for things to go right . . .
>
> NATALIE: Right.
>
> HARLENE: And how hard you are on yourself in terms of judging yourself as a mother.
>
> NATALIE: Yes.
>
> HARLENE: So you say things that you wish you could take back at times.
>
> NATALIE: Yeah, I think, you know, "Why don't I just let her say whatever she's saying and then just not say . . . you know, just go ahead and . . . that's the child, I'm the adult and why should I get in to her thing, you know, doing that?" Then why don't I just say, "Oh, that's the way kids are and that doesn't hurt my feelings," you know, "I'll just not even listen to it." But I *do* listen to it.
>
> HARLENE [agrees]: And take it very seriously because, again, I think you're very sensitive to how you're . . . as you said to how you're doing as a mother and not only evaluating yourself but other people you feel are evaluating you and . . . plus, you're concerned about your *daughter*, I mean, heavens, you *are*, yeah.
>
> NATALIE: She doesn't seem to need me right now but, I feel . . . you know it's hard for me to believe that some time . . . if she goes and stays for four years that there won't be some time that I won't be there and I will need to be there.
>
> HARLENE: So, it's not only things that you've already done, but you're already starting to worry about things that you might not do . . .

Comment: Natalie's worried about past failure and future failure.

NATALIE: Yeah, and the other thing is I'm jealous of her step-mother and my sister-in-law who lives there that she just adores that does *everything* perfect and that has a *perfect* life and that is going to be the mother. My sister-in-law will be more of the mother than . . .

HARLENE: Than the stepmother. Okay.

NATALIE: Than the stepmother. But, they're going to be the mothers. I mean, I'm not going to *be* there; *they'll* be the mothers. Well, I don't want my *place* being taken . . .

HARLENE: So what are you thinking, Sue? It looks like you seem . . .

Comment: Although Sue chooses primarily to listen, I consider her an active member of our conversation. I glance at Sue as Natalie and I talk because I want her to feel included. Sue, like any listener, is having her own inner dialogue and I am curious about it. (This is twenty-five minutes into the conversation.)

Possibilities Emerge for Salvaging a Relationship

I learn what Sue's been thinking. I learn that Natalie was previously in therapy for two years dealing with feeling "unworthy" and "depression" and that she was on antidepressants for six months. Natalie joined in, "I kind of divorced myself from my internal feelings." In addition, she had attended numerous workshops "about self-acceptance." Despite all of this, Natalie said, "I feel terrible."

Sue does not disagree with Natalie that perhaps these previous experiences did not help her self-esteem problem, but maybe they allowed her to be open to herself about all of her feelings and ideas. Sue commented on how honest she thinks Natalie is with herself. We talk about how it might have been a whole lot easier not to be so honest and not to acknowledge and analyze the things she's done or not done.

Natalie told me that her worst fear is that everything will be okay with Alicia, that Alicia will then never call or need her, and that her fear that she has been a bad mother will be confirmed. Sue commented that she has been trying to imagine how Alicia would be listening to this conversation. As we continued, I learned that an equally big fear for Natalie is that she might become as depressed and miserable as she had been. As we see next, Natalie began to talk more about herself and less about her relationship with her daughter.

HARLENE: So, it sounds like you're *really* miserable.

NATALIE: Oh yeah, I know what it was . . . my worth. It's just I don't feel worthy and when we . . . before we moved here I was . . . I really *was* depressed, not like I am now. I was really depressed [laughs] to where I couldn't even move hardly. Well, I was like that for a long time before I realized something was really wrong, and so I finally went . . . I thought I should go to a medical doctor. Something was just terribly wrong with me. Well, I went to a psychologist and then I went to a psychiatrist and I took medication for about six months, but I went to see the psychologist every week . . . and I *was* depr[essed] . . . and that was after laying in . . . it was just everything together, you know, after my son had left, and I just felt . . . that's when I kept thinking was, "I feel so unworthy," and I feel that way a little bit now. I don't feel like I did then.

HARLENE: Not as much unworthy, but still some . . .

NATALIE: But I'm scared; I don't want to *be* like that again.

HARLENE: What did the psychologist tell you? I mean, what did he think was going on?

NATALIE: I don't think he went far enough. I think it was sort of like a fix of . . . a lot of things, my husband was traveling in his job, and we had financial problems, and then, you know, I think . . . *I* don't know, I don't know really. We worked with my husband and I some and some of the things got resolved, but I think mainly more just time helped to heal, and I . . . I don't know . . .

HARLENE: This was how long ago?

NATALIE: A couple of years.

HARLENE: So one of your real *big* fears right now is that you might get that bad, that depressed, that miserable, again.

NATALIE [agrees]: Right, and then I feel kind o' like fighting, like just "kick 'em all out and I'll be okay." You know, if you have a . . . I still have a little bit of, you know, determination . . .

HARLENE: Determination, yeah.

NATALIE: . . . to be okay instead of just lie down and say, "Okay, I'm depressed," you know.

HARLENE: And so you think if you just kind of kicked . . .

NATALIE [laughs]: Knocked 'em off a cliff and just . . .

HARLENE: . . . everybody out of your life or your house that that way you could kind of protect yourself and hold on?

NATALIE: . . . and just let her go ahead and go, and then just put myself into my job and things that *I* enjoy and, you know it's really not a bad deal because she causes such misery, and it's not a bad deal. I ... the stress in the house would be so much less. I'd have more time to do things I want to do [laughs] ... it's really *not* a bad deal [laughs]. If I can look at it that way.

HARLENE: But you can't, it sounds like.

NATALIE: Sometimes I can't, no.

HARLENE: So when you first said that kind of where you are is worrying about how *you* would handle it when she left ... this is what you're really talking about.

NATALIE: [agrees]

HARLENE: Would you really get really depressed and almost nonfunctional, is the way you were describing it.

NATALIE: [agrees] [long pause]

SUE: Or on the other side where you would find, "Oh, I have all this time and less stress," and I mean, sounds like both have crossed your mind, but more of the concern is about the depression, obviously. Uh huh [agrees].

NATALIE: So I guess we'll just have to wait and see what happens.

HARLENE: But what happens now in terms of feeling depressed and miserable? I mean you ...

NATALIE: Well, I cry a lot at night ...

HARLENE: [agrees]

NATALIE: ... and the last few days she's been a lot nicer and like, yes, that makes me sad, *too* [laughs]. Yesterday she didn't have school because of the ice and everybody else did, and we ... she stayed home and she went out ... the ice was bending the limbs of these trees down and she went out and got hot water and threw it on 'em trying to make the trees be okay and there wasn't no electricity in the house. She'd go in and put her hands in hot water and she'd cleaned up, and she did all these things, then last night she talked to me late, real nicely, you know, we just had this *nice* conversation, and *that* makes me sad, *too*. I ... you know, I can't ... because what am I ... and I just sat in my bed thinking, "What am I going to do ... [begins to cry] ... when she's gone?" [long pause]

Comment: Natalie was crying. Since the beginning of the interview, the room has been filled with feelings and emotions. Both are very much a part of this way of working. As with the tenseness in the air, the sadness, the pain, the sense of desperation, the humor, and the misery, I do not search for or highlight them. They are there. They come. They are a natural part of the conversation.

There is a shift back to the relationship with her daughter.

HARLENE: And so then you started even feeling *worse* about yourself I guess when in your times like this . . .

NATALIE: I don't *know*. Is that, is that not normal or something to hold on to some . . . I don't know if I want to hold on so much because I want to be *with* her or, or *what*.

HARLENE: Do we have a . . . ?

SUE: Yeah.

HARLENE: And there's not, there's never been a way that you and your daughter have been able to talk about *any* of these things, concerns, caring, problems, that it just . . . or at least that's what I'm hearing.

NATALIE: Then I end up begging her to stay or something, and then she has us over a barrel, you know like, "Well, if you don't do what I say then I'll go to my dad's." You know, it's just . . .

HARLENE: So it's always kind of a tug of war . . .

NATALIE: *Yeah.*

HARLENE: . . . or some kind of . . .

NATALIE: "I'll just go to my dad's" if she doesn't like what we say, and you can't *parent* like that.

SUE: I think that there are some times where you have been able to talk, if I heard your question, and I don't know.

HARLENE: I'm just thinking it sounds like they struggle with a lot of things, and I hear a lot of tension, a lot of friction, a lot of . . . blackmailing, trying to shame.

NATALIE: Yeah.

HARLENE: I was just wondering, has there ever been a time or any way in which they could talk about any of this in any productive way or has it just started going *downhill*?

NATALIE: I don't know . . . I wish . . . well maybe if we take our sessions together or something, yeah, I'll be able to tell her. I think we have, and what is so *strange* is she's always told me that she would never leave me, that when . . . you know, "I'll never leave you, even when I go to college I want to stay . . . ," you know, and all that, and I *told* her that the other night and she said, "I, yeah, I remember saying that" [laughs].

Comment: Posing a thought and wondering out loud, I continue.

HARLENE: I guess what I'm thinking is that, at least where my mind is right now, is that it's not like a question of "Is she with you or is she with her dad?" Although to me that's an *important* question, important issue, it seems like the most *burning* issue is "Is there any way, is there any hope, is there any chance that the two of you can *salvage* something in your relationship and have more the kind of relationship that I would imagine both of you would like to have?" I mean, she's *there*, she hasn't gone away, she hasn't gone to live with her dad at this point in time, and there's sort of all of this, sort of erratic unpredictable behavior . . . there are the times like last night where you feel close and you're talking and there are other times where she's, where you feel like she's, you said, had you over a barrel. So I guess that's what I'm thinking, that . . .

NATALIE: That's more the question rather than where she lives . . .

HARLENE: Well that's what I'm wondering . . .

NATALIE: Probably, it's what . . . yeah . . .

HARLENE: . . . if that's what's really, I mean it sounds like you really desperately would *like* to have a relationship with your daughter, you would like for that to go *smoother*, and of course you punctuate that with "good mother/bad mother," which I think most mothers probably *do*, so I don't think that's that unusual. So that's what I'm wondering, I mean, what do you think it would take for you and your daughter to be able to talk about anything or try to . . .

NATALIE: Well, what I want . . . I don't . . .

HARLENE: . . . see anything there to capture or repair.

NATALIE: Well, what I'm thinking is what will make it *impossible* is if I just send her off *angry*, you know, like, "Well just go ahead and go and don't call *me*" and all that and, you know, well that could be *mean*, I mean, I . . .

HARLENE: Well, it's also your biggest fear, that she's going to go *there* and everything will be hunky-dory and that that will really close the *door*, and maybe when she's thirty-five she'll come back, but I don't know, but it sounds like you're . . . that that's what you're grasping for.

NATALIE: That I'll have a normal relationship with her, yeah.

HARLENE: Maybe I'm totally wrong, but . . .

NATALIE: Yeah, that's probably . . .

HARLENE: Well, I don't know. What are you thinking? I mean, you know her daughter. Do you think that's something that

Alicia's also miserable about, that she and her mother don't have the kind of relationship that maybe she would like to have?

SUE: Yeah, I think your punctuation of that being tied to the good mother/bad mother thing . . . I was also thinking that there seems to be a punctuation about if there was a good relationship, then she would live with me, or that living with me indicates the good mother/bad mother.

NATALIE: Yes.

SUE: That there's, that it is tied to that in a way even though I know you said, "Well," you know, "it seems like it's a bigger issue than where she lives," so . . .

HARLENE: Well, I'm thinking that that's sort of, we think, built into this drama. I mean there are many, so many, complex pieces and there's so many pieces that one could look at and say, "Well, given this list of all of these things that you've done wrong *according to you*, *no way* you and your daughter could have a relationship or that you could all of a sudden make a U-turn and be a good mother," and I'm just thinking, "Is that really what we're talking about?" I mean, it's like those *are all*, I think, strikes *against* things. I mean certainly divorce can be very difficult on children. Lots of these things, custody battles, can be very difficult on children. What do you call it, being more partial to one child than another, all of those kinds of things can be very difficult and very *trying*, but shouldn't get in the way of it not *happening*, and I don't know maybe . . . and I guess the other thing that maybe I'm cuing in on is the references that you made to your own mother and your relationship with her and I'm not sure how much ya'll have talked about that and where that is *in* it, but in terms of how you're trying not to replicate that or what you might like to have with your mother that you don't . . .

Comment: To summarize, the conversation shifted to Natalie's son, who had earlier moved in with his father. I asked, "How is your relationship with your son, how is it different or similar to your relationship with your daughter?" Through my curiosity, I learned how she had "salvaged" her relationship with him. I also learned a little more about the aunts Natalie fears will become more like mothers, the "good guys," and make her look like the "bad guy."

I learned that Sue's been meeting with mother and daughter in combination and alone. And I learned that the managed health care company has tried to regulate the people whom Sue can or cannot include in her sessions.

Natalie has become more visibly relaxed and has laughed. Aware of the time and my promise to Natalie that we would finish by noon so she could get back to work, I once again share my inner thoughts.

HARLENE: I guess if I had any idea at all at this time to . . . that that would be what I'd be most curious about, meeting with the two of you and talking about kind of mother–daughter things, maybe what also . . . did she have any dreams that haven't been fulfilled, or . . . what does she want? What does she need? If she was the mother of a fourteen-year-old, how . . .

NATALIE: That's what I tried to . . . because she said I couldn't relate and I said, "That's right, I don't," but I try to relate because that's her whole deal . . . "I want to have a baby and I want to," you know, "have a family and all that" . . . that's her dream. "So imagine if you had a daughter and she was fourteen," and she was trying to relate to that, but she didn't. She's off there someplace . . .

SUE: She's not going to get divorced.

NATALIE: Oh, that's right . . . *never.*

HARLENE: Yeah.

NATALIE: I don't care *what* happens. But, of course, nothing's going to happen if she's going to choose the right husband. Her life's going to be, you know, in a . . .

HARLENE: She says, yeah. So she has *lots* of strong opinions and *lots* of strong feelings . . .

NATALIE: Very, very, very, very.

HARLENE: . . . about the divorce, and when . . .

NATALIE: Other people think she is a *dream* child. Her friends' mothers . . . she goes to visit somebody and the mother will call me and say, "You have done such a . . . this happened this week, you have done a *wonderful* job with your daughter, she's *so* confident, she knows what she *thinks.* . . . "

HARLENE: Does she just fake it when she's around people? Make you look good or what?

NATALIE: She *is* confident. She *does* know what she thinks . . .

HARLENE: She is? Hmmm.

NATALIE: . . . and she's . . . I don't know what else she described but how she . . . she is *so* bright and she just knows exactly what she's doing, she does it so well, thanks very *much* [laughs].

HARLENE: Well, I was thinking that must have made you feel really good and really bad, both at the same time, yeah . . . [laughs].

NATALIE: And, she'll write *letters* to some of . . . a couple . . . a family that's friends of ours that we've been friends for a long time, "Oh, you just so, I love you, you're just like a part of my family" to the . . . to the whole family, to the mother and dad, and . . .

HARLENE: So if you've been such a *bad* mother . . .

NATALIE: . . . why is she so nice? Yeah.

HARLENE: . . . where did she get, where did all this come from? Yeah. Maybe another question we'll leave in the air.

NATALIE [laughs]: Time to go?

Comment: We had a short discussion about the time and I offered Natalie my appreciation for letting us videotape.

HARLENE: Do you have any questions that you would like to ask *me*?

NATALIE: What's going to happen now with this tape?

Comment: I answered her question and thanked her. I always thank people for letting me momentarily participate in their lives, for their sharing. And, I acknowledge that they have given me something.

This was the end of our talking with each other. Questions were left in the air. A conversation is never finished. Each conversation, like this one, becomes a springboard for future ones.

ONE CONVERSATION LEADS TO ANOTHER AND TO A RENEWED SENSE OF SELF-AGENCY

I am often asked questions about the transferability of conversations like this one to the outside of the therapy room, to a client's ordinary daily life, and in this case to Sue and Natalie's work together.

Just as we each take our familiar narratives into the therapy room, we carry new ones out with us. Each therapy conversation becomes an invitation to, a springboard for, other conversations. Each becomes part of the ongoing dialogues that a client and a therapist participate in outside the therapy room and, in turn, we each take to the next therapy conversation. Each conversation is part of, is influenced by, and influences other conversations.

Our new narratives achieve new meaning through a different relationship to the larger narrative context. As we accommodate new versions of experience to older ones, we are able to impose a new unity, a new meaning, a new understanding that is the liberating experience of a new sense of *self-agency*.

What Happened Next?

In the next two months, there were three sessions. First, Sue, Natalie, and Alicia met and talked about the kind of relationship each of them wanted and how to get there. In the meantime, Natalie began talking more with Alicia's father, and that led to their meeting with Sue together to talk about parenting Alicia and planning the move. After this session, mother and father together talked with Alicia to make plans and choose schools.

Sue then met with Natalie to review the videotape to see whether she would give us permission to use it. In this session Natalie was much more relaxed and confident as she reviewed what had happened over the last two months. Here is a brief excerpt from the beginning of this session:

Natalie said that for the first time she was able to speak with friends at a school function about her daughter's going to Baton Rouge to attend school and to live with her dad. She said that she was not bothered as much as she used to be. Sue asked her to say more about not being bothered and more about the two months since the interview with me.

Natalie responded emphatically that she had decided, "We can't live like this anymore in our house, constant conflict, like terrorism."

Sue asked her to say more about "the start you feel you've made with that. What do you think has changed in terms of the control that you felt?"

NATALIE: Something's different, with her especially and with me. I'm not afraid to go home like I was.
SUE: Is there anything else you want to say about where you are now?
NATALIE: Self-esteem, what I want to do with my life, how I'm judged by others.

Comment: Natalie talked about working on her sensitivity to being judged by others. She shared some thoughts about herself at work and said that she had decided, "I need to tell them how much I can do."

Sue referred to Natalie's decision to give us permission to use this videotape: "This is a big step for you to share yourself with others." To which Natalie replied, referring to being self-critical, "I need to catch myself." Sue asked, "So, how can you 'catch your-self?'" And the conversation shifted and continued.

This session concluded the therapy. Natalie no longer needed Sue to be part of her continuing conversations.

The Problem Dissolved

In a follow-up phone call six months later, Natalie told Sue that Alicia had moved to her father's at the beginning of the summer. The move, however, had developed a different meaning. After two months, she asked to return home. Mother, daughter, and step-father negotiated new rules, and some months later mother and daughter still are doing fine.

This different way of being in relationship, this kind of talking, which dissolves not only what you talk about, but the way you talk about it, is the essence of my collaborative approach. In the words of the Swedish therapists Britta Lödgö and Gunilla Ström as they viewed this videotape, "When you bring the trolls into the sunshine, they will disappear."

The essence of a conversation is difficult to convey. What I have described and commented on is based on my experience, my position in the conversation, and has been influenced by conversations with others about this conversation. The conversation could have other descriptions and explanations and could have taken many forms. This is only one. And the conversation itself is only one of many conversations that the three of us could have had.

In Part III, I present two "floating islands": the postmodern concepts knowledge and language, and *self*. Because historically they have proved so pivotal and remain central to my ideas about therapy conversations and therapy relationships, I want to give them adequate attention as I understand them.

PART III

Searching for Meanings in Meanings

"IF MY STORY MAY BE OF ANY HELP . . ." CONTINUED

After the long pause that followed my reading the Swedish mother's words, I was cautiously eager to learn more about them, to understand their experiences, and to see more of the picture that her words sketched. I asked the daughters, who both had remarked that they agreed the doctors and therapists should also talk with them, "So, help me. When you said that you agreed with your mother that the doctors should also talk with you, would they talk about you like you weren't there?"

The younger softly answered, "Yes, I don't think they thought it was like that."

I said, "But that's what you felt and what's important. And so, you had some of the feelings your mother was talking about. You felt humiliated and not respected?"

Both girls expressed feeling that the doctors and therapists did not "trust" them, "listen" to them, or let them "speak"; that they considered the sisters "manipulative." I puzzled, "Why didn't they give you a chance to speak? Were they suspicious that you were being manipulative and really didn't want to get better? They thought you liked being sick?"

193

They told about the doctors who "tried to get our parents to force us to get better." They thought, however, that the doctors wanted to be helpful and had good intentions. I wondered whether anyone in the family had ever offered any opinions to the doctors or the therapists.

"Yes, we did," the daughters responded simultaneously.

"And, what happened?"

They said that they still thought they were right, the older softly said.

"Was is that what they were doing had been helpful to other girls, other young women, and they thought that if you cooperated more you would get well?"

"Yes."

When I talk with more than one person at a time, I always watch the others' faces. It helps me stay connected with them and have a sense of when they want to say something. And I think it is critical to giving them the sense that I am acknowledging each person and his or her contributions to the story as important. The father appeared to be considering what the daughters were saying. I was curious about what he was thinking and turned to him.

"What about you, Dad? Would you like to add to this or say something else?"

"They said we were an uncooperative family, and they were not altogether wrong."

"So, one of the ways . . . do you think you did some other things? Are you a critical family in general, or . . . ?"

"In the beginning, you think all the doctors are right. They guess. They're lucky in their guesses."

"So, when things were not helpful you became critical?"

The mother joined in, "I agreed and thought that the doctors were right. When they talked about support, they meant we should force them [the daughters to eat]. It was quite natural they would rebel."

I learned more about the family's experiences with the doctors and therapists. I learned about the numerous treatment programs that the girls had been in and about the individual and family therapies. I learned about the strained relationship between the sisters and how when one's eating problem got worse, the parents tried to tend more to her, but not neglect the other. I learned that occasionally there were some improvements, but they never seemed to last. I learned that the younger daughter had been home for four months now, after an eight-month course of treatment in a private clinic.

The sisters continued to talk about feeling humiliated and not respected. They thought, however, that the doctors were trying to be helpful even though they did not listen to them or their parents. I asked, "If someone would listen, what would you like to tell them? What do you think they should know? What are they missing?"

Both talked more about being forced to eat, the doctors believing they were manipulative, and needing encouragement. The elder talked about not understanding at first what was "going on with my body" and how she now understands but still has psychological questions. Dad said that they took the younger daughter to a private hospital that "had a good reputation" but that when they got there "still no one would talk with us." The conversation hovered around treating the "physical" while neglecting the "psychological" aspects of the problem. I asked them if they had met other girls with the same problem; did they get any help; what made the difference; were the other girls forced to eat? They believed that those who "*dared* to ask" got more help.

As I talked with the family members, I kept the visiting therapists, Gustaf and Kerstin, in my peripheral vision, sometimes having eye contact so that I would have a sense of them and that they would feel included in the conversation. Both seemed heavily absorbed in the talking and looked a little surprised when I turned to check in with them about what they were thinking. After a pause, Gustaf began, "I'm thinking of how important it is to give the right help at the right time and how difficult it is to be of help in a case like this." Kerstin hesitantly and awkwardly said, "That letter got to me—just the feeling of not being heard, it's a very heavy feeling. There is never enough, either too much or too late."

I expressed my amazement to all that "given all the struggles and disappointments" they had come to meet with me. The mother responded to my amazement with, "I can always hope that it can help a few people to think . . . there is no one solution to this sickness." She again shares her advice that the professionals need "more humbleness . . . need to try other methods when the ones they use don't help . . . they should try to listen."

I returned to something the mother said earlier, that the younger daughter had improved at the clinic she was most recently in and that she worries that they [the professionals] will destroy the gains.

I wondered, "What are you doing not to lose the improvements? It sounds like things go backward and then forward. What have you done to stay better? Would you give me some examples?"

As we continued talking, the daughters' voices were increasingly audible. They were not chatty but candidly engaged in sharing their experiences and opinions. Both said what had been most helpful was that the parents now talked with them more, "Both as parents and as friends at the same time," the younger offered.

I offered my sense that she sounded a little hopeful. She agreed. I wondered, "Is there anything you would like them to do in addition to what they're doing now? Anything you would like them to do more of?" I asked her sister, "What needs to happen now?"

The older daughter said that she wanted to go home or at least get out of the hospital more often and do the things that other girls her age do. She told us that today was the first time that she had been out "in this way" in a long time. The mother and she then told me they had spent the afternoon together that day, going to a shopping area and to McDonald's.

The conversation returned to her earlier mention of manipulation. I said, "Let me ask you a hard question, may I? When they say you're just trying to manipulate, what do you tell them?" I also asked, "Do you think there's any way to get them to believe you?" She talked about how hard and depressing it is. She mentioned a dilemma of the doctors saying, on one hand, that she needs to "get better" to have time out of the hospital but, on the other, that when she improves they think she is manipulative and still will not let her have a pass to leave the hospital. I agreed. "A real dilemma: When you improve they think that you are manipulating."

We talked about what she thinks the doctors mean when they say she must get better and what their measurement is. She again referred to the focus on physical signs, commenting that they only measure physical signs and not psychological signs. "If I gained ten pounds but was still depressed, I could go home," she said.

I paused to ask the father, "What are you thinking now?" He said, "I think in the beginning they didn't have a method, but later they had a method but I never knew what it was."

"Do you know their current method or plan?"

He said that the professionals do not talk to him and referred back to the magical age of 18 that the mother mentioned in her letter.

The mother added, "They don't consider us as resources."

The elder daughter joined in, "They tell me they don't want my parents to be involved."

"Do they tell you why?" I asked.

"They're afraid we might manipulate them."

The mother said that in the past, when both girls were at home they were manipulative but that the doctors were "wrong" because "it is not that way anymore."

The talk turned to the relationship between the sisters and between them and the parents. I learned that the two daughters used to fight a lot, but now cherished their brief weekly visits together, when the mother would bring the younger daughter to visit the hospital.

I asked, "What do you do when you visit?"

"We talk," said the younger.

"I look forward to these visits," said the elder.

They said they were learning how to talk as sisters and be friends again. We explored ways to nurture this new relationship. I wondered if anyone had ever talked with the two sisters together. "No," they said, so I further wondered, addressing all four of them, "Do you think it would be helpful?"

At that point our conversation focused on family members talking more with each other. Soon, and quite naturally, this talk led back to their frustrations with the doctors and the therapists. I asked, "What do the doctors need to know? How can we help the doctors know what they need to know, because they can't read your mind?"

Wondering what Gustaf and Kerstin were thinking, I turned to them. Did they have any ideas? Were they feeling as "heavy" and "amazed" as they were earlier? Kerstin said, "I'm not so heavy now; the atmosphere lifted in the room." Gustaf said, "I feel a bit different too, the talking about possibilities."

I shared my thoughts. "What I've been thinking about is that these four people have been dealing with this for a long time. There have been lots of heartaches, disappointments, hopes, improvements, and backslides." I asked, "How can we capture their ideas about and experiences with what is helpful for the girls and share those with the professionals?" I openly commented, "Of course, I'm very biased in the direction of combining the professionals' and the family's expertise . . . taking the best of both . . . and developing a method that would uniquely fit." I agreed that "professionals can have a good idea but that the timing has to be right . . . you have to dare to ask." I summarized the things that were getting better and asked how we could nurture those things.

I looked at the clock and realized that it was late. I turned to tomorrow's workshop. Did the family still agree that we could use the videotape? I inquired. They did. I then asked Gustaf, who agreed, to make some notes on tomorrow's discussion so that we could share any ideas or questions that the participants might have with the family.

I generously thanked them for joining us, sharing their struggles with us, and agreeing to let the workshop participants watch the videotape. The family took the older daughter back to the hospital and then went home. Gustaf, Kerstin, and I looked at the videotape.

As we went our separate ways, even though it seemed like days since I had last slept, I felt energized. I remained intrigued with this family's plight. I had some lingering thoughts: "I would really like to talk more with the sisters; it seemed odd that no one had ever met with the two of them and that the next chapters of the family's story seemed to dangle." I asked Kerstin and Gustaf their opinions about my inviting the girls to meet with me tomorrow. They looked perplexed but intrigued. For logistical reasons, we decided to invite only the older daughter. But first, remembering the parents' frustration that the professionals no longer talked to them, we decided to call and discuss our plan. They were surprised, yet pleased, to hear from us so quickly. They said they knew that their daughter would be honest with us about whether she wanted to talk with us again. So, we called the daughter and without hesitation she agreed to meet.

We met the next day at lunch. Kerstin and Gustaf again joined us. The workshop participants, who had already seen video segments of the family meeting, observed our meeting on closed-circuit television. Some had been stunned by the family's story, some perplexed, and some disbelieving. All were eager to hear more.

As we exchanged greetings, the daughter seemed more comfortable than the day before and her voice was stronger. I told her how much I appreciated her coming to talk with us. I continued, "I'm very occupied by your wish to talk more. If you had that opportunity, what would you really wish to talk about? What would you want the doctors to hear?"

"I want them to listen to me and to believe in what I say. And, that I'm not trying to manipulate all the time."

"Well, it's sort of like you're two persons, and one is trying to get well, and they should listen to that part and try to encourage it."

"I'm the one who knows myself best and what would be best for me."

"Two persons—one really sincere—you want them to know and believe that. Do you think you are saying some things that they're not hearing?"

As we continued, she shared more of her frustration with not being trusted or listened to. She said she wanted to be able to talk with her doctor directly and not communicate through the nurse. We explored ways that she could talk with the people that she wanted to talk with and the ways in which Gustaf and Kerstin might be helpful with this. She ended by reiterating, "I want to be normal."

It Was Inevitable That I Would Tell Their Story

On the plane home from Sweden I had the sense that it was inevitable that I would tell their story. Six months later my meeting with this family and their voices were still vivid in my head. Feeling compelled to share their story and their understanding with others, I wrote to ask their permission. The mother responded. Here is part of her letter.

> I am both glad and proud if our story can be of any use for other people in a similar situation. I am aware of that each person and every family has a history of its own, but somehow and somewhere one can detect a pattern that makes it possible to see similarities and parallels. . . . Of course it is not easy to describe our experiences from almost three years in the near vicinity of purgatory in a short letter and some of the nuances might have been lost on the way, but on the whole it is the true story from our daughters' point of view. Of course we have not lived in an ordeal all the time; there have been many wonderful moments and we have grown very close to each other, but, even when things are getting better (which they do from time to time), you can never feel certain that the battle is won—the achievements can be very precarious and fragile and backlashes are never far away. . . . I wish I could tell you that everything was just great, but I'm afraid it is not quite so.

She said that her younger daughter's life was "still going on pretty well." She was back in school and doing well academically:

> If she could find a best friend she would probably be completely recovered within a short period of time. It is not very easy for me just witnessing her troubles without being able to give her some real help in this matter.

The situation for the older daughter had been more "toilsome," she said.

> Things grew worse at the hospital. She was treated in the same way, if not worse, as before with no regard to her integrity and

human value. During her five months at the hospital there was not much treatment at all; she was mostly left on her own and became more restless and depressed. Nobody seemed to take any notice or care. We tried in every way to make them change their methods, from punishment and limitations of the tiny part of freedom which was left to her, to encouragement and collaboration with the healthy part of her instead—but our efforts were in vain. ... After a lot of agony we decided to run away and were immensely relieved when we learned that no one was forcing us back to the hospital. Now she lives at home and is immensely happy for that. But at the same time we are now alone in this struggle and of course that means both a never ending work and a very heavy responsibility.... Anyhow, one learns by experience (and from a basic instinct of self-preservation) always to struggle on and never to yield. I still believe that we will succeed, but I think that it would have been much more easier if we have been met with more understanding by unprejudiced doctors and therapists and that more efforts had been done to gain our daughter's confidence. If my story may be of any help to therapists, that would be a great comfort to me and perhaps even make me hope that our struggle and sufferings have not been completely in vain.

As the mother's words express, when the members of this family became *partners in dialogue*, they took back the responsibility for their own treatment, and slowly they achieved self-agency and a sense of freedom and hope. I wish each of them well. And I believe they will succeed.

CHAPTER 9

Knowledge and Language

The limits of language mean the limits of my world.
—Ludwig Wittgenstein

POSTMODERNISM EMPHASIZES the *relational nature of knowledge* and the *generative nature of language*—referring to a way of conceptualizing and describing and to the changing characteristics of what we know or think we know. We generate knowledge with each other through language. Language—spoken and unspoken words, sounds, utterances, gestures, signs, and other forms of speech and action used to communicate—is the primary vehicle through which, in which, we construct our worlds, give order and meaning to our lives, and relate to each other.

THE RELATIONAL NATURE OF KNOWLEDGE

Postmodernism, to reiterate, challenges the representational and dualistic nature of knowledge—the notion of a knowing individual mind that internally constructs knowledge of a real world that is out there to know. In contrast, postmodernism views knowledge as a social phenomenon of culture, communication, and language. Knowledge is socially constructed: it evolves from interactions and communications between persons. It is the creation of social beings, not the representation or mirroring (either flawed or unflawed) of nature or reality (Rorty, 1979). Knowledge is "a matter of conversation and of social practice, rather than . . . an attempt to mirror nature" (p. 171). What we know, or think we know (knowledge, feelings, emotions, thoughts, and perceptions), is discerned through our constructions and is communicated in language. Knowledge and the knower are interdependent; the knower is a contributor. But where is knowledge located? How is it transmitted? How is it mastered?

Knowledge Is Communal

Gergen (1994), a strong proponent of communal knowledge, suggests, "*The terms and forms by which we achieve understanding* [knowledge] *of the world and ourselves are social artifacts, products of historically and culturally situated interchanges among people* . . . and *are not dictated by the* . . . *object* [of the account]" (p. 49). Reality, including our experiences, our descriptions, and our explanations of reality, is a product of social dialogue—exchange and interaction—and represents an agreement between people. Accounts, thought of as realities, are sustained because they are consensually negotiated and deemed useful, not because they are true. The *perceived objective validity* (my emphasis) of the account influences whether it is sustained across time (Gergen, 1994, pp. 44–54). Or, as Rorty (1979) stated, knowledge is the "social justification of belief" (p. 170). Psychological knowledge or psychological reality is, for instance, "largely guided by the way we construct the world" (Semin, 1990, p. 170). This makes all knowledge, including psychological knowledge derived from research, simply "*consensus-in-dialogue*" (Groeben, 1990, p. 38).

Knowledge Is Culture-Bound

Bruner (1990) used the term *enculturated knowledge* (p. 21) to emphasize the "cultural nature of knowledge acquisition" as well as the "cultural nature of knowledge" (p. 106). If knowledge is culture-bound, what is this culture that limits it? Is it not itself "consensus-in-dialogue"? The anthropologist Clifford Geertz (1973) defined culture as "an historically transmitted pattern of meanings embodied in symbols, a system of inherited conceptions expressed in symbolic form by means of which men communicate, perpetuate, and develop their knowledge about and attitudes towards life" (p. 89). Knowledge, whether local or universal knowledge, is embedded within a context of contexts, within local contexts embedded within larger contexts (for example, dyads within family, family within community, community within national culture).

Knowledge Is a Fluid, Ongoing Process

Knowledge is continually changing; it is not final. It is, therefore, discontinuous and not cumulative. This is not to say that *new* knowledge does not have roots in, does not incorporate, *old* knowledge. There is, however, no knowledge foundation on which new knowledge is pyramidally based or from which deductions can be drawn. In therapy, for instance, a therapist does not find fragments that eventually add up to a meaningful whole, filling in the missing pieces with knowledge. The quest is not a passive process with an endpoint of discovering or understanding truth or convincing others of the therapists' knowledge. A therapist actively participates with a client in language and in this process of partnership creates what can be thought of as new knowledge, for instance, new ways to think about problems, new meanings to life events, and new ways to act.

This approach contrasts with the more familiar way of thinking about psychological knowledge, which is based largely on observations. Our observations tell us what is. And we often pay more attention, and give more credibility, to our observations of the person than to what the person tells us. Postmodernism warns us that we cannot observe the inner life, the inner thoughts of another person. Psychological knowledge, terms, and descriptions, including diagnoses, personality traits, and family patterns, are "configured in the medium of language" and are "no more or no less than idealized abstractions capturing decontextualized semantic relationships" (Semin, 1990, p. 161). Said differently, "the language one uses in categorizing observable action is itself a human product" (Shapiro & Sica, 1984, p. 17). The limitations and risks of any knowledge as private, objectifiable, universal, and generalizable have been questioned by postmodern feminist scholars who cautioned against metanarratives, including those perpetuated by feminists themselves, that ignore or blur diversity among women, which includes but is not limited to cultural, historical, racial, ethnic, and age differences (Belenky, Clinchy, Goldberger, & Taruel, 1986; Code, 1988; Fraser & Nicholson, 1990; M. Gergen, 1988; Kitzinger, 1987).

THE GENERATIVE NATURE OF LANGUAGE

We are born into language and inherit all that comes with it: history, culture, tradition, and so on. Language is the vehicle through which we exist and share with each other and with ourselves. It is the primary way in which we construct our realities, our worlds, our observations, and our understandings, through actions with others. It is the vehicle through which we ascribe meaning, make sense of our lives, give order to our world, and relate our stories. We act and react through language, using it to relate, to influence, and to change. We could not think of love, cooperation, power, or envy, nor of such complex social activities as marriage or psychotherapy without the appropriate language, vocabulary, and narrative.

Wittgenstein offered one of the most profound challenges to the modernist notion of language and its function as representational of empirical facts, reality, and our experiences of such. Academicians van der Merwe and Voestermans (1995) summarized Wittgenstein's notion that language as the symbolic representation of sensory experience is self-refuting:

> If the logical grammar of language necessitates that the propositional content of our expressions should be logical pictures of possible sensory facts, and only that, for our expressions to be meaningful, then the entire articulation and justification of this understanding of language are indeed devoid of any meaning and cognitive content, because they cannot themselves be verified with reference to possible sensory facts. The assumption of an isomorphic resemblance between the structures of language and experience, and the definition of meaning as symbolic representation, expresses a philosophical (mis)understanding of the relation between language and experience and not a verifiable perception of any empirical facts. Therefore, the very conception of language as the symbolic representation of sensory experience fails to comply with the criteria of meaningfulness that it prescribes. (pp. 31–32)

Language and Experience Go Hand in Hand

Wittgenstein instead suggested the *active* and *creative* aspect of language. He was interested primarily in the relationship between language and experience, the ways people together in their everyday lives construct and make sense of their experiences, the ways they relate linguistically to each other. Communicating Wittgenstein's position, van der Merwe and Voestermans (1995) suggested that language and "meaning-giving (and -taking, for that matter) is an experiential affair . . . [and] belong to people's way of going about things in the world they inhabit" (p. 37). From this perspective "language is thus no longer an outer expression of inner states, but is social in its origins, uses and implications" (Gergen & Semin, 1990, p. 14). And it does not exist independently of the people who use it.

Ricoeur, among others, talked about the relation "between language and lived experience" (as cited in Madison, 1988, p. 86), implying that "action and discourse are inseparable" (Madison, 1988, p. 98). Madison suggested,

> Language is the way in which, as humans, we *experience* what we call reality. . . . Expressed experience is experience which has settled down and become something "of substance." Experience is not really meaningful until it has found a home in language, and without lived experience to inhabit it, language is an empty, lifeless shell. (p. 165)

Language Is Active

Language changes and is changed over time. Hermeneutic scholar Brice Wachterhauser (1986a) reflected Heidegger's viewpoint: "Changes in the world necessitate changes in language, and changes in language affect what we are able to grasp about the world. . . . By searching for new ways to speak about new situations and experiences language develops" (p. 29). For instance, our overarching social, cultural, and historical narratives change over time. Historical periods are narrative eras in which descriptive vocabularies are developed; in turn, language is influenced by our stories, histories, cultures, and traditions.

Shotter (1993b) referred to Wittgenstein's thoughts on language "as *formative* . . . [as functioning] to formulate the situations in which we are involved *as* situations." Shotter himself talked about the *constitutive* and *formative* nature of language (p. 72), proposing that it is our "major 'prosthetic device'" (p. 27). All suggest the active, the generative nature of language.

Language Creates Social Reality

What we know (knowledge, feelings, emotions, thoughts, and perceptions) is known through, is formed in, and is communicated in language. Language is reality. I do not suggest that *real* events don't happen or that you can't kiss the Blarney stone. Children fall off tricycles, drugs affect people, people get fired from their jobs, and couples file petitions for divorce. Events happen, but the meanings we attribute to them are constructed in language. Madison challenged that reality is not the product or referent of language but its creative source. He suggested, for instance, that what we think to be literal truths are simply "metaphorical truths which are taken literally, for instance, believed in" (p. 87).

Meaning

We give meaning to—interpret and understand—our experiences through language. What we think and believe is real, what we assume is real, is construed, accounted for, and sustained in language. Meaning (our interpretations and our understandings) is linguistically and jointly constructed through spoken and unspoken language. It is more than representational, more than what is defined and thought to be out there in the physical world. Whether touchable or untouchable, physical or nonphysical, the meaning attached exists in language; that is, one can see and feel an object such as a table or an egg, but one cannot touch an entity or institution such as an educational program or an art museum, or a concept such as neutrality. There is no meaning outside the meanings we create and give to things. As well, those meanings are context-dependent and can differ from one person to another.

The meanings we attribute to things, people, and events—the way we talk about them—allow us to be connected to or disconnected from others. Meanings influence the way we are in relationship with the other; according to Bateson (1972), they do not emerge on the basis of the essence, the thingness; instead, they emerge rather paradoxically from the difference. They emerge from nonpresence—what is absent, not there; the space, the interval between. "*New* meanings are simply new ways of relating to things by means of new or unusual usages of *words* [my emphasis] (or their semiotic equivalent in other expressive media)" (Madison, 1988, p. 188).

Words

We use words to develop and convey meaning. Words do not have essential meanings; their use is "always individual and contextualized in nature" (Bakhtin, 1986, p. 88). Their meanings are derived in language, not just in our spoken utterances but in the way we use them with each other. Although a word is an "expression of some evaluative position of an individual person" (p. 88), that person cannot determine how that word affects another person, what it expresses for that person. We, both speaker and listener, inhabit the word.

Gergen (1988a) expresses the concept as follows:

> The meaning of a word is not to be found in its underlying intention or locked deeply within the unconscious. Rather, the meanings of words as well as actions are realized within the unfolding patterns of relationship. The problem is thus not to look inward to an interior region for the meaning of a *word or action* [my emphasis], but outward into the continuously expanding horizon of the relationship. (p. 46)

The other person, Gergen (1988a) suggests, allows the word to make sense. The word and its use do not belong to one person or another but to all those who use it. Bakhtin (1986) describes words as "interindividual" (p. 121): there is no such thing as a private language; language is public and relational. A word within a sentence and the sentence itself derive their meaning from the relationship of each to the other and to the context. I find interesting the ways the nature of words varies and some words cannot be translated from one language to another. In effect, the conception *word* is determined afresh with the system of every language, and as a result the word-as-element-of-speech is language-specific, not language-universal (McArthur, 1992, p. 1120). Although words in these senses do not have fixed meanings, they do carry embedded assumptions. Words, warned Heidegger, "always contain a preshaped way of seeing." Similarly, Foucault warned that they have "hidden mechanisms of coercion and predefinition of relationships of power, sexuality, the body, transgression, pleasures" (cited in Palmer, 1985, p. 20).

Language Determines and Generates Understanding

Social constructionists like Shotter (1993a) believe that shared understandings are rare. Shotter himself is more concerned with "how conversation and dialogue can still proceed, *before* shared understandings" (p. 120) are realized, the process in which people try to understand each other. Gergen (1994), likewise, is interested in how we understand and how we misunderstand. Both challenge the belief that one can reach into the interior of another and truly understand him or her. Gergen specifically disputes that such a state of "intersubjectivity transparency" can be achieved (p. 256). Critical of the hermeneutic focus on the individual, Gergen suggests that

> rather than commence with individual subjectivity and work deductively toward an account of human understanding through language, we may begin our analysis at the level of the *human relationship* as it generates both language and understanding [suggesting that it is the] conventions of relationship that enable understanding to be achieved. (p. 263)

Language and Coordination

The way we think about language influences the way we position or locate ourselves in a discourse or in a relationship and make *space* for each other. Language is a communal, not an individual product, used for its meaning within the community (Gergen, 1991a). Language is "primarily for the coordination of diverse social action, with its representational function working *from within* a set of linguistically constituted social relations" (Shotter, 1993b, p. 20). Our constructions, descriptions, and explanations are the result of human coordination of action through language (Shotter, 1991b).

Vygotsky's "Language" and "Thought"

In talking about language, it is important to note the influence of the Russian developmental psychologist L. S. Vygotsky, who viewed humans as a product of nature and culture. The acquisition and use of language were central in his study of the "sociogenesis of the higher forms of behavior" (1966, p. 45), or in Shotter's (1993b) characterization of the ideas of Vygotsky, "how people, through the use of their own social activities, by changing their own conditions of existence can change themselves" (p. 111). Vygotsky viewed language as a "tool" for negotiating meanings and for influencing people's behaviors (p. 111), one that shapes, though not in an instrumental sense. Gergen and Semin (1990) note

> Vygotsky plays a central role because, as he proposed, not only are the cognitive categories social in origin, but so are the forms of ratiocination in which these categories are embedded. Thus everyday understanding is inherently social rather than a biolog-

ical act; it cannot be cut away from the sociocultural circumstances of the agent. (p. 10)

Vygotsky (1986) also made important contributions with his ideas about the process through which thoughts are formed in language through words, which he terms *inner speech*:

> The relation of thought to word is not a thing but a process, a continual movement backward and forth from thought to word and from word to thought. In that process, the relation of thought to word undergoes changes that themselves may be regarded as developmental in the functional sense. Thought is not merely expressed in words; it comes into existence through them. Every thought tends to connect something with something else, to establish a relation between things. Every thought moves, grows and develops, fulfills a function, solves a problem. (p. 218)

Shotter (1993a), in discussing Vygotsky's notion of inner speech, elucidates, "Unformulated in words, a thoughtseed remains vague and provides only the possibility of having a meaning" (p. 44). Quoting Vygotsky,

> The relation between thought and word is a living process; thought is born through words. A word devoid of thought is a dead thing. ... But thought that fails to realize itself in words remains a "Stygian shadow" [O. Mandelstam]. ... The connection between thought and word, however, is neither preformed nor constant. It emerges in the course of development, and itself evolves. (p. 255)

In Shotter's words,

> The voiced utterance-flower, which can move us and guide us in our actions, emerges in the course of a dialogic process of what Vygotsky calls "inner speech," a process which can vary in its character according to the "others" involved in the thought's "development"—those with whom, about whom, and to whom, in one's inner speech one speaks. ... Thus, people's attempts to realize their thoughts—to formulate their thoughts to themselves in ways which make those thoughts socially *usable*, so to speak— must be *negotiated* in an inner back-and-forth process, in which they must attempt to understand and challenge their own proposed formulations as the others around them might. (p. 44)

Among the most important formulations or knowledges that we are involved in creating and coordinating with ourselves and others through language are the notions of *self*. Let me now turn to the question, What is self? What is a postmodern concept of *self*, including self-narrative, self-identity, and self-agency? Whatever happened to the notion that a human being is a knowable, fixed self? Who are all the possible "mes"? How do some selves become heroes and heroines and some become victims? As therapists, how can we participate in our clients' becoming their own heroes and heroines? Is it possible to transform our self-identities, and if so how? What challenges does a postmodern concept of self have for therapy: its theory, practice, research, and education of therapists?

CHAPTER 10

Self: Narrative, Identity, and Agency

There is no such thing as the self that thinks and entertains ideas.
—LUDWIG WITTGENSTEIN

We are voices in a chorus that transforms lived life into narrated
life
and then returns narrative to life, not in order to reflect life,
but rather to add something else, not a copy, but a new measure
of life;
to add, with each novel, something new, something more, to life.
—CARLOS FUENTES

TO ASK THE QUESTION, What is *self?* surrenders and leaves us in the mire of traditional Western foundationalist and reductionist objectivity: the notion of self as autonomous, given, and discoverable. From a postmodern perspective, objective reality disappears as an organizing concept, and thus, the question, in the sense of discovering the *self* and its essence, becomes a nonquestion. Postmodernism challenges the idea of a single, fixed core self that we can reveal if we peel away the layers. Rather, it invites a shift from a

211

modernist logical understanding (verifiable reality) of self to a narrative social understanding (constructed reality) of self—it invites a shift from a focus on unquestioned universal givens such as self and self-identity as the things themselves to a focus on understanding how these givens, these meanings, emerge from human understanding. In this linguistic view, the self becomes a *narrative self* and identities exist in relation to a perspective, to a point of view that is related to our purposes. Postmodernism does not suggest that we give up trying to understand self, but that self can be described and understood in an infinite variety of ways.

Before turning to the wonderment of the postmodern narrative self, I want to consider two questions: What is narrative? And how is it used in the context of this book?

NARRATIVE: A STORYTELLING
METAPHOR AND BEYOND

Narrative is a storytelling metaphor that frequently appears in contemporary psychotherapy literature and discourse, not in the literary sense, but in the sense of narrative in everyday life, the way we compose our lives (W. J. Anderson, 1989; Bruner, 1986, 1990; Labov, 1972; Mair, 1988; Sarbin, 1986; Schafer, 1981; Spence, 1984; White, 1980; White & Epston, 1990). Narrative refers to a form of discourse, the discursive way in which we organize, account for, give meaning to, and understand, that is, give structure and coherence to, the circumstances and events in our lives, to the fragments of our experiences, and to our self-identities, for and with ourselves and others. Narrative is a dynamic process that constitutes both the way that we organize the events and experiences of our lives to make sense of them and the way we participate in creating the things we make sense of, including ourselves. In a narrative view, our descriptions, our vocabularies, and our stories constitute our understanding of human nature and behavior. Our views of human nature and behavior are only a matter of our descriptive vocabularies, our language conversations, and our stories and narratives. Our stories form, inform, and re-form our sources of knowledge, our views of reality. I am not, therefore, using the narrative metaphor as another template or map for understanding, interpreting, or predicting human behavior, but as a metaphor for what we do and what we do with each other.

For me, however, narrative is more than a storytelling metaphor;[1]

it is a reflexive two-way discursive process. It constructs our experiences and, in turn, is used to understand our experiences. Language is the vehicle of this process: We use it to construct, to organize, and to attribute meaning to our stories. What we create is an expression of our language use: our vocabularies and our actions achieve meaning through our semantics. Meaning and action cannot be separated; they are reflexive and cannot be thought of in causal terms. The limits of our language constrain what can be expressed—our narrative structures and stories and, thus, our futures. As discursive practices, our narratives are in continuing evolution and change. Stories, thus, are not accomplished facts but are entities in the process of being made. Narrative becomes the way we imagine alternatives and create possibilities and the way we actualize these options.[2] Narrative is the source of transformation.

Narratives are created, experienced, and shared by individuals in conversation and action with one another and with the self. They are the ways we use language and relate to others and ourselves through it. The psychologist Jerome Bruner (1990), among others (Dunn, 1988; Nelson, 1989), suggests that children learn at an early age to organize their experiences narratively through the stories they hear and learn to tell. We construct meaning in everyday life, we account for how and why we think our world is and how and why it ought to be, through narrative. Narratives are the "stories [that] serve as communal resources that people use in ongoing relationships" (Gergen, 1994, p. 189). Similarly, the postmodernist Lyotard (1984) holds that narratives are our "social bonds" (however, he ardently confronts the notion of metanarrative as privileging and oppressing, especially grand social theory narratives). That is, both the individual and society are, as writer Anthony Giddens (1984) suggests, *"constituted in and through recurrent practices"* (p. 222).

Narrative as a Discursive Schema

Narrative is a discursive schema located within local individual and broader contexts and within culturally driven rules and conventions. Both local individual and broader cultural narratives are situated in and interact with each other. The human narrative, according to Bruner (1990), "mediates between the canonical world of culture and the more idiosyncratic world of beliefs, desires, and hopes" (p. 52). Narratives are created, told, and heard against this contextual and cultural schema. What may appear as orderly or disorderly is culturally influenced, jointly shared, and agreed upon. In this sense and to serve these functions, narratives must be comprehensible, coherent, and connected. Toward this aim, in our Western culture, we organize our stories temporally, with beginnings, middles, and ends. They relate to the past, present, and future. And they both connect in sequential fashion and intertwine over time.

Stories are always situated in a history because without a history that changes over time our lives would be unintelligible. We share ourselves and our lives with others by assembling the bits and pieces of our narratives into viable storied versions influenced by memory, context, and intention. For instance, when we try to make sense of a dream, tell a friend about a vacation experience, or recount a childhood event, we do so in narrative form. Bruner (1986), long interested in the relationship of narrative and meaning, suggests, "Narrative deals with the vicissitudes of human intention" (p. 16); he (1990) refers to this way of using language to "frame" our experiences as well as our memories of our experiences as a "narrative mode of thought" and as "narrative structures." In Bruner's (1990) analysis,[3]

> People do not deal with the world event by event or with text sentence by sentence. They frame events and sentences in larger structures.... The larger structures [narrative structure] provide an interpretive context for the components they encompass. (p. 64)

Bruner (1990) distinguishes the necessary characteristics of narrative as (a) sequential: "composed of a unique sequence of events, mental states ... that do not ... have a life or meaning of their own" (p. 43) except in a narrative structure; (b) factually indifferent: "it can be 'real' or 'imaginary' ... it has a structure that is internal to discourse ... the sequence of its sentences, rather than the truth or falsity of any of those sentences is what determines its overall configuration or plot" (p. 44); and (c) uniquely managing departure from the canonical: giving an account of, linking, the exceptional and extraordinary in a manner that mitigates, makes possible, or at least comprehensible, a deviation from a standard cultural pattern (p. 47).

Gergen (1994) chooses to focus on narrative intelligibility: "Narratives are forms of intelligibility that furnish accounts of events across time. Individual actions ... gain their significance from the way in which they are embedded within the narrative" (p. 224).

Gergen suggests that a well-formed or intelligible narrative generally meets certain criteria: (a) it has an established, valued endpoint; (b) the events recounted are relevant to and serve the endpoint; (c) the events are temporally ordered; (d) its characters have a continuous and coherent identity across time; (e) its events are causally linked and serve as an explanation for the outcome; and (f) it has a beginning and an end. He likewise cautions that we must keep in mind that narratives are contingent upon both the local and universal cultural, social, political, and historical narratives in which they are embedded.

In this narrative view a *postmodern self* is considered an expression of this capacity in language and narration: the self telling the story is, through the storytelling process, being formed, informed, and re-formed. As human beings we have always related to each other by telling and listening to stories about ourselves and others. We have always understood who and what we are and might be from the stories we tell one another: "Understanding . . . through language, is a primary form of being-in-the-world. . . . This process of self-formation and self-understanding can never be final or complete" (Woolfolk, Sass, & Messer, 1988, p. 17).

The philosphy professor G. B. Madison (1988), influenced by Paul Ricoeur, says we understand and give meaning and intelligibility to our lived experiences through narrative, through storytelling:

> The self is the way we relate, account for, speak about our actions. . . . The self is the unity of an ongoing narrative, a narrative which lasts a thousand and one nights and more—until, as Proust might say, that night arrives which is followed by no dawn. (pp. 161–162)

These ongoing narratives are embedded within and intertwined with other narratives. Both self- and other-stories determine who we are. At best, we are no more than one of the multiauthors of the constantly changing narrative that becomes our self, and we are always embedded in the local and universal multiple historical pasts and the cultural, social, and political contexts of our narrative making.

Shifting Identities and Continuity Through Change

The self in this postmodern narrative view is not a stable and enduring entity that is limited to or fixed in geographical place or time; it is not the simple accumulation of experience; nor is it an expression of neurophysiological characteristics. Identity, thus, is not based on some kind of psychological continuity or discontinuity of selfhood but on the constancy of an ongoing narrative. As Rorty (1979) indicated, humans are the continuing generators of new descriptions and new narratives rather than beings one can describe accurately in a fixed fashion. The self is an ongoing autobiography; or, to be more exact, it is a self–other, multifaceted biography that we constantly pen and edit. The self is an ever-changing expression of our narratives, a being-and-becoming through language and storytelling as we continually attempt to make sense of the world and of ourselves. Self, therefore, is always engaged in conversational becoming, constructed and reconstructed through continuous interactions, through relationships (Anderson & Goolishian, 1988a; Goolishian & Anderson, 1994). We live our narratives and our narratives become our living; our realities become our stories and our stories become our realities. Like past, present, and future these are reflexive processes and cannot be separated. This reflexivity provides continuity to the ongoing process of composing and recomposing our lives.

Ricoeur suggests that

> unlike the abstract identity of the Same, this narrative identity, constitutive of self constancy, can include change, mutability, within the cohesion of one lifetime. The subject then appears both as a reader and the writer of its own life, as Proust would have it. As the literary analysis of autobiography confirms, the story of a life continues to be refigured by all the truthful or fictive stories a subject tells about himself or herself. This refiguration makes this life itself a cloth woven of stories told. (Ricoeur as cited in Joy, 1993, p. 297)

Similarly, the Canadian psychologist Morny Joy (1993) exemplifies this constant revision position in her proposal that a person's life is not a static narrative with one plot but a process, a "dynamic mosaic."

> We can talk of a person's life as a composite of many different narrative plots. Each plot lends cohesion and coherence to the manifold influences that ceaselessly threaten to overwhelm us. So it is that a particular plot is constructed by a person as a response to a specific situation or experience that needs clarification. This plot can help a person establish a bridgehead from which he/she can thematize a set of events that may otherwise be either too chaotic or too distressing. It can also assist in the expression of strategic

actions of a political or ethical kind in response to the same situation. (pp. 296–297)

If we follow this premise that narrative is dynamic and ongoing, then how do we develop a self-identity? Is self-identity synonymous with self-continuity? In other words, if we are always engaged in conversational becoming, how do we have continuity at the same time we are involved in transformation?

In a postmodern view the problem of *identity* and *continuity* or what we think of as our *selfhood* becomes maintaining coherence and continuity in the stories we tell about ourselves, constructing narratives that make sense of our lack of coherence with both ourselves and the chaos of life. Our narratives of identity become a matter of forming and performing the *I* that we are always telling ourselves and others that we are, have been, and will be. The self becomes the person or persons our stories demand (Gergen, 1994), I believe, whether the self becomes a hero or a victim. We are always as many potential selves as are embedded in and created by our conversations. In this vein, the psychoanalyst Roy Schafer describes self as an "experiential phenomenon, a set of more or less stable and emotionally felt ways of telling oneself about one's being and one's continuity through change" (as cited in Madison, 1988, p. 160).

Narrative theory in this discursive sense was one of the early avenues of challenge to the modern view of self and of exploration of the implications of defining the self as a storyteller—an outcome of the human process of producing meaning by language activity. To help us understand some of the wonderment of the postmodern socially created and relational *narrative self*, it would be useful to pause and take a look at the contrasting modernist understandings of self and identity.

A MODERN KNOWABLE SELF

In the twentieth century, Western philosophical tradition has developed vocabularies and narratives of the self in which the person is a being who is consistent, observable, and knowable by him- or herself and by others. This notion of self and the conception of the person as a bounded, unique, integrated, motivational, and cognitive system and as the center of emotion, awareness, and judgment have been powerful forces in modern psychological theory and practice.

They are steeped in the Cartesian dualism that mind is a closed space sufficient unto itself and that mind and body are separate. In a metaphysical sense, this notion of self implies that there is something central to the human being, an essential core that is particular to humanness. In an epistemological sense, the notion of self implies that self is an entity that exists, endures over time, and can be known—observed, measured, and quantified. Self possesses quality and quantity.

What is *self*? has long been a central question of psychology and psychotherapy. The languages of psychotherapy, of the analytic writers who describe the person as having a biologically based and impulsive unconscious as well as the family therapists who have created the family as the cradle of our identities, are embedded in modernist narratives. All contain the element of the knowable human story—selves that can be discovered, identified, and described by others as well as ourselves/oneself. The self becomes the overarching entity that somehow underlies, supports, and is the basis of all that selves engage in—emotions, feelings, thinking, and acting. The person in charge of self, the *underlying* self of self, is seen as the owner of his or her actions and capacities.

In this modern perspective, the self is a taken-for-granted abstract entity, distinct and apart from other psychological constructs. Each person is an independent event in the universe; an autonomous, self-determining individual; and a bounded, unique, integrated motivational and cognitive system that is the center of awareness, emotion, and judgment—an encapsulated self (Anderson & Goolishian, 1988a; Goolishian, 1989; Goolishian & Anderson, 1992, 1994). Self and nonself, and self and other, are clearly demarcated. The individual or family or, more precisely, the interior of the individual or family is the psychological subject of inquiry. Most psychological phenomena, like self, can be traced to some causal, essentialist, foundationalist explanation. Historically, psychological classifications of behavior are based on this modernist notion of self and self-identity.

Current cognitive psychology, for instance, explains the psychological phenomena of the human mind, including self and consciousness, as the internal actions of the central nervous system. Like a computer, the mental operations of mind and self process information against some criterion or syntax built into the system. In this view the self connects the inner experience and the outer world. I include cybernetic systems theory and its mechanical metaphor as applied to human systems and family therapy, and even some forms of radical constructivism and personal construct theory, under this rubric of cognitive psychology. In these theories, human meaning and understanding are often reduced to biological structure and functioning of physiological systems, or to system components that cybernetically compute and thus give rise to a psychological process called the *self*—or the interactional process called the *family*.

What happens to self and self-identity if we pursue the notion that language does not represent the self but is part and parcel of it, weaving in and out the *I*s, the *Me*s, and the *You*s?

SELF AS A CONCEPT

Linguistic and Socially Created Selves: Many Is

Our language possesses ambiguities. Take the word *self*, for instance. It is as if the word refers to an object. The linguistic scholar Emile Benveniste was one of the earliest to challenge the traditional Western philosophical notion of self. He argued in his classic paper "Subjectivity in Language" (1971) that the self is constructed and understood in language. According to Benveniste, language is responsible for the notion of self and language without personal pronouns is inconceivable. "*I* refers to the act of individual discourse in which it is pronounced, and by this it designates the speaker" (as cited in Madison, 1988, p. 161). As Madison interprets Benveniste, "The I exists in and by means of saying 'I'; the I is not a subject . . . a preexistent substance, which speaks; it is as subject a speaking subject" (p. 161). The *I* does not exist outside language, outside discourse; it is created and maintained in language and in discourse. In other words, it is in and through language that a person constructs a personal account of the self: who we believe ourselves to be is a linguistic construction. The *I* is not a preexisting subject or substance in the epistemological or metaphysical sense; it is a speaking subject (Gadamer, 1975). For Benveniste,

> Consciousness of self is only possible if it is experienced by contrast. I use *I* only when I am speaking to someone who will be a *you* in my address. It is this condition of dialogue that is constitutive of *person*, for it implies that reciprocally, *I* becomes *you* in the address of the one who in his turn designates himself as *I*. (As cited in Madison, 1988, p. 162)

Postmodernism proposes that the self is not an entity nor a single being. There is no sole core *I*, no fixed tangible thing inside someone that can be arrived at by peeling away layers. Even though it can be argued that the self is made up of many components, for instance, many narratives, many experiences, many relationships, these do not add up to or constitute a single self or a core self. Rather self (and other) is a created concept, a created narrative, linguistically constructed and existing in dialogue and in relationship (Benveniste, 1971; Bruner, 1986, 1990; Gadamer, 1975; Gergen, 1989, 1991b, 1994; Harré, 1995; Rorty, 1979; Shotter, 1989). In this view, *the self is a dialogical–narrative self* and *identity is a dialogical–narrative identity.* Self-knowledge, *Who am I?*, according to Gergen (1989), in a postmodern sense "is not, as is commonly assumed, the product of in-depth probing of the inner recesses of the psyche. . . . Rather, it is a mastery of discourse—a 'knowing how' rather than a 'knowing that'" (p. 75). Similarly, according to Shotter (1995a),

> instead of immediately adopting the Cartesian focus upon how we as isolated individuals might come to know the objects and entities in the world around us, or to express our inner experiences, we [social constructionists] have become more interested in how we first develop and sustain certain *ways* of relating ourselves to each other in our talk, and then, from within such talk-sustained relationships, come to make sense of our surroundings. (p. 385)

All in all, identities are now in relationship to a perspective, to a point of view that is relative to our purposes. The self now can be described in an infinite variety of ways. And implicit in this is that any one self, any one mind is not exactly like another (Harré, 1995, p. 372).

In this narrative perspective the self, the narrator, is many *Is*, occupies many positions, and has many voices. In the view of Hermans and his colleagues:

> The voices function like interacting characters in a story. Once a character is set in motion in a story, the character takes on a life of its own and thus assumes a certain narrative necessity. Each character has a story to tell about experiences from its own stance. As different voices these characters exchange information about their respective *Mes* and their worlds, resulting in a complex, narratively structured self. (Hermans, Kempen, & Van Loon, 1992, pp. 28–29)

Critics of postmodernism, of social constructionism in particular, often fear that in these views the individual is lost: the person loses individual rights, becomes the puppet of a society that threatens or takes away human rights, and is no longer personally responsible. In my opinion it is the opposite. The individual and individual responsibility have a position of primary importance. The difference is in how the individual and responsibility are conceived. As individuals absorbed in others, as nonsolitary selves, as relational beings we are confronted even more, not less, with issues of responsibility. Responsibility, as discussed in chapter 5, however, becomes shared.

Another critique is that the view of socially constructed multiple selves results in a fragmented self. The response of Hermans et al. (1992) to this concern is that

> the multiplicity of the self does not result in fragmentation, because it is *the same I* that is *moving back and forth* [my emphasis] between several positions. Thanks to this identity . . . variance and invariance, or continuity and discontinuity, coexist in the functioning self. (pp. 28–29)

Rather, the wonder is that change and continuity exist side by side. This is fittingly illustrated by the character King George III in *The Madness of King George* (Evans & Hyther, 1995). Commenting on mad King George's performance of lines from Shakespeare's *King Lear*, the lord chancellor remarks, "Your Master seems more yourself." To which King George replies, "Do I?, yes, I do. Yeh, I've always been myself even when I was ill. Only now I *seem* [my emphasis] myself and that's the important thing. I have remembered how to *seem*." Later when the populace is celebrating his return, "Our old King is back," King George retorts, "Do not presume I am the person I was. The King is himself again." In other words, what others experienced as two different King Georges was the same King George *moving back and forth*.

It seems important at this time to return to the notion of narrative and its emergence within psychotherapy and where it fits within the modern–postmodern *self* shift.

NARRATIVE ACCOUNTS AND VIEWS OF IDENTITY IN PSYCHOTHERAPY

The Self as Storyteller

About twenty years ago, some psychotherapists and clinical theorists began to move away from the constraints of a modernist, cognitive psychology and its view of the self as a computing machine and to take on an interpretive perspective.[4] The common characteristic of this new direction is the notion of the individual or the self as narrator and storyteller. This move, this interpretive turn, evolved from two distinct yet overlapping paths. One path represents the emergence of narrative as storytelling and weaves around the notion of the self as a storyteller and the story as created inside the self; psychotherapy from this perspective is a storied event. The other path represents the emergence of an interest in language and dialogue and centers on the self as a social, dialogical process. Here, the narrative is thought of as being created "outside" the self and therapy is perceived as a dialogical event.

Perhaps the earliest attempt at outlining the role of narrative in psychotherapy arose from the psychoanalytic movement; interestingly enough it dates back to Freud and is related to the primacy he gave discovering one's past or discovering the *why*. In his 1937 paper "Constructions in Analysis" Freud (1964) suggested that when the requisite childhood oedipal memories are not recovered by the process of free association and analysis of ego defenses, it is permissible for the analyst to "construct" a story close to what it would be if it could be remembered.[5]

> The path that starts from the analyst's construction ought to end in the patient's recollection. . . . Quite often we do not succeed in bringing the patient to recollect what has been repressed. Instead of that, if the analysis is carried out correctly, we produce in him an assured conviction of the truth of the construction [analysis created] which achieves the same therapeutic result as a recaptured memory . . . how it is possible that what appears to be an incomplete substitute should produce a complete result. (pp. 265–266)

Most, however, would credit the writings of Roy Schafer (1981) and Donald Spence (1984) in the psychoanalytic literature and of Donald Polkinghorne (1988) and Jerome Bruner (1986, 1990) in the psychology literature as the first to pique psychotherapists' interest in narrative by introducing the notion of the self as the narrator or storyteller, and by delineating the role of narrative in psychotherapy. According to Spence (1984), and extending Freud's notion, all an analyst can do when a patient's memories are unrecoverable is to construct a story as similar as possible to the childhood events related to the problem so that the newly constructed narrative is approximately what it *might* be. For Spence a therapist's task was not the archaeological discovery of a hidden and unrecoverable reality, but a matter of narrative development, of construction of a life story that fit a patient's current circumstance without regard for the "archaeological trueness" of the construction. He introduced the term *narrative truth* to refer to the analyst-influenced new narrative constructed in psychoanalysis. Whether that narrative is true is less important than whether it fits the patient's real story. That is, the constructed story should have external and internal coherence, livability, and adequacy, and yet somehow remain congruent with the real but unrecoverable memories of childhood. This could partially explain why some psychotherapists working with adults are attempting to make sense of present life difficulties by linking them to repressed memories of childhood sexual abuse (Crews, 1995).

Schafer in *Language and Insight* (1978) took a more Wittgensteinian and social construction perspective. For Schafer the self is a manifestation of human action, the action of speaking about oneself. In his view we are always telling stories about who we are to ourselves and to others, always enclosing one story within another. The self, then, becomes more or less stable and emotional ways of telling oneself and others about one's being and one's continuity through continuous and random change (as discussed in Madison, 1988, p. 160). Like Spence, Schafer was concerned with the content of the constructed narrative, but he was equally occupied with the storytelling process, the method of construction, the narrative talking. For him, the process of the telling of the story holds the opportunity for change. A therapist's challenge, in his perspective, is to help patients retell the stories of their lives in a way that makes change narratively conceivable, believable, and attainable. A therapist, in this relationship, is similar to a helpful editor. Narrative used in these psychoanalytic arenas focuses on the narrative content and its usefulness, not the narrating process. Writer Kevin Murray (1995) highlighted a difference between the content path and the process path: "One sees narrative as a mental space which serves the progress of an individual through the world, whereas the other makes narrative part of that very world" (p. 187).

The latter path that this interpretive turn in psychotherapy took led to the emergence of an interest in language and dialogue in which the self as a dialogical self and psychotherapy as a dialogical event became pivotal. Let me now address this interpretive turn. How are the meanings we attribute to ourselves and the events of our lives dialogically created, preserved, and altered over time? And in therapy how does the therapist participate in this process?

A Relational View of Self and Narrative Identity

Central to the many linguistic and socially derived narratives that emerge in behavioral organization are those that contain the elements articulated as *self-stories*, *self-descriptions*, or *first-person narratives*. These self-stories influence our self-identities: they take a narrative form. Of this linguistic narrative realm, the philosopher Anthony Kerby (1991) suggests,

> On a narrative account the self is to be construed not as a prelinguistic given that merely employs language, much as we might employ a tool, but rather as a product of language—what might be called the *implied self* of self-referring utterances. The self, or subject, then becomes a result of discursive praxis rather than either a substantial entity having ontological priority over praxis or a self with epistemological priority, an originator of meaning. (p. 4)

For Polkinghorne (1988), stories are the way we achieve our "narrative identities":

> We achieve our personal identities and self-concept through the use of the narrative configuration, and make our existence into a whole by understanding it as an expression of a single unfolding and developing story. We are in the middle of our stories and cannot be sure how they will end; we are constantly having to revise the plot as new events are added to our lives. Self, then, is not a static thing or a substance, but a configuring of personal events into an historical unity which includes not only what one has been but also anticipations of what one will be. (p. 150)

Like that of other narratives, the development of these self-defining narratives takes place in a social and local context involving conversation and action with significant others, including one's self. A linguistic and dialogic view emphasizes this social nature of the self—as emerging in and embodied in relationships—and it emphasizes our capacity to create meaning through conversation. This is the *linguistic relational view* of self proposed by Gergen (1987, 1989, 1991b), in which the self (and other) is realized in language and dialogue and becomes a linguistic dialogical self. Inherent in this view, as suggested earlier, is that a narrative never represents a single voice, but rather a multiauthored self, and because we are constituted in dialogue, we are ever-changing. In this vein, Sarbin (1990) interestingly suggests that because our self-narratives occur in a social context they are the products of "enforced collaboration" (p. 60).

I do not mean to minimize what seems like a characteristic of human nature—our constant search for self and self-understanding, or what Madison (1988) refers to as "desiring selves." In his words, self "is a function of the conversation with similar, desiring selves, a function of the self-reinforcing narratives they pursue together in their occasional, casual conversations as well as those more serious ones which last to all hours of the night" (p. 166). By desiring Madison means self-enhancement, the self we want to be and have the potential to realize. His emphasis too is on conversation with others: "We are constantly pursuing and constantly desiring with other selves that we can become the self we desire to be and can be who we are" (p. 166).

This storytelling self in the view of Bakhtin (1981) also takes a dialogic form. Bakhtin was partially yet significantly influenced by Dostoyevsky's literary form, in which the story was not singly narrated by *an* author but told by multiple authors, as each character gave a separate account of the story. In his analysis of Dostoyevsky's character constructions, Bakhtin suggested that each character (or an author) is a plurality of independent voices (which could be, for example, another character, a conscience, one's inner thoughts, or an imagined other) in dialogue, or what he called a *polyphony*. Bakhtin characterized the self as like a polyphonic novel, in which the self is not a single entity, one voice or one position, but a multiplicity of each. As Hermans et al. (1992) indicate, "The conception of the self as a polyphonic novel . . . permits one individual to live in a multiplicity of worlds, with each world having its own author telling a story relatively independent of the authors of the other worlds" (p. 28). I question, however, that they emerge *relatively independent* of each other.

The physician Rita Charon (1993) similarly refers to this kind of polyphony or narrating selves when she talks about patient narratives that emerge, and those that do not emerge, in medical settings:

> To tell about oneself in a therapeutic setting, whether medical or psychotherapeutic, posits a self who tells and a self about whom the teller tells, the therapeutic telling [like any telling] generating an author, an implied author, and a character. . . . Although patients' accounts of themselves are based on *true* events, by nature of the narrating situation patients will produce a certain version of the *true* events [emphasis added]. . . . Contrary to commonly held assumptions, then, the patient is not the person . . . multiple contradictory voices must be heard and recognized [who] together compose the person who suffers. (p. 89)

Self-stories, and notions of self, are simply one version of many versions that are influenced by the narrating situation. People's selves that emerge and the stories they tell about themselves vary in relation to the social context and conversations with other individuals in that context.

This linguistic relational view of self is in sharp contrast with psychology's more usual definition of self, which Bruner (1990) chides for being "whatever is measured by tests of self-concepts" (p. 101). In terms of the narrative metaphor, stories (self and other) determine who we are or who we or others think we are (Bruner, 1986, 1990; Gergen, 1994; Gergen & Gergen, 1986, 1988; Kitzinger, 1987; Shotter, 1988, 1991a; Surrey, 1991). From Bruner's (1990) narrative perspective,

> Selves we construct are the outcomes of this [narrative, story-telling, and language] process of meaning construction. . . . Selves are not isolated nuclei of consciousness locked in the head, but are "distributed" interpersonally. Nor do Selves arise rootlessly in response only to the present; they take meaning as well from the historical circumstances that gave shape to the culture of which they are an expression. (p. 138)[6]

We must remember then that the self-stories we hear in therapy are not the only story or necessarily *truer* than other stories.

"Edges" Where Change Occurred

It was within the ranks of social psychology and among social construction theorists in particular that "an increasing concern with personhood—with person, agency, and action (rather than with causes, behaviour and objects) built and that the notion of the social construction of the self fully emerged" (Shotter, 1989, p. 135). Although several (Gergen, 1982, 1989; Harré, 1979, 1983; Harré & Secord, 1972; Polkinghorne, 1988; Potter & Wetherell, 1987; Shotter, 1975, 1989) can be given credit for taking this notion to the edge in suggesting that the self, and self-identity, are socially constructed in language, Gergen, Harré, and Shotter have made pivotal contributions, and in different ways; all focus on the *process* of identity creation and not its structure.[7]

Gergen's (1977) research on how people's self-concepts and self-esteem vary in relation to the social context and the comments of the individuals within that context has been perhaps the most visible early effort to assign primary influence to the social and relational aspects of self-construction. From this he advanced the notion of relational authorship and suggested that the self and self-identity are narrative realities socially constructed in language. Self-identities are the function of the socially constructed stories we continually narrate to ourselves and others. One's self-identities are a manifestation of and are generated by persons in conversation and action with one another and with themselves. These socially constructed narrative realities give meaning and organization not only to the events and experiences of our lives but also to our self-identities, which are always subject to shifting definitions and a variety of explications as the social interaction shifts. This process is similar to what Bruner (1990) referred to as "meaning-making" (p. 12).

Arriving at what he calls a socially constructed "relational self," Gergen (1973, 1985, 1991b) moves beyond the concepts of individual authorship and coauthorship (Gergen, 1973; Gergen & Taylor, 1969; Morse & Gergen, 1970), to the self as a multiauthored social construction:

> Narrative accounts are embedded within social action. Events are rendered socially visible ... and are typically used to establish expectations for future events. ... Narratives of the self are not fundamentally possessions of the individual; rather they are products of social interchange—possessions of the socius. (Gergen & Gergen, 1988, p. 18)[8]

That is, a narrative never represents a single voice. We are always as many selves and potential selves as are embedded in our conversations and our relationships. These self-identities, who we are or who we believe ourselves to be, like the notion of self, Gergen (1994) distinguishes "are not personal impulses made social, but social processes realized on the site of the personal" (p. 210). In fact, Gergen (1988b) goes so far as to say,

> We need not assume that human nature is a property of single, isolated individuals with relatedness a secondary and problematic byproduct. Invited is an analysis in which the individual is an emergent property of community—in which relationship precedes identity. If such were broadly realized, conflict might not be a necessary antecedent to communion. (p. 405)

Shotter (1989) emphasizes that we must pay attention not only to the construction of the *I* but also to the construction of, and the importance of, the other—the *you:* "I act not simply 'out of' my own plans and desires, unrestricted by the social circumstances of my performances, but in some sense also 'in to' the opportunities offered me to act. . . . The relationship is ours, not just mine" (p. 144). Shotter talks of the formative nature of the *you* in communication (and relationship) as "a process by which people can, in communication with one another, literally in-form one another's being, that is, help to make each other persons of this or that kind" (p. 145). Thus, the narratives *I* tell about *you* are part of the process of your identity, and vice versa. Harré (1983), like Gergen and Shotter, argues for the conversational construction of the person as well as institutions and organizations.[9]

This linguistic, dialogical, and relational path takes us beyond the view of narrative therapy as storytelling and story making and the self as the narrator. Because unless we extend this view, we succumb to the risks and concerns associated with modernist objectivity: who chooses and who directs the story to be told, how it is told, and what emerges from it.

The Narrating Process: A Caveat

Narrative theory, of course, has been conceptually useful in a variety of social science arenas besides psychotherapy: medicine, anthropology, law, culture theory, and organizational development and management (Brody, 1987; Bruner, 1990; Charon, 1993; Coles, 1989; Davis, 1992; Feldman, 1990; Kleinman, 1988a, 1988b; Sachs, 1985; Sherwin, 1993; Turner, 1980; Wilkins, 1983). Common to all these writers is that our socially arrived at narratives are the only human nature and behavior that we know—our understandings, our descriptions, our methods of observing social organization, the tools through which we understand problems, and our modes of action are all nothing more than expressions of our language use, vocabularies, and stories. Whether in the legal process, the medical process, the anthropological process, or the psychotherapeutic process, the professional participates with the client in a *narrating process* of the telling, retelling, and creating—or inventing and reinventing—of the client's past, present, and future.

The way we participate as professionals in this narrating process, our position in it and our mode of action, marks the distinction between a modern and a postmodern process. In this participation, professionals have special responsibility for the way they position themselves and the choices they make in the narrative telling, hearing, and creating process—in the relational means of joint construction of the new narrative. As therapists, for instance, we choose how we talk with and about clients, what we select to talk about with them, and how we participate in the way they tell their story. And, whether we believe that language is representational or formative, we are responsible for the way we use language, the language choices we make, and how these influence the account that emerges, the account that is privileged, the account that is deemed the true one. How we choose, for example, to ask about a father's behavior with a daughter can attribute different judgments about the same event: good, bad, or questionable behavior. How we choose, for example, to learn about, and what we choose to learn about it, can influence the way a story about a conflict between a man and his boss is shaped: where blame is posited, who should have done what, and who should do what. It can also signal whose side we are on, indicating what we think the solution should be.

In another professional area, culture of law and lawyering, Sherwin (1993) talks about how legal practices and institutions are socially created and maintained through professional discursive practices and narrative constructions. He critiques the use of dominant legal discourse to serve as a tool for people in positions of power to guide or tell another's story, thus giving the professional's version (and usually in the dominant community's discourse) more emphasis than a client's. A lawyer, like a therapist, can dominate the interaction and therefore the story that emerges by controlling the flow of topics and setting the pace. Using divorce cases as an example, Sherwin showed how "lawyers constructed the identity of their clients . . . and retold their clients' stories in a way that reflected and facilitated the attorney's sense of legal reality" (p. 46). Sherwin encourages the legal professional to take a serious look at how laws are created and how legal ideologies are maintained through the dominant discourse; this process would be equally applicable to psychotherapy theories and practices (including diagnoses).

Similarly, some feminist scholars within philosophy and psychology have expressed a critique of mainstream social science in general and psychology in particular in relation to the modernist scientific modes on which they are based. Through these modes, the professional operates under an "aura of objectivity" (Kitzinger, 1987, p. 24), in which the individual is the unit of study and conceptualization and through which normative definitions—in the feminist case, normative definitions of oppressed and socially marginalized peoples—are generated. Such perceived professional expertise intrinsically acts to perpetuate a discipline's legitimacy. Drawing upon, critiquing, and contributing to postmodern notions of self and self-identity as constructed and interpreted within and influenced by sociocultural, historical, and political discourses, these scholars resonate with the notions of individual narrative accounts of identity and the self as always open to constant revision (for other work compatible with this definition of self see: Flax, 1990; M. Gergen, 1994, 1995; Grimshaw, 1988; hooks, 1984; Joy, 1993; Kerby, 1991; Kitzinger, 1987; Ricoeur, 1988, 1991). And, like Ricoeur, they warn about confusing self-identity and core-self (Flax, 1990; Kitzinger, 1989). From the perspectives of the socially, dialogically constructed *I* and the constant rewriting of self-identity, a core narrating *I*, a core-self is a myth.[10] The narrating *I* and the socially and dialogically constructed *I* are reflexive—the narrator, in the process of narrating, is becoming.

Cecelia Kitzinger (1987), feminist psychologist and scholar, for instance, challenges *lesbianism* as a psychological category. She claims that the individualistic, humanistic focus of contemporary liberal psychology approaches personalizes the political, promoting a reality of a "private and depoliticized identity" (p. 45) and avoids and ignores what she believes is an institutional, sociopolitical, and sociocultural position.[11] In marked contrast, and in a provocative and compelling argument, Kitzinger bids for a social constructionist alternative and proposes what she calls "'accounts' of lesbian identity" (p. 90), emphasizing that the observer has no direct access to the individual experience and that the *identity account* is the unit of analysis, not the individual.

When, as in this study, the *account* is defined as the primary unit of study, then, although account gathering must depend initially on individual account providers, these people's psychologies are incidental to the research: because the account is no longer tied to the individual who provided it, the researcher can pursue her study of the account per se, broadening the research to find evidence of these accounts in the sociocultural milieu, to discover the ideologies with which they are associated and the political interest that dictates their promotion or suppression. This approach serves to draw attention to the political, rather than the personal, features of lesbian accounts of identity (p. 90).

Self-Agency and Change: "The Stories We Tell Ourselves"

It is through these self-narratives that we become actors, performers, or agents and that we derive a sense of social or self-agency. By *self-agency* I refer to a personal perception of competency for action.

To act or take action, Sarbin (1990), among others, suggests, indicates intentionality: "that human actors engage in conduct for some reason, to satisfy some purpose, to make sense of" (p. 50). Having self-agency or a sense of it means having the ability to behave, feel, think, and *choose* in a way that is liberating, that opens up new possibilities or simply allows us to see that new possibilities exist. Agency refers not only to making choices but to participating in the creation of the expansion of possible choices. The concept of agency can be likened to having a voice and being free to use that voice or not to use it.

I believe that self-agency is inherent in all of us and is self-accessed. It is not given to us. As therapists we cannot give it to someone, just as we cannot empower someone else; we can only participate in a process that maximizes the opportunity for it to emerge. Harré (1995) refers to this inherent competency as "potential asserting. . . . People are born as potential persons, and social constructionists offer an account of how potential personhood becomes actual personhood, and of how in that development some important variety can be discerned" (p. 372). In Shotter's (1995a) words, people's agency is "exhibited in their two-way ability to give shape or form to their lives while remaining rooted in their culture" (p. 387).

When I think of self-agency, I think of two words that clients often use to describe the results of successful therapy: *freedom* (from the imprisoning past, present, and future) and *hope* (for a different future) (Anderson, 1991b, 1992, 1995). New self-stories, new first-person narratives that permit the telling of a new history that is more tolerable, coherent, and continuous with present intention and agency, evolve. This is similar to what Shotter (1991a) means when he speaks of providing "new and empowering accounts of ourselves instead of disabling ones." It is like the British oral historian Ronald Frazier's response to his analyst's question, "What exactly are you hoping for?" Frazier said, "To find, to re-create a past with a certain certainty that I can put it behind me and go on with my life" (cited in Shotter, 1991a). Both Shotter and Frazier refer to a sense of agency, a sense of freedom, a sense of hope.

I like Freeman's (1993) suggestion that what seems like seeking freedom from a past is in fact seeking freedom from an "expected course of things" (p. 216). The prison is the imagined future, not the (imagined) history.[12]

I am reminded of Tom, the unemployed high school coach and English teacher in rural South Carolina in Pat Conroy's *The Prince of Tides*, who tries to free himself of his past, his present, and his future as he searches for who he can be. He looks back in reflection on his troubled "defenseless, humiliated, and dishonored" family, and his abusive and turbulent childhood—as he tries to untangle, make sense of, and reconcile his life.

> I wish I had no history to report. I've pretended for so long that my childhood did not happen. I had to keep it tight, up near the chest. I could not let it out. I followed the redoubtable example of my mother. It's an act of will to have a memory or not, and I chose not to have one. Because I needed to love my mother and father in all their flawed, outrageous humanity, I could not afford to address them directly about the felonies committed against all of us. I could not hold them accountable or indict them for crimes they could not help. They, too, had a history—one that I remembered with both tenderness and pain, one that made me forgive their transgressions against their own children. In families there are no crimes beyond forgiveness. . . .
>
> Though I hated my father, I expressed that hate eloquently by imitating his life, by becoming more and more ineffectual daily. . . . I had figured out how to live a perfectly meaningless life, but one that could imperceptibly and inevitably destroy the lives of those around me. (Conroy, 1987, pp. 8, 101)

At one point, he describes the still empty pages of the leather journals stacked on his shelves that his sister sent him each Christmas as "an eloquent metaphor of my life as a man" (p. 614): "I lived with the terrible knowledge that one day I would be an old man still waiting for my real life to start" (p. 634).

For Tom, forgiveness took the place of the tyranny of the past as indicated in his words "through the procedure of remembrance, I would try to heal myself" (p. 101). It allowed him to take the journals off the shelf, so to speak, and like Frazier to "go on with his life." And, as Shotter proposes, he was able to give shape and form to his life while remaining rooted in his culture:

> My life did not really begin until I summoned the power to forgive my father for making my childhood a long march of terror. . . . I think we began to forgive our parents for being exactly what they were meant to be. We would begin our talks with memories of brutality or treachery and end them by affirming over and over again our troubled but authentic love of Henry and Lila. At last, we were old enough to forgive them for not having been born perfect. (Conroy, 1987, pp. 282, 631–632)

Our self-narratives can permit or hinder self-agency. That is, they create identities that permit us to do or hinder us from doing what we need or want to do, or they simply allow us to feel that we could or could not act if we so chose (Anderson & Goolishian, 1988a; Goolishian, 1989; Goolishian & Anderson, 1994). In therapy we meet people whose "problems" can be thought of as emanating from social narratives and self-definitions or self-stories that do not yield an effective agency for the tasks defined. Women, for example, who are either self-labeled or labeled by others as "adult survivors of childhood incest" can develop narratives that fix a self-identity that is inherently self-limiting (Anderson, 1992). I am reminded of Rita,[13] who grew up in an incestuous family, and who was in anguish for years as she tried to live with, in her words, "the Rita others saw and liked" and "the Rita I saw and didn't like."[14] Reflecting on her experience in therapy, she said, "I now feel free to get on with my life. When I realized that I could be both of those people, I'm still me. I'm still both of those people, but I like me now." Through therapy Rita developed a new identity that included among other things two previously conflicting identities: "me"/"not me." The new identity, "Both are me," freed Rita from anguish and allowed her to get on with her life. Rita's dilemma illustrates how such labels can keep the past alive in a way that maintains the woman's identity as victim or survivor, and forms an obstacle to her more viable and liberating self-definitions. This is similar to Freeman's (1993) notion of "rewriting the self," referring to "the process by which one's past and indeed oneself is figured anew through interpretation" (p. 3).

From an interpretive, meaning-generating perspective, change is inherent in dialogue: change is the telling and retelling of familiar stories; it is the redescriptions that accrue through conversation; it is the different meanings that are conferred on past, present, and imagined future events and experiences. Change becomes developing future selves. What becomes important in therapy are the individuals' first-person narratives (Gergen, 1994; Gergen & Gergen, 1983, 1986, 1988; Kitzinger, 1987; Shotter, 1991b, 1993a; Surrey, 1991). In Shotter's words,

> The conduct of social life is based upon a right we assign to first-persons to *tell* us about themselves and their experience, and to have what they say taken seriously. . . . All our valid forms of inquiry are based upon such a right. . . . The authority of first-persons [Shotter later uses the term *ordinary people*] has been usurped in recent times by the third-person, external observer position [Shotter later prefers *experts*]. (Shotter, 1984, as cited in Shotter, 1995a, p. 387)

When familiar ways of conceptualizing the individual no longer fit with my shifting experiences of relationships and conversations with and about clients, these views of self, self-narrative, self-identity, and thus, self-transformation were a welcomed conceptual tool. They partly inspired the shift (described in chapter 4) from thinking of systems as a people collective—as a contained entity that acts, feels, thinks, and believes—to considering systems as consisting of individuals who coalesced around a particular relevance (Anderson, 1990; Anderson & Goolishian, 1988a; Anderson, Goolishian, & Winderman, 1986a, 1986b; Goolishian & Anderson, 1987a). This renewed interest in the individual was not in terms of the Western psychological sense of the individual as bounded by and possessing a core self, but rather the individual in relationship. These alternative views were also part of a shift to thinking differently about change in therapy: self was no longer the subject of the verb change; a client was no longer the subject that a therapist changed. And these views constitute a major distinguisher between a collaborative language systems approach to therapy and other narratively informed postmodern therapies.

In my view the purpose of therapy is to help people tell their first-person narratives so that they may transform their self-identities to ones that permit them to develop understandings of their lives and its events, that allow multiple possibilities for ways of being in and acting in the world at any given time and in any given circumstance, and that help them gain an access to and express or execute agency or a sense of self-agency. To restore or achieve self-competency, one must transform one's self-story. It is exactly this self-story transformation that allowed what Rita experienced as contradicting selves—constraining selves—to say, "I can be both of those persons." Such freeing descriptions lead to a transformation of self. Therapy becomes a transformative event—the natural consequence of dialogic conversation and collaborative relationship.

In the next chapter, I address what a postmodern therapy philosophy looks like in two other domains: educating therapists and consulting with organizations.

PART IV

Broadening the Space

"DISSOLVING TIDAL WAVES"

Twenty therapists who call themselves the Learning Consortium invited me to spend a day with them. They meet twice a year to share their work, to connect, and to nurture each other as part of their professional and personal growth. One of the therapists, whom I will call Lee Ann, requested consultation on what she described as "an uncomfortable dilemma" that had arisen in her work with a couple. I asked Lee Ann and her colleagues to join me in an experiential exercise. Since it was just after lunch, they welcomed activity. I will intertwine my recollection of this consultation, a discussion of the experiential exercise, and Lee Ann's reflections two weeks and five months later. In describing the consultation I focus on its process and Lee Ann's experience, not the content of the couple's life situation or the therapy.

"AS IF"

In keeping with my philosophical stance and my aim of creating a space that encourages internal and external dialogue, I have designed an experiential exercise that I call "As If" to help participants address dilemmas, concerns, problems, struggles, or issues presented in supervision, teaching, or business consultations (Anderson, 1991a; Anderson & Burney, in press; Anderson & Rambo, 1988; St. George, 1994). The exercise has both a consultation and learning agenda: it allows participants to experience the kinds of conversations I talk about and to take part in a "problem dissolving" process.

I want to give participants an opportunity to develop an awareness of the way each member of a system experiences and thinks about the same information or event, experience the diversity of individual perceptions and points of view, discuss ideas in a public forum instead of a private setting, develop an awareness of the influence of professional language, experience the generation of meanings and shifts in perspectives, and observe the style and types of questions and comments that invite the other into conversation, as well as those that impede it. In addition, participants experience that a dialogue may take many shapes and its outcome cannot be predicted.

The exercise combines four processes that provide a skeletal framework: presentation, listening, reflections, and discussion. It is individually tailored to the context of the consultation and the situation addressed, a presenter's agenda, a group's agenda, and a group's size. Any number of people, whether a two-student supervision group, a six-person therapy team, a twenty-member business department, or a hundred-participant conference, may be involved in the exercise. A presenter may be an individual therapist, members of a therapy team, or a department staff.

"As If" Positions

Asking Lee Ann to list the characters in the drama began the consultation. She listed herself, a husband, Larry, a wife, Carol, the wife's dead brother, and the wife's daughter from her first marriage, who had died at age three. I asked her colleagues (nineteen total) to listen to her story "as if" they were one of the people on Lee Ann's list or a consultant to her, putting "on hold" any emerging questions, comments, or suggestions. Those in each of the six "as if" positions were asked to cluster together and to take a moment to situate themselves mentally in their positions. I requested that they listen to Lee Ann silently.

Presenter's Story

I asked Lee Ann to address three questions, imagining that the characters in her story were present and listening to its telling:

1. Tell *us* why *you* selected this situation. For example, does it present a particular kind of clinical dilemma, is it a therapy impasse, or is it a familiar problem in your work?
2. Tell *us your* hope, agenda, or goal. For example, what are your expectations of the consultation? Do you have a particular question that you want us to address? What do you want help with?
3. Tell *us* what *you* think *we* need to know. For example, what is your story? What do you think is important for us to know in order to address your agenda and meet your expectations?

These questions, combined with the silent "as if" listener position, enable the presenter to lead with what she or he deems relevant, not what others consider important. My use of language such as "What do *you* want *us* to know?" emphasizes this distinction. I purposely use pronouns to emphasize the importance of the teller and the listener and their roles in a dialogic process. For instance, the pronouns in "Tell *us* what *you* think *we* need to know" underscore that the presenter will tell his or her story, selecting what he or she wants the others to hear. I use the collective pronoun *us* because I want to include myself as one of the listeners. This maximizes the likelihood that the presentation is made to all present and not only to the consultant as the designated expert. My role throughout was facilitative. I listened silently, only speaking to indicate the next step of the exercise.

Lee Ann, a soft-spoken, unpretentious southern woman with a quiet yet strong passion for learning, calmly and slightly apologetically expressed her discomfort with the wife, Carol, and her sympathy for the husband. She described Carol as "angry and overbearing" and as an "anxious monologue of complaints and whirl of emotions." She was exasperated by Carol's "relentless laundry list" of her husband's "ten evils." She thought the wife, who had recently left the husband in what Lee Ann deemed a "blackmailing attempt to get him to change," was hopeless. Encounters with Carol were like being hit by a "tidal wave of over rushing drowning water." Fearful of being "swallowed-up by the verbal and emotional wave," Lee Ann was ready to abandon the wife and refer her to another therapist at the next appointment. Such strong negative feelings and intolerance for a client were unfamiliar to Lee Ann, and although seemingly embarrassed by her reaction as well as by her self-declared failure with this couple, she was eager to examine her dilemma with her colleagues and me.

"As If" Listeners' Reflections

When Lee Ann finished her story, I asked the listeners to maintain their "as if" positions and in those voices to share their thoughts and experiences of Lee Ann's story with the others in their clusters. For example, what piqued their curiosity, what did they hear that invited them into conversation, what made them feel misunderstood, and what recommendations, if any, did they have for Lee Ann? As they reflected with each other, I asked Lee Ann to visit each cluster as a silent listener.

The listeners in each cluster represented the multiple inner voices that an individual may have at any time. Each voice embodied a perspective, sometimes harmonious, sometimes conflictual. The exercise relied on the imagination of the listeners since they only knew the members of Lee Ann's story as she portrayed them and her story's content as she introduced it. The listeners did not need command of the content. The content was simply one vehicle for the process.

After each cluster had ample time to share reflections, I asked a member of each to speak as a collective "as if" voice, sharing his or her multiple voiced reflections with the rest of us. I recorded their words and phrases on a board for all to see. Recording these for all to see highlighted the fact that I listened carefully to each person's comments and considered them important. Equally important, Lee Ann and the "as if" members were able to listen more attentively when freed of taking notes.

Afterward Lee Ann wrote down some of the voiced fragments that caught her curiosity, which she later shared with me. Her notes illustrate that when we speak we never know what the other person attends to, how he or she hears, and what it means to him or her. Lee Ann's notes included these fragments: From the "as if" husband—"I have difficulty being the husband," "I'm happy to be understood . . . I want help for my wife . . . I'm tired of carrying her anger"; from the "as if" wife—"I want someone to understand the depth of my suffering . . . no one has ever given me the depth of my pain. . . . I don't want to deal with another loss. I'm alienating him now because my parents are about to die. . . . I have no control"; from the "as if " deceased brother—"I'm concerned for my sister . . . angel of death . . . I want her [Carol] to 'get a life'"; the "as if " dead daughter—"It's abusive to keep her from the dying . . . I'd stand up for you . . . it's hard to see you alone . . . I'm confused"; and the "as if " consultant—"trying to find a way to connect . . . I can agree Carol's been injured . . . trying to learn more about Carol's experience of abuse without agreeing with her . . . flip the ten evils . . . get something partial on each area." Scribbled at the top of Lee Ann's note page was "Gadamer—Wittgenstein—Shotter."

Reflections on Reflections

I asked Lee Ann to reflect on the "as if " listeners' ideas, comments, questions, and suggestions. For example, what intrigued her, what made her feel understood and respected, what made her feel misunderstood and frustrated? Then all participants shared their continuing reflections on the others' reflections or Lee Ann's.

Participants' Discussion

I invited everyone to share his or her experiences of the consultation process. Some commented on the difficulty of giving up their therapist role and staying in a silent listening position while holding back questions and comments. Others expressed surprise at how many ideas could be generated without access to all of the usually deemed necessary details—the content. And others wondered how a problem can be dissolved without a solution. Several voiced what it was like to be talked about and to hear another's description of oneself (for example, one's attributions, intentions, and feelings); some discussed what encouraged conversation and what erected barriers to it. Both Lee Ann and her colleagues noticed the way, the manner, the tone, and the attitude in which perceived delicate and dichotomous content was addressed and questioned influenced the way it was heard.

How the Tidal Wave Dissolved

All, including Lee Ann, were surprised at how relieved she now felt even though she left the consultation without a list of strategies. Instead, Lee Ann acquired a different perception of Carol and Larry and her relationship with them. She said, "I don't know what

I will do when I see Carol and Larry again, but I feel comfortable and confident that I will know that when the time comes." She identified this difference and this new sense of agency in a letter that she sent to me two weeks after the consultation.

> I felt much better after the consultation. I had been carrying around a sort of grimness anticipating Carol's next appointment. But much of that had washed away by the time of our appointment. I was able to listen without cutting off (interrupting) her usual laundry list of the ten "evils" that Larry supposedly perpetuates. I began asking questions about the ten "evils" in a different way from how I have done before the consultation. I found that I could let Carol's intense, critical, battering language flow over or around me without my feeling crushed or pierced by it and I was able to pick up (hear) a thread (almost an invisible one) of ambivalence on her part. Indeed while Carol left Larry for a month, most recently this week, she is saying that she doesn't want a divorce, and he has said so too. . . . One by one I am asking more questions of the 10 evils . . . it feels like untying complicated knots, one by one. But she seems to be liking (I know I am) our new way of relating. I feel more confident of myself in relation to Carol and less cowed by her ways of self-expression.

Five months later, Lee Ann wrote to share her "stream of consciousness" as she looked back on the consultation. She highlighted the influence of "presence" and "silence" and her subsequent thoughts.

> I think one essential part of your presence in the room was your sitting on my right side. That simple, "felt" presence of you *with* me, not directing me or correcting my thinking about the couple, was refreshing.
>
> As I think of it, you "took" a position of silence like a friendly comrade or companion. I have thought about that so many times in sessions with the couple. Both the verbal reflections of my colleagues (the "said" reflections from their minds) and your nonverbal reflections (the "unsaid" reflections from your mind) have been powerfully helpful. I have thought about that position of silence as a room, an invitation for further unraveling the knottiness of Carol and Larry's lives together, of room for mystery, what they and I have yet to come to understand, some kind of abiding constancy, like an assurance for this search for greater understanding. Perhaps by being open, accepting, and silent, we offer great gifts to our clients and students.
>
> I have a memory of seeing you in my peripheral vision from my right eye. My eyes and my mind are gentler as I look at Carol and

think of her. I have been freer to see Larry's and especially Carol's concerns from a greater number of points of view.

In mentioning your experiences and referring to writers (Gadamer, Wittgenstein, and Shotter) in an elliptical way, you gave me and my colleagues clues and trails to follow. We have a sense of being connected to a larger community of learners. This sense is freeing, liberating, and life affirming. By the way, I have borrowed a copy of Ray Monk's incredible biography *Ludwig Wittgenstein: The Duty of Genius*. I am finding it wonderful and am looking for what he and the others you mentioned say about understanding that comes through listening and being in conversation in such an open-hearted manner.

I believe Lee Ann speaks to the difference between creating a space and relationship for encountering: being invited into a conversation and respected by the other versus being shut out and prejudged by the other. She speaks to what it is to be heard and understood as well as to be unheard and misunderstood. She speaks to the options that are both limited and expanded through interactions. She speaks to the richness of different voices—what is lost when only the expert's voice is heard, what is lost when voices are moved toward consensus, and what is lost when we believe we know what the other should say and what his or her unsaid is. She speaks to Mary Catherine Bateson's (1994) stories about the meanings and learnings that are accessible to us through our *peripheral vision* when we dare to dance with the unfamiliar other.

> A certain amount of friction is inevitable whenever people with different customs and assumptions meet. . . . What is miraculous is how often it is possible to work together to sustain joint performances in spite of disparate codes, evolving different belief systems to affirm that possibility. . . . In all learning, one is changed, becoming someone slightly—or profoundly—different. . . . What is learned then becomes a part of that system of self-definition that filters all future perceptions and possibilities of learning. (pp. 23, 79)

Moreover, I believe she speaks to the depth, power, and emotion of dialogue.

After Words

We often forget that we and our clients carry other people's voices around with us and that these voices become part of who we are, part of our thoughts and actions. They may be the voices of others currently in our lives or voices from the past. In this "as if" consultation process, the dead family members' voices illustrated the importance of these voices.

The experiential activity and discussion provide a chance for all participants to experience making room for an other and its relevance to dialogue. Silently listening enables both "as if" members and presenters to hear differently than when listening and speaking simultaneously. That is, when the "as if" members are prohibited from asking questions, sharing ideas, or making suggestions, they sense the difference between listening to what a presenter wants them to hear and what they think they should hear. They grasp how premature knowing (for example, ideas that inform questions) can impede access to another person's experience. Silently moving among "as if" clusters as they talk gives presenters an opportunity to listen more fully because they are not engaged in clarifying or defending their views and actions. When the "as if" voices are then shared with the larger group, members gain an understanding of the difficulty of preserving and duplicating the richness of prior conversations in their reporting.

Through the process participants become aware of the multiplicity of self voices that each of us may have at any one time and how these voices may be in harmony or disharmony. Hearing the several "as if" voices of each character in the story gives presenters and other participants an opportunity to gain the awareness that as we talk with the people we meet in therapy or other contexts (outer dialogue), each of us silently and concurrently interacts internally with the spoken words (inner dialogue). Presenters and participants also experience the usefulness of accessing and bringing the inner thoughts and vocalized voices into the outer conversation. As they hear each other's reflections, they experience the shifting of perspectives that occurs in a dialogic process. They also experience that ideas are not fixed, discrete pieces that are simply transferred from one person to another, but that each person interacts in his or her own way with what the others offer. The "as if" voices do not offer new "information" for the presenter; this is not the intent. The newness and future possibilities come from the fluidity of the ongoing, back-and-forth interactions as each conversation (within and outside the consultation room) becomes part of and leads to others. Tidal waves dissolve.

CHAPTER 11

Beyond Postmodern Therapy

I have spent my life . . . trying to learn how to share enough
with strangers to make learning possible, learning to identify
divergent premises instead of taking my own for granted, and to
accept a broader or more ambiguous view than common sense.
The basic challenge we face today in an interdependent world is
to disconnect the notion of difference from the notion of superior-
ity, to turn the unfamiliar into a resource rather than a threat.
                                          —MARY CATHERINE BATESON

THE SOCIAL RELEVANCE of a postmodern philosophy extends beyond
the psychotherapy arena to a boundless realm of social systems
and their unique requirements, offering new possibilities.[1] The
postmodernism that informs my biases about therapy, including
the therapist's stance, the process of therapy, and the therapy system, informs all my work, with individuals and groups of individuals in therapy, learning, research, or consultation contexts (Anderson & Burney, in press; Anderson & Goolishian, 1990c; Anderson &
Rambo, 1988; Anderson & Swim, 1993, 1995). It also permeates the
events and relationships of my private life.

The actualization of this philosophy inherently varies from one
setting to another because each setting has its unique purposes and
demands that the process tailor itself to the needs and goals of its

participants. As in therapy, each encounter is conceptualized as a linguistic event in which people with different types of expertise interact, mutually exploring and addressing that which brings them together. As each system coalesces around a particular relevance (dilemma, challenge, task, or goal), its form, format, and lifetime are shaped by that significance and are specific to the internal and external reasons for its existence. Each system and its members exist within larger contextual parameters of agendas and goals that influence local objectives and strategies.

LEARNING TO BE A THERAPIST

At the heart of my biases about learning is a belief that it is a dynamic, continuing, daily, lifelong process. Our everyday professional and personal contexts and experiences, both formal and informal, constitute our learning systems and frame our learning circumstances. They are our knowledge communities. Some systems and circumstances allow for the maximization of professional and personal enhancement and possibilities; others minimize it. What are the characteristics of those systems and circumstances that maximize opportunity for learning? How can learning have significance for a learner and the world in which he or she lives? How can a teacher create environments for learning? How can a person learn to be a therapist in these contexts? How can the personal and professional development fostered in organized learning environments be made relevant, be translated, or be continued outside the learning arena in a participant's unique clinical setting and everyday life? How can we be open to learning from our everyday life experiences?

Dialogical Learning Communities

Given the premise that learning—the development and acquisition of knowledge—is a social and interactive event, a joint action that takes place through dialogue, dialogue is the essence of the learning process. Inherent in the notion of dialogue is that learning to be a therapist is eminently learnable but not teachable. Shotter (1993a, 1993b) questions, "Can you teach someone how to *be* [my emphasis]?" I do not believe that I can teach a person to be a therapist, but I can create a space and foster a generative conversational process in which he or she can learn to be (Anderson & Goolishian, 1990c).

A designated learning community (whether seminar, workshop, or therapy supervision), like any other human system, is one in which people relate to each other in and through language. The premise that dialogue is generative and that transformation occurs in and through it serves as the foundation for my thoughts and actions about collaborative learning communities. It informs the way I conceptualize my role and the kinds of relationships and processes that I want to foster and imbues my intentions and actions. One of my intentions is to create and facilitate a learning environment and process whose participants can access, elaborate on, and produce their own unique competencies. I want each person to generate his or her individual seeds of newness and to cultivate them in the personal and professional lives that take place outside the organized learning context. I want to invite and encourage participants to take responsibility for and to be the architects of their own learning. To these ends, I want to ensure that each participant has a voice, contributes, questions, explores, is uncertain, and experiments. I hold these premises and intentions whether I am contracted to teach a university class, supervise a clinical team, or conduct a workshop and whether the learning situation is more structured and formal or less structured and informal.

The Role of Difference

From a postmodern perspective there are many ways to know. People learn in different ways and this variety is reflected in postmodern approaches to teaching and supervising. Any group of students, even if homogeneously organized, has diverse learning styles, agendas, and kinds of expertise. All members contribute what is characteristic of them; no contribution is better or more important than another. All differences are valued, considered equally important, and viewed as the seeds of newness.

Working within differences is not easy, especially when teachers and students are pulled by complex issues, dilemmas, and challenges offered by the situation and circumstance. A postmodern teacher requires himself or herself, for instance, to pay attention to and adapt to the diverse needs, conflicts, and discomforts of students, as well as those imposed externally by licensing boards, credentialing commissions, and professional associations.

Central to creating opportunities for novel learning communities, processes, and relationships, as in therapy, is a teacher's philosophical stance. Dialogical learning begins when a teacher welcomes, shows an openness to, and encourages each person to present and explore his or her view. The aim is—through shared inquiry that entails mutual puzzling, curiosity, and exchange—to explore, clarify, and use differences, not to ignore, negotiate, or dissolve them. Similarly, the responsibility of a classroom teacher, a seminar leader, or a clinical team supervisor is to provide room for and encourage all voices in this process. As in therapy, this responsibility entails the ability to participate simultaneously in multiple, sometimes contradictory expressions of viewpoints. The opportunity for learning—for newness and change—resides in this capacity of all participants continually to tell and retell, write and rewrite their unique narratives.

The dialogic process, not its content, as in therapy, becomes the primary agenda. A teacher's agenda is not to export by rote what he or she knows (predetermined content) or provide a recipe for how to do therapy (cookbook skills), or tell a student what to do, or correct errors. Instead, a teacher's challenge is to give a student an opportunity to join in a shared inquiry into, and conclusion to, the issues at hand. As in therapy, this requires a trust in the other person's capacity for self-agency and an inherent trust in the process and in the relationship. Tolstoy suggests one aspect of this constant challenge:

> Every teacher must ... by regarding every imperfection in the pupil's comprehension, not as a defect of the pupil, but as a defect of his own instruction, endeavor to develop in himself the ability of discovering new methods. (Tolstoy quoted in Schön, 1983, p. 65)

One student shared her thoughts about differences within her clinical team.[2]

> We were from such a wide variety of backgrounds, and it was not always easy to deal with our differences. But we could talk about all of this. It felt as if the supervisors modeled how to deal with differences. They acted like the process they talked about. We didn't feel we had to defend a position.

Another student talked about the way her supervisors approached differences between team members and supervisors.

> It's the way [the supervisors'] questions are asked. The questions seem spontaneous, to come from curiosity, the here and now, and the experience. They don't seem like questions the supervisors

take from their question box, like part of an agenda, like techniques, or manipulative. They ask questions in a nonthreatening, nonjudgmental way. It's more like the questions prompt us to reflect on our position rather than challenge it. They enable us to see the unseen, to see in colors rather than just black and white. The question doesn't imply I'm wrong but allows me to provide my own conflict and ask new questions.

All was not rosy, though, for another student grappling with paradigmatic differences between her teammates: "I feel that at this point I'm in a state of 'cognitive dissonance' and the road to 'cognitive harmony' looks to be uphill."

Not only students have varying expectations and styles; postmodern teachers, like other teachers, have their own unique predispositions. An often inherent tension between a postmodern teacher and a student is a teacher's desire to be less hierarchical and authoritarian and a student's expectation of hierarchy and authority. One student in a course on supervision and consultation reflected on this difference: "Some students, I think, may not want an egalitarian relationship with someone they see as an authority . . . they expect more structure, more lecture." Another student in the same course said of students' propensity for the familiar and awkwardness with the unfamiliar, "I think the silence that sometimes follows your invitations for comments and feedback is because we, as students, are not used to such openness for freedom of the type of conversations that you allow."

I hold the not-knowing position in teaching as I do in therapy. A teacher does not preknow, for instance, what is important to a student or what a student's goals may be (standardized learning). Premature knowing can oppose and interfere with the development of a collaborative and participatory learning environment. This caveat does not suggest that a teacher discards what he or she knows or passively goes along with a student's agenda. A teacher is sensitive to and accepts what each student contributes to and wants of a situation: an active process involving connecting, interacting, negotiating, and adjusting.

I do not want my not-knowing position to be misperceived as knowing nothing or withholding knowledge. Rather, it is related to what I do with what I know or think I know. I, too, am entitled to have a preference or to express an opinion about theoretical content, clinical process, or learning format. I am open to sharing my expertise, wisdom, biases, and experiences. Preferences and opinions, however, do not come from a position of privileged knowing, of assumptions about what is best for a learner, or of assurance of how and what another person ought to learn. What I am preoccupied by or value is submitted with humility, tentativeness, and openness to alternatives. I expect myself to remain as open to change as I expect a learner to be whether that is through challenge or disregard.

I am often asked, "Isn't it nihilistic to say you're not an expert? Aren't you responsible for being, and expected to be, the expert?" Some question my naivete: "How can you deny you know more than the people you teach?" I do have expertise: That expertise is in creating a space for and facilitating a learning process. Through my expertise, I elicit others' expertise, which in turn intertwines, dissipates, and blends, creating increased competence for each of us in our own way. All participants—teacher and student, supervisor and supervisee—are learners and are subject to change as they share and explore each other's voice, as voices connect and intertwine, constructing something new and different for each.

For me, the learning process is not about providing information or withholding it, or telling or not telling a student what to do. It is about how I encourage a learner to participate with me, and others, in learning as an active two-way enterprise. Information, of course, is shared in any dialogical endeavor, but one person cannot assume how another person hears, reads, or incorporates that information. What another learns can be totally surprising.

"You Never Know How the Other Person Learns What You Think You're Teaching"

One day in a supervision and consultation course, as we talked about the dialogical and constructionist nature of teaching and learning a student gave a beautiful example of the unexpected.[3] Beginning with "My daughter taught me that you never know how the other person learns what you think you're teaching," she told a story about her five-year-old daughter, who was taking piano lessons and preparing for her first recital. Because the daughter had leg braces and was a little unsteady, the piano teacher asked the mother to coach her on how to curtsey after her performance. So after each practice session at home the mother coached the daughter. At each practice, she told her, "When you finish, stand up, face the audience, smile, and curtsey, and they will clap."

At the recital the daughter played perfectly. Then as taught, she stood up, faced the audience with a beaming smile, and curtseyed perfectly. The audience clapped. The daughter curtseyed again, and the audience clapped again. She curtseyed again, and had a standing ovation. The mother rushed to the stage to retrieve her daughter just as she was about to curtsey once more. At the reception afterward, a woman complimented the girl on her performance and on her curtsey, but, puzzled, asked, "Honey, why did you curtsey so many times?" "Because my mother taught me how to get you to clap," the daughter proudly responded.

I do not assume that I can interact effectively as an instructor—give knowledge or determine what newness will occur for the other, as the child's mother did with her coaching (Maturana, 1978). A teacher is not an overflowing pitcher from which a student sips information that fills him or her with duplicate knowledge. Teaching and supervising are not done to somebody; they are interactional processes that involve mutual interpreting and understanding. A drama teacher, Viola Spolin (1963), captures the essence of this point in her analysis of improvisation in the theater.

> We learn through experience and experiencing, and no one teaches anyone anything. . . . If the environment permits it, anyone can learn whatever he [she] chooses to learn; and if he [she] permits it, the environment will teach him [her] everything it has to teach. . . . Moreover, the teacher cannot truly judge good or bad for another, for there is no absolutely right or wrong way to solve a problem.

Learning, from this perspective, is not standardized. Rather, as it becomes collaborative and participatory, it also becomes individualized and self-directed. Students begin to experience, recognize, and value their expertise, competencies, and talents. They become more thoughtful and active in delineating what they want to learn, in determining how they best learn, and in requesting a teacher's and fellow students' participation in their learning. They develop a sense of confidence.

Students who have participated in collaborative learning systems and processes note a sense of freedom and competence, as expressed in this chorus of voices:

> I'm leaving my anxiety behind. I'm seeing life in different ways. It's funny, but I realize I'm more ignorant than ever. [To which the interviewer asked, "Does that make you anxious?"] Sometimes, but it depends on the situation. I don't have to have the answers, and that's okay.

There's a feeling of being connected . . . she's [the supervisor] present . . . she asks questions in such a way that I start thinking about another way of looking at it, or I think about other questions . . . my question becomes a nonquestion . . . and when I go back to my counseling center what I do flows naturally from this process.

It's not that they [the teachers] didn't have ideas or thoughts, but they never pushed their ideas on us. I never felt guilty if I didn't like their ideas. I was pleasantly surprised that they let us question their opinions. What surprised me most is that sometimes they liked mine better than theirs. But most important they gave us a lot of power.

I never felt what I was thinking was wrong. They were interested in whatever I said, and somehow seemed to stretch it, to knead it.

I've got it! If I can't possibly change my thoughts about something, how can I expect my client to?

I am often asked, "How do you deal with power differentials?" My response is simple. Of course, cultural discourses and organizational institutions bestow authority on us as teachers. I have, however, a great deal of personal freedom in how I choose to accept and exercise that authority in all arenas. I am often challenged, "This sounds fine for a small seminar where students expect this format, but what about large classrooms where students expect a lecture or in supervision where the supervisee says, 'Tell me what to do'?" I do not underestimate the perceived hierarchy in our cultural, political, and social discourses and practices. I maintain my philosophical stance, however, on all occasions, but I am always operating along a continuum—accommodating to what each occasion, circumstance, and relationship calls for. And, in my experience, the actualization of my philosophical stance continuously creates a learning environment that is less hierarchical, more egalitarian, and more mutually rewarding.

Certainty

In our pragmatic Western world, most therapy students begin their study with a need and a quest for certainty. Influenced by empirical thought and methods in which a teacher is a master knower of a subject and the way a learner masters it and knowledge is equated with certainty, we have come to expect therapists to be experts in human behavior and to expect teachers of therapists to be able to tell them how to do therapy. Students want skills and techniques and are eager for a foolproof recipe. Skills and techniques, like certainty, are often confused with competence.[4] When students expect certainty and predictability, there is always a period of discomfort with a process that entails uncertainty and randomness. Moving toward comfort occurs slowly as they experience a collaborative and connected way of constructing meaning, and thus learning, with others. As students experience and recognize their own voice and authority to generate knowledge, certainty becomes a nonissue and their need for it dissolves. Students often experience this shift before they have words to make sense of it. Roberto, a Central American psychiatrist, reflected on his struggle with uncertainty and the freedom he eventually experienced in it.

> I had doubts in the beginning that this [a collaborative language approach to therapy] would work. It seemed so abstract and I had so many questions and so much frustration with not knowing. What was I to do with my previous ideas? I had an internal battle to be open to others' ideas. Then one day I realized that I had changed and my therapeutic possibilities had changed. I no longer felt that I had or needed to have wisdom; I didn't need to direct the conversation. I didn't feel a need to change the client. Working with really difficult cases forced me to realize that I am not the key to change, but that the key is through the dialogue, through the process. I don't know what it is or how to explain it, but I know that when I become worried about a troublesome case, when I leave supervision it will be all right. I will feel relieved, not that I will have an answer to my question but that the question will no longer be a question and that if I am capable what to do will come.
>
> No, I haven't had to leave behind all of my previous learning. All of what I've learned can be catalogued in my memory and is there to use. It's all just possibilities. The difference is my intention.

Self-Reflection

Learning and professional competency are enhanced for teachers and students when they become the architects of their own learning (McKeachie & Kaplan, 1996; Neufeldt, Karno, & Nelson, 1996; Schön, 1983, 1987, 1991). Self and reflection are the critical elements of this experience.

In learning contexts, just as in therapy, being in silent conversation with oneself is as important as being in spoken conversation with others. This self-dialogue, or self-reflection, involves the ability to talk with oneself in a dialogical manner. The dialogue we have with ourselves, the thoughts we have, the questions we ask, involve continuous puzzling over and checking out our interpretive understandings against what has been said and not yet said, and against what has been done and not yet done. Self-dialogue involves thinking about and comparing our sense and understanding with those of the people with whom we are in conversation. Self-reflection, which may occur inside or outside the classroom, allows a student to think about, to expand, to reconsider, to understand differently, or to give up the familiar and dominant therapy narratives. The purpose is not self-discovery or, for instance, insight; rather, it is a process of development and transformation of knowledge.

To encourage learners to reflect on their learning and to examine and improve my teaching and consulting, I consistently invite feedback and evaluation from all participants. In a class or team practice format I ask students to provide me with their reflections on our work together by responding to printed questions that I hand out at each meeting. The prompt question may be related to that day's agenda or to future agendas. Questions that I have posed include "What suggestions do you have for making our team practice more relevant to your everyday practice?" "What would you like added to our agenda next week?" "What are you learning?" "What do you wish you were learning?" and "What are you learning about yourself and how you learn?" In addition, students are invited to share any other comments they wish. They consistently choose to share their personal learning experiences and the meaning of the learning to them. I take their reflections seriously, using them to learn more about each participant, address his or her needs, and refine my teaching. Students are both surprised and appreciative: "You take feedback that you request very seriously and so demonstrate it by moving in the desired direction of the students on the team."

Equally important, teacher or supervisor must be aware of whether he or she is involved in self-monologue or other-monologue rather than self-dialogue or other-dialogue. When self- or other-monologue dominates, a teacher and student, or a supervisor and supervisee, may find themselves engaged in parallel or dueling monologues. When this happens, thinking ruts develop and opportunities for new learning narrow. Both teacher and student become unproductive. Clues that might alert a teacher or supervisor to this kind of dialogical collapse include feeling frustrated by a student or supervisee, favoring one person's opinions and actions over another's, dwelling on one idea or event, assuming too quickly that he or she knows what the problem is and what the solution should be, not liking a student, or blaming a therapy's lack of progress on a supervisee's ineptitude or personality. Making private thoughts public and inviting student feedback are antidotes to monologue.

Professional and Personal Transformation

Professional learning involves a reflexivity between professional and personal growth. "How does the conversation, the learning, that occurs inside a learning room transfer to a student's everyday work and personal context?" is often asked. First, generativeness and transformation are inherent in a dialogical conversational process. A conversation does not have beginnings or endings and is not self-contained. Each conversation is part of previous and future conversations. Like an in-the-room therapy conversation, a learning conversation is not a self-contained entity separate to itself. Second, a conversation itself does not cause something to happen or cause someone to be different outside a learning room. It does not create a new idea, change an attitude, perform a new behavior, execute an intervention, or develop a homework assignment. What happens inside and outside a supervision room is part of a two-way mutual influence as learner and teacher and any others involved bring, take, and interact with each other and others. It is a trap, I believe, to think that we can predict and ensure the transferability and durability of a conversation by steering or reinforcing it, for instance, through designing tasks for a supervisee to perform outside a supervision arena. Although in my opinion, most learning takes place outside formal learning arenas, what happens inside that arena simply serves as a springboard, an invitation, a catalyst for continued learning. As one supervisee put it, "I find that my internal conversation does not end when I leave here. What begins here continues outside. It's like now I'm always in a learning mode with no end."

Students learning a collaborative approach report that the most significant outcome of their learning is that their professional knowledge begins to permeate their everyday personal lives:

> Each week when I would leave the externship, my world perception was always quite different than when I arrived. I felt less judgmental and more accepting of people's differences. As a result, I also felt more accepting of myself.

> I now give myself permission to be flexible. I have acted in ways that surprised me, done things that I had never imagined before. I also have a lot more faith and confidence in others' abilities and in my own.

> In learning to listen to other people I have learned to listen to myself.

I am continually amazed by how creative clients, students, and consultees, given the chance, can be; by the new learning they can create with each other, and the thirst they develop for more. A student in a supervision seminar reflected, "I left feeling I learned a lot, which is paradoxical, given the fact that I seemed to accumulate more questions in my notes than prescriptions!" Another student in the same seminar reflected at the end on her ongoing learning:

> It now seems like I'm in a constant state of reflection of inner dialogue about my work with others. . . . [I] search for ways I can be different. . . . I still struggle with hearing what someone else wants you to hear, no matter how clearly stated or how embedded it is in their way of communicating, and happily now I see the struggle as close to the core of the process I'm in. I like searching for a way of fitting with the person I'm talking with . . . some days it happens more easily than others. . . . Maybe there's a turn in the road up ahead, beyond which my search for the "fit" won't be so awkward.

CONSULTING WITH ORGANIZATIONAL SYSTEMS

An organizational system is yet another purposeful social system that has formed around a particular relevance.[5] Such systems share the complexities of systems that we meet in therapy and in teaching. I approach consulting with organizational systems such as private businesses, public mental health agencies, or educational institutions just as I do therapy and teaching. I maintain the same philosophical stance and possess the same process expertise. I have the same aim: I want to help an organization with what it wants help with, whether its request is in the business (strategic planning, customer satisfaction, or program evaluation), team (productivity, group dynamics, or enhancing of strengths), or the individual (supervisory skills and managerial stress) realm.

Organizations, like other social systems, are complex structures whose traditions and rituals can contribute to monological states and problems in search of solutions. One organization's dilemma might be increasing its capacity to be creative and innovative in dealing with ever-changing external business and work environments. Another organization's dilemma might be improving communications among its members. Another's might be developing strategic goal setting that produces results. Whatever the case, organizations search for ways to strengthen employees'—teams', staffs', managers', and executives'—ability to address problems and work together more effectively and productively. In this context, my approach aims to integrate people and business strategies in a collegial and egalitarian manner in building pathways to change and success.

Collaborative Inquiry

Like therapy and teaching, organizational consultation involves connecting, collaborating, and constructing in the way I have discussed, and dialogue remains the essence of the consultation process. Toward this, I want to provide a conversational space and facilitate a conversational process in which a client(s) can engage in dialogue with himself or herself and with others in defining the questions to be addressed and grappling with the answers to be created. Such collaborative inquiry moves from a top-down elite problem-solving process to a shared process that involves multiple problem solvers. It provides the tools, the building blocks, and the pathways to problem definition and dissolution and to development and achievement of the designated goals. When employees, managers, or some combination of both mutually inquire into a problem, codefining, redefining, and designing its solutions, links are built between people. Individual and group accountability and commitment to managing their own environment are enhanced, thereby facilitating ownership of the solution and its implementation.

Among the most critical considerations in organizational consultation that values and relies on collaborative inquiry are admitting all relevant voices to the conversation and acknowledging their expertise. This consideration presupposes that regardless of the reason for the consultation (the dilemma, the problem, the challenge, or the goal), the bottom line is that people are an organization's and a consultant's first and foremost resource and hope.

Typically, a person in authority (for instance, a company's president, a division manager, or a board of directors) who has defined something as creating a problem or requiring attention extends the invitation for consultation. Such a client may request an individual consultation around issues such as his or her management style, personnel decisions, or conflict management.[6] Or he or she may want a consultation that will include other members of the organization in an examination of issues such as work group conflict, managerial skills, or strategic planning. The actual people whom a consultant will work with in an organization system may or may not be willing participants and may or may not accept the problem definition of the person seeking the consultation. Hence, to create a space for and facilitate dialogue, it becomes important to acknowledge and access these relevant voices as early as possible. Their inclusion—and the manner in which they are included—signals their importance in a consultation and inevitably leads to active and enthusiastic engagement in its process—dialogical conversation.

Windows of access to the relevant voices, including the timing, appear in each consultation.[7]

Perhaps a brief description of a consultation with a community organization will help illustrate this sensitiveness of accessing and including these multiple voices. In this consultation, as in any, decisions about format, structure, phases, and participants evolved from, and were mutually determined in, the initial and subsequent conversations (Anderson & Burney, in press). Here we designed a beginning agenda and format to serve as a skeletal working frame for a process, but, as in any consultation, we considered it tentative and were poised to change it if needed.

"Our Growth Presents Both Opportunities and Problems"

Collaborative Inquiry Begins with the President's Invitation

A colleague[8] and I were asked by the president of the board of directors of a chamber of commerce to consult with the volunteer board of directors and the paid office personnel. In her call she expressed the chamber's dilemma: "Our growth presents both opportunities and problems." Her consultation agenda included a nontangible product: in her words, to "create energy among the board members," to develop a "working board" attitude, and to facilitate "communication and cooperation" between the board and the staff. She also wanted a tangible product—a "strategic plan" for the next year. We arranged to meet to learn more about her perceived dilemma, what she wanted to accomplish, the circumstances of the request for consultation, and her story of the chamber's organization, its history, and its relationship to the community. To help ground the consultation process, I will offer a brief synopsis of what we learned in our meeting.

The chamber was highly visible and perceived as an aggressive advocate for a rapidly growing tourist and residential community. The board included forty influential business representatives recruited from the community and six ex officio public servants (for instance, the city mayor, the city administrator, the school superintendent). Although all board members were high-profile community leaders, the chamber's office personnel, a thirteen-member staff including an executive director, a convention director, an economic development director, and ten administrative staff, were the people the community's businesses dealt with on a daily basis. About 50 percent of the board members were active in all chamber endeavors, about 40 percent only attended chamber meetings, and the other 10 percent were inactive.

The chamber office had been in a period of upheaval and transition during the last year. Most personnel were new, including the executive director, who was hired six months earlier to replace the previous director, fired a year before under what the president described as "messy circumstances." The economic development director had been on board for three months in his newly created position. Because this position and its separate budget were funded by the city, the development director reported directly to the mayor. She said—and we later learned that the new executive director concurred—that the staff had "performed extraordinarily . . . holding down the fort" during this transition. We learned a great deal more about the organization that I will not elaborate on since my intention is to focus on a consultation process, not its content.

The Next Conversation

An idea developed in our meeting with the president that we would design a one-and-a-half-day out-of-town retreat for the board and staff. Having asked the president whom we should consult about planning the retreat and its objectives, we next met with her, the vice chair, the executive director, and the economic development director. In this meeting we clarified the retreat's objectives and outlined the content areas to be addressed, and the president reiterated her desire to have a retreat in which people could be inspired and connect with each other. Another idea that developed in this meeting was that my colleague and I would spend a day before the retreat with the chamber office personnel as a step toward creating a bridge between the two groups at the retreat. The executive director's agenda for the staff day was to nurture the relationships among staff and to promote in each participant a feeling of being valued in his or her role in relation to the chamber's mission. Following this meeting, my colleague and I sent a letter of introduction to the staff (including the executive director, convention director, and financial development director). We enclosed four "food for thought" questions that had evolved from the two previous conversations that we wanted them to address to help us learn a little about them, their roles, and their views of the chamber before the staff day. We told them that responding to the questionnaire and identifying themselves on it were optional and confidential. All thirteen members responded to our questions and identified themselves.

Our four questions were as follows: What do you think are the most important things that your team members at the chamber office need to know about you? What are the most important challenges or dilemmas that you face in *your* position at the chamber? What do you think are the most important challenges or dilemmas that confront the chamber? and What do you think are the obstacles or challenges, if any, that impede the chamber's ability to address these successfully? As in therapy, we do not place emphasis on problem over solution, or vice versa. We begin with where a client is and with what is important to him or her. A question process serves as one way to invite the other voices and their expertise into the conversation, to continue to set the tone for collaboration, and to begin crisscrossing dialogues.

We organized the staff day as we do any single-phase or multiphase consultation. Each step of a consultation informs the next, including what will be talked about and who will be involved in the talking. We designed an agenda that provided a preliminary structured guideline that we thought would continue to ensure a collaborative tone, to enhance participation (see Anderson & Burney, in press, for an expanded discussion of a similar consultation). The design included introductions, partner interviews, small group inquiries, large group exchanges, consultant reflections, and experiential activities.

Each consultation conversation begins with consultant introductions, summarizing what they know, at that time, about the members, the organization, and the assumed reasons for the consultation. In this vein, consultants want to make their understanding—what they know and think—public. In each encounter, they express a genuine appreciation for the opportunity to work with the organization and its members and their wish that their work together be productive and helpful.[9] Consultants are always explicit about their nonexpert concept: As consultants they are not experts who preknow the dilemmas or the solutions to the dilemmas but are present as collaborative partners in a process of mutual discovery—"a process we do with you rather than to you" (Anderson, 1990, 1993; Anderson & Burney, in press; Anderson & Goolishian, 1992). This public nature and theme continue as the person who requested the consultation, in this case, the executive director's request for a staff day, is given an opportunity to share his or her thoughts about and expectations for the consultation (or that phase of it) with all present. In this consultation, the president joined the staff for the introduction but, as planned, did not stay.

Group Games

Introductions are often followed by an experiential activity, typically a group game—a physical metaphor—in which all members, including the consultants, participate on an equal basis, further facilitating the establishment of a collaborative tone. The game in this consultation served as a process vehicle for inviting people to connect with us and with each other, and as a content vehicle for identifying characteristics of seamless and effective working teams.

Partner Interviews

The next step, and one that is often included in a consultation at some point, entailed members forming teams of two and interviewing each other. The suggested content of the interviews—usually in the form of questions—is informed by the previous conversations. Each member then introduces his or her partner to the large group.[10] Each introducee is encouraged to listen to and reflect on the manner in which his or her partner makes the introduction and interprets and expresses answers to the questions. During the introductions, a consultant records responses, using members' words and phrases, on a large pad. The partner interviews allow each participant an opportunity to talk and contribute from the beginning, easing those who might otherwise not speak into conversation, and lessening the chance that those who usually do all of the talking will dominate the discussion. The interviews continue to reinforce the public nature of the consultation as people begin to talk out loud and listen to each other.

Small Group Inquiry

An important part of consultation from a collaborative perspective is small group inquiry. Members are divided into groups and each group is asked to discuss selected issues and/or questions. The membership of each group is determined by the circumstances of the consultation. In the chamber consultation, we simply randomly placed people. Again, the content (for instance, the issues and questions) evolves from and is informed by all of the conversations up to that point. The content is always thought of and presented as a springboard from which to generate and develop ideas about a dilemma and possibilities for addressing it. In this instance, one of the small group inquiries focused on the questions "What are the most important things for the board to know about the staff and what you do?" and "How can the board be more helpful to you in your daily work?" Depending on the particular consultation and its circumstances, the person requesting the consultation may be asked to rotate from group to group as a silent observer.[11] This gives participants an opportunity to talk without that person's involvement, and allows the person to listen to the discussions firsthand since it is difficult to capture and recreate the richness and nuances of a conversation. Most important, the listener can choose, not someone else, what he or she is interested in, puzzled by, or wants to ignore. We gave each group a large writing pad on which to record their ideas and any new questions. A consultation may include one or many small group inquiries.

Large Group Reflections

After each small group, members reconvene to the large group, reporting their small group's accomplishments and exchanging general reflections. The reporting process can take many forms. A consultant may ask the group to have one member summarize or may ask groups to determine the manner in which they would like to share with the larger group. The reflection process that follows—offerings, questions, and curiosities—is usually spontaneous and unstructured. As in all phases of a consultation, a consultant records the words and phrases for all to see. What emerged in the large group reflections was a creative staff plan for introducing themselves to the board and for participating in the retreat, which they thought would enhance two-way communication between them and the board.

Throughout a consultation, as in a therapy or learning event, collaboration is reinforced by a consultant's stance—the manner in which a consultant positions himself or herself, including introducing ideas, asking questions, making comments, and trying to understand what has been said and not said. Whether a consultant is more or less active during any phase of a consultation is determined by the demands of the occasion.

Closing Reflections

The last phase of a consultation typically includes an opportunity for both client and consultant to reflect on the consultation—reviewing and evaluating it and highlighting the next steps. The reflections may take many forms; they may be offered individually or a consultant and a client may have a reflecting conversation in front of the other participants. In this instance, the staff day was one phase of the consultation. The next phase was the board–staff retreat, in which we provided a space and process for collaboratively analyzing and developing strategies for addressing the four concerns that the president initially offered and with which the other three members of the "next conversation" concurred and expanded on.

Briefly, the retreat included the following components: introductions, experiential exercise, four small group/large group discussion sequences around the four content areas, a group dinner, and a group lunch. We also built in an opportunity to periodically touch base and reflect with the four organizers.

A consultation thus consists of several back-and-forth, criss-crossing conversations. Through this process problems are defined and redefined; options are created and recreated. Problems either have dissolved or are in the process of dissolving. Participants leave with meaningful and durable results that they, not the consultants, have produced.

Recording the consultees' ideas and suggestions, their words and phrases, is an important part of the process as it makes all information continually available to everyone. After the consultation, all recordings are typed out and sent to the person requesting the consultation. That person is also interviewed for follow-up on his or her reflections on what happened and feedback for the consultant. Consultation clients report experiencing the process in both a conversational and an informal style while feeling that they have worked hard and produced useful results. Once introduced to a new way of communicating with and experiencing each other and approaching the task during a consultation, members of organizations discover that the consultation conversations become opportunities for a different way of working together and addressing problems in their everyday organizational life. As in therapy and learning contexts, conversations inside the consultation room continue, invite, and become part of conversations outside it. Likewise, the potential for self-agency and possibilities endures.

Reflecting Back and Forward

We shall not ease from exploration
And the end of all our exploring
Will be to arrive where we started
And know the place for the first time.

—T. S. ELIOT

People often ask me how long it takes me to write a play,
and I tell them "all my life." I know that's not the answer
they're after—what they really want is some sense of the time
between the first glimmer of the play in my mind, and the
writing down, and perhaps the duration of the writing down—
but "all my life" is the truest answer I can give.

—EDWARD ALBEE

When I began this book I hoped to share, explore, and expand my version of an emerging dynamic postmodern therapy, including what I believe distinguishes it from others. I have offered one window of understanding into the language and conversation environment that is created between client and therapist: one way of understanding how strangers in a contrived context—therapy—

can form a transient relationship that approximates and enhances self-agency within everyday life.

Psychotherapy involves consulting with people around their life dilemmas. Such dilemmas range from the complexities of everyday ordinary living—child-related, adult relationship-related, family-related, school-related, work-related—to the more relentless complexities of the exceptional—psychotic, substance abuse, and eating disorder behaviors. How are these complexities seen within a non-pathological context? Psychotherapy itself is a social construction of modernism. The mental health professions are a social construction. Are these still helpful, viable constructions? Are they outdated? Should any or all of them be covered by health insurance? Given the rapid and unpredictable social, technological, and scientific changes—postmodernism offers a breakthrough in terms of a new narrative that challenges the future of psychotherapy as we know it, including the way we think about these questions. Postmodernism places therapists who embrace it swimming against the tide in unfamiliar and uncharted waters.

Postmodern thinking has the same risks as any other product of discourse, history, or culture. The very act of advancing a postmodern therapy entails the risk of stumbling back into empiricism: encouraging another taken-for-granted therapy metaphor, promoting certain thoughts and actions and prohibiting others. As Gergen (1991b) warns,

> To the extent that any given paradigm gains adherents to its discursive procedures and related practices, it may be said to generate enclaves of power. That is, the reigning system of intelligibility promotes certain patterns of organized social action and at the same time forbids or discourages a range of competitors. In effect, each paradigm operates simultaneously as a productive and repressive force. (p. 212)

I suspect that some readers may conclude that, notwithstanding my claim to a postmodern worldview, I believe that I have found the reality, the truth, about therapy. My belief, for instance, that dialogical conversation is generative and its natural consequence is change can be heard as the reality, the truth. I do not believe and do not mean to imply that this is the truth; it is simply a current description and explanation of my experience. I use the language tools available to me at this moment to describe and explain my experience. My experiences and my ideas about them will change in the future, as they have in the past.

I hope the reader will not conclude that I have presented a new model. Instead, I suggest a way to think about human beings, their life dilemmas, and a professional's relationship in their lives. My strong focus on dialogue and language should not be inferred to presuppose a cognitive approach that only fits people with mature verbal skills. Each person, no matter how limited a professional may perceive his or her verbal skills or intelligence potential to be, has thoughts, feelings, and opinions that are accessible and expressible in dialogical conversation. In the therapy relationship, a therapist has the responsibility to help each person to find means to express his or her own narrative versions.

I hesitate now, as I did when I began, to use the word *therapy* as if it is objectively definable, since each person involved in it has his or her own definition. I reject the accepted culturally ascertained meanings of therapy that decry remedial treatment designed or serving to bring about social compliance. My apprehension centers on the convention of dysfunction aptly expressed, I think, in Nancy Milford's (1970) *Zelda: A Biography*: Was she mad or did F. Scott Fitzgerald usurp her narrative? Therapy can usurp first-person narratives.

I am brought back full-circle to my earlier amazement about the multiplicity of ways in which others have heard the Swedish mother's passionate narrative about her family's desperate struggle with anorexia. I have experienced similar diversity as others watched videotaped examples of my work: "I don't see anything postmodern," "That doesn't look different from what I already do," "Refreshingly innovative," and "Imperceptible." People will always take diverse experiences and meanings from the same events. A therapist's job is to ensure that there is room for each voice to express and to facilitate conversation among the voices.

Conversations are reflective. Writing this book has involved numerous reflective conversations that I have had with myself and with others. I have heard the authors Edward Albee and Horton Foote say, in effect, that writing begins with thinking long before the words are put on a page. Likewise, thinking continues after writing. Thinking is writing; writing is thinking. As a postmodern therapist, classroom teacher, seminar leader, supervisor, or business consultant I must remain open to the twists and turns, to the uncertainty, unknown futures, and newness to which they lead. As I face new encounters and mysteries in my everyday life, I am forced to make sense of them as they challenge my own dearly held familiar views and biases. I always wonder what I am becoming that I have not yet been.

I hope that I have provoked your internal conversations and reflections, and have stimulated you to analyze and question your own clinical theory and practice. I will continue to examine mine. You, the reader, have been and will be part of the conversations I participate in as each new experience summons me to describe, explain, and understand it, and as I reflect on all the things that I said and did not say. I am grateful for these conversations and anticipate with pleasure the places I will know for the first time.

NOTES

PREFACE
1. I make no distinctions among theory, research, clinical practice, teaching, and organization consultation. I approach all from the same philosophical base. All are collaborative efforts.

CHAPTER 1
1. I would add that it is also tensions between the ways we experience and the available means through which we can account for our experiences.

2. I think this is a difference in the emergence of new ideas within family therapy and psychology over the past forty years. In family therapy the innovators are theoretical practitioners, whereas in psychology they are mainly theoreticians.

3. Gregory Bateson, Donald Jackson, Jay Haley, and John Weakland along with their later colleagues are often referred to as the Mental Research Institute (MRI) associates, although the research began before MRI was formed in 1958 (Bateson, Jackson, Haley, & Weakland, 1956, 1963).

4. The initial and later contributions of the MRI associates cannot be overemphasized. Their exciting, provocative ideas, often in the vanguard, have been adopted and expanded by virtually everyone in the field. Although the group included several others, it is usually associated with the early work of Bateson, Jackson, Haley, and Weakland. For those who are unfamiliar with their earlier writings, and early clinical and theoretical developments, or who may not have experienced their enthusiasm, I suggest Jackson (1968a, 1968b) and Watzlawick (1977).

5. Interestingly enough, Bateson's communication theory was related to meaning and the way by which the transmitted information was thought to occur.

6. In transgenerational theory, for example, the paradigm is described in terms of blurred generational boundaries; symptoms are related to the triangulation of a third person by members of a dyad who are unable to handle relationship tensions and change. The symptomatic behavior in the third or triangulated person is sufficient to prevent change and thus maintain stability (homeostasis) in the dyad. Structural family theory, for example, focuses on the relationship of dysfunctional family structure to symptom function; theorists conceptualize symptomatic behavior as representing collusions across generations. The appearance of the symptom (pathology) is required by the family to maintain current family structure in the face of pressure to change.

In still another example, the Multiple Impact Therapy group conceptualized symptom development in terms of collusions across generational boundaries that left individuals open to dysfunction during later stress. The symptom was characterized by the problem requirements of the developmental period in which the collusion took place. Further, strategic therapists assumed communication becomes the social organization and viewed symptom development as a way a family member indulges in the self-sacrifice required to maintain family stability without undergoing organizational change. The work of Carl Whitaker, Lyman Wynne, and Virginia Satir, for instance, can also be analyzed from this same perspective.

Even psychoanalytic theory can be seen as based on a cyberneticlike theory. The interpretation of symptoms by classical individual psychoanalysis is quite explainable in homeostatic terms, requiring only a shift from psychic to interpersonal structure. For instance, a symptom occurs at a time when a weakened ego is not able to maintain a balance between the id and superego; thus it is developed in order to maintain the balance.

7. The focus here is on the cybernetic metaphor. A challenge to, or even acknowledgment of, Parsonian-like social systems theory is almost nonexistent (Anderson & Goolishian, 1988b; Goldner, 1988). Interesting, however, the early MRI theory replaced the family role concept with family rules because role is *individual* in origin and orientation and suggests a reliance on a priori theoretical and cultural definitions that exist independently of behavioral data, and therefore, no allowance is made for the relationship (Jackson, 1965).

8. *Morphogenesis:* From the Greek roots *morphe*, meaning "form," and *genesis*, meaning "coming into being"; a theory of how things change.

9. In this vein, Bateson suggested that therapists were dealing with family beliefs, not pathology.

10. The MRI group's interest in and contributions to the use of language in therapy also significantly influenced the field.

11. Lynn Hoffman (1985) called therapies informed by second-order cybernetics "second-order" family therapy.

12. Although this move away from knowing as a "search for an iconic representation of ontological reality" (von Glasersfeld, 1984) predates

these references, it was these challenges that caught the attention of psychotherapists.

13. The characterization *radical* is used to emphasize constructivism's breaking away from conventional theories and philosophies of knowledge (von Glasersfeld, 1984, p. 20). Von Glasersfeld's (1984) essay provides an excellent analysis.

14. *See* Hoffman's *Foundations of Family Therapy: A Conceptual Framework for Systems Change* (1981), in my opinion the best description and explanation of the history of family therapy through the 1970s.

15. The physicist Ilya Prigogene called these far-from-equilibrium systems "dissipative structures." To maintain stability, they must constantly change. According to Prigogene, reality, and therefore change, is multidimensional and does not result in or arise from a pyramidlike foundation. Rather, it evolves in a nonhierarchical, weblike manner, with the web of descriptions becoming more and more complex (see Briggs & Peat, 1984, pp. 167–178).

16. The Galveston group's interest in language was first inspired by Watzlawick, Beaven, and Jackson's (1967) *Pragmatics of Human Communication.* We later were influenced by Maturana's (1975) "The Organization of the Living" and "Biology of Language: Epistemology of Reality" (1978), and, from the early 1980s, by language as conceptualized in hermeneutic and social constructionist theories.

17. I recognize that there is a debate about whether family therapy is an ideology or a process centered on the number of persons in a room, and likewise whether it is a separate and distinct discipline or a subspecialty, for example, of psychology. I believe that these debates obscure the essence of family therapy as a paradigmatic shift. *See* Shields, Wynne, McDaniel, and Gawinski (1994); Anderson (1994); and Hardy (1994).

18. *See* Lynn Hoffman's *Foundations of Family Therapy: A Conceptual Framework for Systems Change* (1981).

CHAPTER 2

1. For the purposes of this chapter I have synthesized the characteristics of modernist or Enlightenment narrative.

2. I embrace Richard Palmer's (1985) distinction between theory and philosophy. Palmer suggests that theory involves contemplation of theoretical knowledge, usually distinguished from practical knowledge; the theorist remains distanced, detached, objective. Philosophy refers to positions one holds, for example, values and standpoints. I will expand on my preference for this distinction when I talk about therapy. John Shotter (1993a, 1993b) also makes this distinction.

3. A complete review of postmodernism (often associated with poststructuralism) is beyond the scope of this book (see Andreas Huyssen in Nicholson, 1990).

4. Although the two positions are often blended, they arise from dif-

ferent traditions. Poststructuralism is usually associated with the French literary critic Jacques Derrida and the social historian Michel Foucault and in general refers to the notion that discourse is driven by underlying structures that are framed in language, not by the internal structure of the objects (Gergen, 1995, p. 39).

5. Richard Palmer (1984) prefers *philosophy of interpretation* to *theory of interpretation* (p. 149).

6. *Lived experience* is a term used by the nineteenth-century hermeneutic philosopher Wilhelm Dilthey to refer to his notion that "understanding itself is a manifestation of life; acts of understanding are lived by us, they constitute 'lived experiences'" (Dilthey, 1984, pp. 25–26).

7. Gergen (1994) also critiques Gadamer's notions of intersubjectivity and shared cultural heritage (pp. 260–263).

8. See Gergen (1994, pp. 66–69) for an expanded comparison and contrast.

PART II

1. This is a clinical narrative of a *Master's Series* interview that I did at the American Association for Marriage and Family Therapy, Annual Conference, October 1992.

2. One of the handicaps of the written word is that a reader can only interact with the author he or she has created. Another is that it is linear. Here I hope the reader can interact with the imagined "me" and with themselves in a reflective fashion.

CHAPTER 3

1. Because of my close collaboration with Harry Goolishian, other colleagues, and students, I shift between singular and plural pronouns.

2. My colleagues and I were greatly influenced by the creative thinkers at the Mental Research Institute and their emphasis on "speaking the client's language" rather than the more traditional therapy methods that focus on "teaching the client the therapist's language" (see Watzlawick et al., 1974).

CHAPTER 4

1. Lynn Hoffman (1990, 1993) thought along the same lines suggesting, "The system doesn't create the problem, the problem creates the system" (1990, pp. 5–6; 1993, p. 40).

CHAPTER 5

1. I hesitate to use the word *change* because of its usual linear and individualistic meaning in psychotherapy discourse: someone changes someone else. I prefer the word *transformative*, which allows more of a sense of co-ever-in-motion, although I tend to use both out of habit.

2. This is an idea developed in my collaboration with my colleague Arlene Katz.

3. I previously have used the notion of coauthor, but it no longer seems to fit. The new narratives are influenced as well by relationships and events outside the therapy room; the therapist is simply one of multiple authors.

4. I thank my colleague Kathy Weingarten for suggesting this term.

5. I tend not to use the word *negotiate* and prefer *encounter*, as in "encountering different realities." For me, negotiating implies an adversarial position: the resolution of conflicting differences, as in bargaining, dickering, arbitrating, interceding, and mediating.

6. Hermans's notion is similar to the notions about Dostoyevsky's characters discussed in chapter 10.

7. Shotter (1990), responding to and expressing strong concern about psychologists' role in what he termed "dubious military projects," charges psychology with using its mechanism as a device to disclaim responsibility, and to avoid accountability for what were, in his mind, obviously politically obnoxious proposals (p. 207).

8. My experiences often determine my choice of words. For instance, I often find in therapy and problem discourses that *determine* has a negative connotation, implying willfulness (as, in fact, does *intentional*). In this book, however, I use *intentional* in the sense that we are all intentional beings. Specifically, I use it here to signify "determined to act in a certain way" as in *Webster's new collegiate dictionary* (1972).

CHAPTER 6

1. Students often use the word *power* to describe their personal and professional experiences of self-transformation when they are immersed in trying to learn the collaborative approach.

2. McCarthy and Byrne (1988) quote Hederman and Kearney: "It was a place where even the most ordinary can be seen in an unusual light. There must be a neutral ground where things can detach themselves from all partisan and prejudiced connection and show themselves for what they really are. . . . This province, this place, this centre is not a political or geographical position, it is more like a dis-position."

3. I like Swedish philosophy student Ullanliina Lehtinen's reiteration of Wittgenstein's caution about subjectivity, which she calls the *subjectivistic fallacy*: the mistake of fusing or confusing *subjectivity* (individual experience) with *subjectivism* (epistemological relativism) (1993, p. 44). She speaks to the idea that inner experience, although it seems to be highly individualized to the person who "possesses" it, is a social construct that should be open to question and doubt. Gergen (1994) talks about the problems of the notion of *intersubjectivity*: one person can enter another person's subjectivity. He challenges the tradition of beginning our analysis of human understanding and social meaning at the indi-

vidual level and suggests instead that we begin at the level of *human rela-tionship* (pp. 258–263).

4. For discussions of the circle of meaning or the hermeneutic circle, see Wachterhauser (1986b, p. 23) and Warneke (1987, pp. 83–87).

5. I agree with Gergen's (1988a) reservations about the notion of "the person as a text": "[T]hat the metaphor of the text places us in a position from which neither reading, intimacy, nor self-knowledge is possible" (p. 43). Gergen further suggests, and again I agree, that neither is cen-tering attention on the reader the answer. Both place the individual in isolation. He continues,

> No valuable account can be given as to how valid inference from external manifestation to the inner region of intent or motive can occur; and there is little means of demonstrating how tests can resist absorption into the reader's forestructure of understanding. Thus, the metaphor of person as text favors the conclusion that valid com-munication, correct interpretation, and genuine intimacy are all beyond human reach. (p. 49)

His alternative, a relational account, "views the interpretative process not as the act of the single individual attempting to locate the inner region of the other, but as a process of mutual collaboration" (p. 49).

6. Vygotsky was an early critic of traditional views of development and psychology. He and his colleagues were interested in a cultural–historical approach to human development, particularly symbolic means of interaction: the acquisition and use of language.

7. For Gergen (1994), to supplement is to respond communicatively to and to coordinate oneself around the other's utterance (p. 265). Words, he suggests, do not have meaning in and of themselves: "They only appear to generate meaning by virtue of their place within the realm of human interaction." And it is this realm of human interaction that Gergen refers to as supplementation, which he believes acts

> both to create and to constrain meaning. . . . It is only by virtue of supplementary signifiers that signified actions gain their capacity to mean, and it is only within the relationship of action-and-supplement that meaning is to be located at all. (p. 265)

Supplementation is an inherently reciprocal and fluid process in that "supplements operate to determine the meaning of actions, while actions create and constrain the possibility of supplementation" (p. 266); and in that each action and each supplementation, as is their relationship to each other, is continually subject to change. The action influences the supple-ment, which in turn influences the action, which in turn, and so on—lead-ing to an infinite number of meanings, with the "possibility for [under-standings and] misunderstandings permanently and pervasively at hand" (p. 270). *See also* chapter 2, p. 42.

8. Stein Braten is a Norwegian sociologist and systems theorist who is questioning the appropriateness of some of the developments and applications of systems theories' ideas about autonomy to the social and psychological sciences (see Braten, 1987).

9. Shotter (1993a) also talks about theories as monologic, suggesting that "following the way of theory, the project of individual researchers becomes that of formulating, monologically, a single framework to function as a 'structured container' for all such events, thus to create a stable, coherent and intelligible order amongst them" (p. 57).

10. I have elsewhere talked about monologue as one way of understanding therapeutic impasses (Anderson, 1986). I do not imply, however, that monologue is wrong; rather, I would suggest that in these moments we are closed to the other and thus there is no "crossing of perspectives" (Braten, 1984).

11. I have described this consultation elsewhere: *See* Anderson (1991b, 1993).

12. When I talk about this kind of dialogue and relationship—this kind of listening—therapists and students often liken it to a psychodynamic-based Rogerian approach. There is a basic difference. The intent of a therapist's comments or questions is not to reflect back but represents attempts to actively be in a shared inquiry that entails checking out if he or she has understood or misunderstood, helping a client expand the said and formulate the unsaid.

CHAPTER 7

1. This is an idea that my colleague Arlene Katz has discussed.

2. All client names and other identifying characteristics have been changed.

3. Shotter (1993a, p. 130n1) talked about what this not-knowing position requires of the therapist. He suggested that a therapist's task is

to "feel" in the course of it, the unique other who confronts him or her, what it is like to be him or her. Thus, as well as rethinking the nature of the communication, a therapist must also re-think the nature of his or her knowledge (of the other) as beginning with a whole sequence of vague, fragmentary feelings that, over time, they must integrate into a "felt" totality, a whole which functions as a "basis" in terms of which a linguistic formulation of its nature can be judged for its adequacy. . . . And perhaps that will be the most difficult for them [therapists], trained as they have been to a high degree as academics, to think and to act autonomously, with a "plan" or "picture" in mind, they must grasp what it is like just to "feel one's way forward", to just creatively respond to their circumstances—as we do in fact do it all the time, in sensing, say the "shape" of a problem in something that someone has just said, and in formulating a question which we hope will clarify things.

4. This client has been mentioned in previous papers; (*see* Anderson, 1995; Anderson & Goolishian, 1992). I use the story here because it so dramatically illustrates the therapist position that I am talking about.

5. By *subjectivity* I mean a client's inner thoughts, the unsaid and the not-yet-said. I do not think of subjectivity as an inner mental state or as something singularly possessed or bounded by a mind or as the real. I think that what goes on in a person's head, so to speak, is relational.

6. I sometimes question, however, whether possibilities can be infinite since any one of us or any combination of us has only a finite number of experiences to draw from. Anyway, the possibilities are measureless.

7. I have talked about Anna elsewhere (*see* Anderson, 1995).

8. A reader might easily think that a note on a folded napkin with a postage stamp mailed from northern Norway to Texas is a bit odd. I did not. I was simply amazed that it arrived without a tear.

9. I want to thank my colleague Karen Parker for introducing me to Anne Rice.

10. Bill's therapist was Harry Goolishian. I have used this example elsewhere and have chosen to include it here because it so poignantly illustrates what I am trying to convey.

11. This quote is attributed to Gregory Bateson but the source is not identified.

12. I do not think of "go slow" in the classic sense of Watzlawick, Weakland, and Fisch (1974) in which they talk about it as "the paradoxical intervention of choice" (p. 135).

13. I have talked about Hans elsewhere (*see* Anderson, 1995). The therapist was Klaus Deissler of the Verband i Internationaler Institute fur Systemische Therapie, Marburg, Germany.

14. I thank my colleague Sylvia London and her client for sharing this transcript (also quoted in chapter 6).

15. Elsewhere I have referred to these as C therapy (Anderson, 1992).

CHAPTER 10

1. I use *narrative* and *story* interchangeably.

2. Bruner (1990) suggests that just as narrative permits, it also constrains: "There is breakdown that results from sheer impoverishment of narrative resources—in the permanent underclass of the urban ghetto, in the second and third generation of the Palestinian refugee compound, in the hunger-occupied villages of semi-permanently drought-stricken villages in sub-Saharan Africa. It is not that there is a total loss in putting story form to experience, but that the 'worst scenario' story comes so to dominate daily life that variation seems no longer to be possible" (pp. 96–97).

3. Bruner (1986) argues that two modes of thought—ways in which we construct and organize experiences—are necessary: the paradigmatic (referring to inductive, objective, and givens) and narrative modes (referring to subjectivity, reflexivity, and fluidity) (pp. 11–43).

4. This emergence of the self as storyteller in the social sciences and in psychotherapy deserves more attention than space permits. The reader is referred to Mitchell (1981) and to Sarbin (1986, 1990).

5. Freud, however, seemed to reject this narrative position later in the paper, when he compared this process to psychotic delusion and warned against it.

6. Bruner's (1986) definition of self sounds very close to a social constructionist view of self; however, he refers to himself as a constructivist (p. 130).

7. Gergen, Harré, and Shotter are also at the forefront of those questioning the modernist traditions of psychology in general and its illusion as a science in particular.

8. Gergen (1994) later amends this to highlight the notion of relationships: "Narratives of the self are not fundamentally possessions of the individual but possessions of relationships—products of social interchange" (pp. 187–188).

9. Others, such as psychologists Jonathan Potter and T. R. Sarbin, are part of a branch of this path known as *narrative psychology* and also are interested in the narrative of psychology itself.

10. The psychiatrist Roderick Anscombe (1989) takes an interesting look at what he refers to as the "myth of the true self." He suggests that the notion of the true self (in this discussion, the core self) serves an important function in psychotherapy. As a figment of the patient and therapist's imaginations, it serves as a starting point for curiosity and a direction or potential to which a patient aspires.

11. Kitzinger (1987) suggests that such a definition of lesbianism in fact serves as a form of social control (p. 39).

12. Freeman (1993) gives a beautiful example of this concept of being imprisoned by the "expected course of things" in his discussion of the Australian author–historian Jill Kerr Conway's struggle with her life relationships and identities (pp. 185–214).

13. Rita is the name I give to a woman in the family with widespread multigenerational sexual abuse that my colleague Arlene Katz and I consulted with.

14. Interestingly, perhaps this is somewhat similar to Laing's (1969) notion of the divided self in his attempt to understand the onset of schizophrenia: the discord betwen the self a person thinks he or she is (the internal concept) and the one that the family acts "as if" he or she is (the external experience). The experience is incongruent with and invalidates the concept.

CHAPTER 11

1. The Public Conversations Project of the Family Institute of Cambridge merits mention. This project aims to engage political adversaries in dialogue around controversial public issues such as abortion.

2. Some of the student voices in this chapter also appear in Anderson and Swim, (1993, 1995).

3. I thank Selia Servin Lopez for this vignette.

4. I do not mean to suggest that I do not value competence; rather I question what is usually deemed competent.

5. For an expanded discussion of consultation, see Anderson and Goolishian (1986); Anderson and Burney (in press).

6. I do not assume when a person requests an individual consultation that it will continue that way; it may or may not. As in therapy, who is involved in any one conversation at any time is determined on a conversation-by-conversation basis.

7. The number of participants in a consultation varies. It may be with a 6-member management team or with a department with 50 or more members. What is important is that each voice is accessed.

8. J. Paul Burney, Ph.D.

9. I want to emphasize that in consultation, as in therapy, I tend to use collective and cooperative language such as "our work together."

10. In this consultation, even though people worked together daily, some for years, we did not assume that they knew each other. The introductions focused on sharing personal information that each thought would be helpful for the others to know.

11. If we had an idea that silently observing would hamper open discussion, we would certainly take that into consideration.

BIBLIOGRAPHY

Agatti, A. P. R. (1993). III. The identity of theoretical psychology. *Theory and Psychology, 3,* 389–393.

Andersen, T. (1987). The reflecting team: Dialogue and meta-dialogue in clinical work. *Family Process, 26,* 415–428.

Andersen, T. (1990). *The reflecting team: Dialogues and dialogues about dialogues.* Broadstairs, Kent, UK: Borgmann.

Andersen, T. (1991, May). *Relationship, language, and pre-understanding in the reflecting process.* Paper presented at the Houston Galveston Narrative and Psychotherapy Conference, New Directions in Psychotherapy, Houston, TX.

Andersen, T. (1995a). Clients and therapists as co-researchers: Enhancing the sensitivity. *Fokus Familie, 1.*

Andersen, T. (1995b). Reflecting processes; acts of informing and forming: You can borrow my eyes, but you must not take them away from me! In S. Friedman (Ed.), *The reflecting team in action: Collaborative practice in family therapy* (pp. 11–37). New York: Guilford.

Andersen, T. (1996). Research on the therapeutic practice: What might such research be—viewpoints for debate. *Fokus Familie, 1,* 3–15.

Anderson, H. (1986). *Therapeutic impasses: A break-down in conversation.* Adapted from paper presented at Grand Rounds, Department of Psychiatry, Massachusetts General Hospital, Boston, MA, April 1986, and at the Society for Family Therapy Research, Boston, MA, October 1986.

Anderson, H. (1990). Then and now: From knowing to not-knowing. *Contemporary Family Therapy Journal, 12,* 193–198.

Anderson, H. (1991a). Opening the door for change through continuing conversations. In T. Todd & M. Selekman (Eds.), *Family therapy approaches with adolescent substance abusers* (pp. 176–189). Needham, MA: Allyn & Bacon.

Anderson, H. (1991b, October). *"Not-knowing": An essential element of therapeutic conversation.* Paper presented at the American Association of

Marriage and Family Therapy Annual Conference Plenary, Creating a Language of Change, Dallas, TX.

Anderson, H. (1992). C therapy and the F word. *American Family Therapy Association Newsletter, 50* (winter), 19–22.

Anderson, H. (1993). On a roller coaster: A collaborative language systems approach to therapy. In S. Friedman (Ed.), *The new language of change: Constructive collaboration in therapy* (pp. 323–344). New York: Guilford.

Anderson, H. (1994). Rethinking family therapy: A delicate balance. *Journal of Marital and Family Therapy, 20,* 145–150.

Anderson, H. (1995). Collaborative language systems: Toward a postmodern therapy. In R. Mikesell, D. D. Lusterman, & S. McDaniel (Eds.), *Integrating family therapy: Family psychology and systems theory* (pp. 27–44). Washington, DC: American Psychological Association.

Anderson, H. (1996a). Collaboration in therapy: Combining the client's expertise on themselves and the therapist's expertise on a process. In T. Keller & N. Greve (Eds.), *Social psychiatry and systems thinking: Cooperation in psychiatry.* Bonn: Psychiatrie Verlag.

Anderson, H. (1996b). A reflection on client–professional collaboration. *Families, Systems & Health, 14,* 193–206.

Anderson, H., & Burney, J. P. (in press). Collaborative inquiry: A postmodern approach to organizational consultation. *Human Systems: The Journal of Systemic Consultation and Management.*

Anderson, H., & Goolishian, H. (1986). Systems consultation to agencies dealing with domestic violence. In L. Wynne, S. McDaniel, & T. Weber (Eds.), *The family therapist as systems consultant* (pp. 284–299). New York: Guilford.

Anderson, H., & Goolishian, H. (1988a). *Changing thoughts on self, agency, questions, narrative and therapy.* Unpublished manuscript.

Anderson, H., & Goolishian, H. (1988b). Human systems as linguistic systems: Evolving ideas about the implications for theory and practice. *Family Process, 27,* 371–393.

Anderson, H., & Goolishian, H. (1989). Conversation at Sulitjelma: A description and reflection. *American Family Therapy Association Newsletter.*

Anderson, H., & Goolishian, H. (1990a). Beyond cybernetics: Some comments on Atkinson and Heath's "Further thoughts on second order family therapy." *Family Process, 29,* 157–163.

Anderson, H., & Goolishian, H. (1990b). Chronic pain: The family's role in the treatment program. *Houston Medicine, 6,* 1–6.

Anderson, H., & Goolishian, H. (1990c). Supervision as collaborative conversation: Questions and reflections. In H. Brandau (Ed.), *Von der supervision zur systemischen vision.* Salzburg: Otto Muller Verlag.

Anderson, H., & Goolishian, H. (1991a). Revisiting history. *Australian–New Zealand Journal of Family Therapy, 12,* iii.

Anderson, H., & Goolishian, H. (1991b). Thinking about multi-agency work with substance abusers and their families. *Journal of Strategic and Systemic Therapies, 10,* 20–35.

Anderson, H., & Goolishian, H. (1992). The client is the expert: A not-knowing approach to therapy. In S. McNamee & K. Gergen (Eds.), *Social construction and the therapeutic process* (pp. 25–39). Newbury Park, CA: Sage.

Anderson, H., Goolishian, H., Pulliam, G., & Winderman, L. (1986). The Galveston Family Institute: A personal and historical perspective. In D. Efron (Ed.), *Journeys: Expansions of the strategic–systemic therapies* (pp. 97–124). New York: Brunner/Mazel.

Anderson, H., Goolishian, H., & Winderman, L. (1986a). Beyond family therapy. *Journal of Strategic and Systemic Therapies, 5*(4), i–iii.

Anderson, H., Goolishian, H., & Winderman, L. (1986b). Problem determined systems: Towards transformation in family therapy. *Journal of Strategic and Systemic Therapies, 5,* 1–13.

Anderson, H., & Rambo, A. (1988). An experiment in systemic family therapy training: A trainer and trainee perspective. *Journal of Strategic and Systemic Therapies, 7,* 54–70.

Anderson, H., & Swim, S. (1993). Learning as collaborative conversation: Combining the student's and the teacher's expertise. *Human Systems: The Journal of Systemic Consultation and Management, 4,* 145–160.

Anderson, H., & Swim, S. (1995). Supervision as collaborative conversation: Combining the supervisor and the supervisee voices. *Journal of Strategic and Systemic Therapies, 14,* 1–13.

Anderson, W. J. (1989). Family therapy in the client-centered tradition: A legacy in the narrative mode. *Person-Centered Review, 4,* 295–307.

Anscombe, R. (1989). The myth of the true self. *Psychiatry, 52,* 209–217.

Atkinson, B. J., & Heath, A. W. (1990). The limits of explanation and evaluation. *Family Process, 29,* 145–155.

Auerswald, E. H. (1968). Interdisciplinary versus ecological approach. *Family Process, 7,* 202–215.

Auerswald, E. H. (1971). Families, change, and the ecological perspective. *Family Process, 10,* 263–280.

Auerswald, E. H. (1985). Thinking about thinking in family therapy. *Family Process, 224,* 1–12.

Auerswald, E. H. (1986). Epistemological confusion in family therapy. *Journal of Marital and Family Therapy, 26,* 317–330.

Ault-Riche, M. (Ed.). (1986). *Women and family therapy.* Rockville, MD: Aspen Systems.

Baker, W. J., Mos, L. P., Rappard, H. V., & Stam, H. J. (Eds.). (1988). *Recent trends in theoretical psychology.* New York: Springer-Verlag.

Bakhtin, M. (1981). *The dialogic imagination* (M. Holquist, Ed., and C. Emerson & M. Holquist, Trans.). Austin: University of Texas Press.

Bakhtin, M. (1986). *Speech genres and other late essays* (W. McGee, Trans.). Austin: University of Texas Press.

Bakhtin, M. (1990). *Art and answerability: Early philosophical essays* (M. Holquist & V. Liapunov, Eds., and V. Liapunov, Trans.). Austin: University of Texas Press.

Bateson, G. (1972). *Steps to an ecology of mind.* New York: Ballantine Books.

Bateson, G., Jackson, D. D., Haley, J., & Weakland, J. H. (1956). Toward a theory of schizophrenia. *Behavioral Science, 1,* 251–264.

Bateson, G., Jackson, D. D., Haley, J., & Weakland, J. H. (1963). A note on the double-bind—1962. *Family Process, 2,* 154–161.

Bateson, M. C. (1994). *Peripheral visions: Learning along the way.* New York: HarperCollins.

Becker, A.L. (1984). The linguistics of particularity: Interpreting super-ordination in a Javanese text (pp. 425–436). Proceedings of the Tenth Annual Meeting of the Berkeley Linguistic Society, Berkeley, CA, Linguistics Department, University of California, Berkeley.

Becker, C., Chasin, L., Chasin, R., Herzig, M., & Roth, S. (1995). From stuck debate to new conversation on controversial issues: A report from the Public Conversations Project. In K. Weingarten (Ed.), *Cultural resistance: Challenging beliefs about men, women, and therapy* (pp. 143–164). New York: Harrington Press.

Beckman, H. B., & Frankel, R. M. (1984). The effects of physician behavior on the collection of data. *Annals of Internal Medicine, 101,* 692–696.

Belenky, M. F., Clinchy, B. M., Goldberger, N. R., & Taruel, J. M. (1986). *Women's ways of knowing.* New York: Basic Books.

Benveniste, E. (1971). *Problems in general linguistics.* (M. Meck, Trans.). Coral Gables, FL: University of Miami Press.

Berger, P. L., & Luckmann, T. (1966). *The social construction of reality: A treatise in the sociology of knowledge.* New York: Doubleday/Anchor Books.

Blackman, L. M. (1994). What is doing history? The use of history to understand the constitution of contemporary psychological objects. *Theory and Psychology, 4,* 485–504.

Bograd, M. (1984). Family systems approaches to wife battering: A feminist critique. *American Journal of Orthopsychiatry, 54,* 558–568.

Braten, S. (1984). The third position: Beyond artificial and autopoietic reduction. *Kybernetes, 13,* 157–163.

Braten, S. (1987). Paradigms of autonomy: Dialogical or monological? In G. Teubner (Ed.), *Autopoietic law: A new approach to law and society.* Berlin: De Gruyter.

Braten, S. (1988). Between dialogic mind and monologic reason: Postulating the virtual other. In M. Campanella (Ed.), *Between rationality and cognition* (pp. 1–31). Turin: Albert Meynier.

Braten, S. (1993). *Law as an autopoietic system.* Oxford: Blackwell.

Briggs, J. P., & Peat, J. P. (1984). *Looking glass universe.* New York: Cornerstone Library, Simon & Schuster.

Brody, H. (1987). *Stories of sickness.* New Haven, CT: Yale University Press.

Bruner, J. (1986). *Actual minds, possible worlds.* Cambridge, MA: Harvard University Press.

Bruner, J. (1990). *Acts of meaning.* Cambridge, MA: Harvard University Press.

Buxton, C. E. (1985). *Points of view in the modern history of psychology.* London: Academic Press.

Carpenter, J. (1992). What's the use of family therapy? Australian Family

Therapy Conference plenary address. *Australian and New Zealand Journal of Family Therapy, 13,* 26–32.

Cecchin, G. (1987). Hypothesizing, circularity, and neutrality revisited: An invitation to curiosity. *Family Process, 26,* 405–414.

Chance, S. (1987, January). Goodbye again. *The Psychiatric Times/Medicine and Behavior,* 11 and 21.

Charon, R. (1993). Medical interpretation: Implications of literary theory of narrative for clinical work. *Journal of Narrative and Life History, 3,* 79–98.

Chessick, R. (1990). Hermeneutics for psychotherapists. *American Journal of Psychotherapy, 44,* 256–273.

Chubb, H. (1990). Looking at systems as process. *Family Process, 29,* 169–175.

Code, L. (1988). Experiences, knowledge and responsibility. In M. Griffiths & M. Whitford (Eds.), *Feminist perspectives in philosophy* (pp. 187–204). Bloomington: Indiana University Press.

Coddou, F., Maturana, H., & Mendez, C. L. (1988). The bringing forth of pathology: Radical constructivism, autopoiesis and psychotherapy. *The Irish Journal of Psychology, Special Issue, 9(1).*

Colapinto, J. (1985). Maturana and the ideology of conformity. *The Family Therapy Networker, 9,* 29–30.

Coles, R. (1989). *The call of stories: Teaching and the moral imagination.* Boston: Houghton Mifflin.

Conroy, P. (1987). *The prince of tides.* Toronto: Bantam Books.

Copeland, W. D., Birmingham, C., De La Cruz, E., & Lewin, B. (1993). The reflective practitioner in teaching: Toward a research agenda. *Teaching and Teacher Education, 9,* 347–359.

Crews, F. C. (1995). *The memory wars: Freud's legacy in dispute.* New York: New York Review of Books.

Danziger, K. (1988). On theory and method in psychology. In W. J. Baker, L. P. Mos, H. V. Rappard, & H. J. Stan (Eds.), *Recent trends in theoretical psychology* (pp. 87–94). New York: Springer-Verlag.

Danziger, K. (1994). Does the history of psychology have a future? *Theory and Psychology, 4,* 467–484.

Davis, P. C. (1992). Law and lawyering: Legal studies with an interactive focus. *New York Law School Law Review, 37,* 185–207.

Dell, P. F. (1980a). The Hopi family therapist and the Aristotelian parents. *Journal of Marital and Family Therapy, 6,* 123–130.

Dell, P. F. (1980b). Researching the family theories of schizophrenia: An exercise in epistemological confusion. *Family Process, 19,* 321–335.

Dell, P. F. (1982). Beyond homeostatis: Toward a concept of coherence. *Family Process, 21,* 21–42.

Dell, P. (1985). Understanding Bateson and Maturana: Toward a biological foundation for the social sciences. *Journal of Marital and Family Therapy, 11,* 1–20.

Dell, P., & Goolishian, H. (1979). *Order through fluctuation: An evolutionary epistemology for human systems.* Paper presented at the Annual Scientific Meetings of the A. K. Rice Institute, Houston, TX.

Dell, P., & Goolishian, H. (1981). Order through fluctuation: An evolutionary epistemology for human systems. *Australian Journal of Family Therapy, 21,* 75–184.

Denzin, N. K. (1989). *Interpretive biography.* Newbury Park, CA: Sage.

Derrida, J. (1978). *Writing and difference* (A. Bass, Trans.). Chicago: University of Chicago Press.

de Shazer, S. (1985). *Keys to solution in brief therapy.* New York: Norton.

de Shazer, S. (1991a). Here we go again: Maps, territories, interpretations, and the distinction between "the" and "a" or "an." *Journal of Marital and Family Therapy, 17,* 193–195.

de Shazer, S. (1991b). Muddles, bewilderment, and practice theory. *Family Process, 30,* 453–458.

Dilthey, W. (1984). *Selected writings.* H. P. Rickman (Ed. and Trans.). Cambridge: Cambridge University Press. (Originally published in 1914)

Doherty, W. J., & Boss, P. G. (1991). Values and ethics in family therapy. In A. S. Gurman & D. P. Knistern (Eds.), *Handbook of Family Therapy* (pp. 606–637). New York: Brunner/Mazel.

Drucker, P. F. (1994, November). The age of social transformation. *The Atlantic Monthly,* 53–80.

Dunn, J. (1988). *The beginnings of social understanding.* Cambridge, MA: Harvard University Press.

Eco, U. (1984). *The name of the rose.* New York: Harcourt Brace.

Elkaim, M. (1980). A propos de thermodynamique des processus irreversibles et de therapie familiale. *Cahiers critiques de Therapie Familiale et de Pratiques de Reseaux, 3,* 6.

Elkaim, M. (1981). Non-equilibrium, chance, and change in family therapy. In Models of Therapeutic Intervention with Families: A Representative World View. *International Issue Journal of Marital and Family Therapy, 7,* 291–297.

Erickson, G. D. (1988). Against the grain: Decentering family therapy. *Journal of Marital and Family Therapy, 14,* 225–236.

Eron, J. B., & Lund, T. W. (1993). How problems evolve and dissolve: Integrating narrative and strategic concepts. *Family Process, 32,* 291–309.

Evans, S. (Producer) and Hyther, N. (Director). (1995). *The madness of King George* (film). (Available from Hallmark Home Entertainment)

Faulconer, J. E., & Williams, R. N. (Eds.). (1990). *Reconsidering psychology: Perspectives from continental philosophy.* Pittsburgh: Duquesne University Press.

Feldman, S. P. (1990). Stories as cultural creativity: On the relation between symbolism and politics in organizational change. *Human Relations, 43,* 809–828.

Fish, V. (1993). Poststructuralism in family therapy: Interrogating the narrative/conversational mode. *Journal of Marital and Family Therapy, 19,* 221–232.

Flaskas, C. (1990). Power and knowledge: The case of the new epistemology. *Australian and New Zealand Journal of Family Therapy, 11*, 207–214.

Flax, J. (1990). *Thinking fragments: Psychoanalysis, feminism, and postmoderism in the contemporary West.* Berkeley: University of California Press.

Foucault, M. (1972). *The archeology of knowledge.* New York: Harper Colophon.

Foucault, M. (1980). *Power/knowledge.* New York: Pantheon.

Fowers, B. J. (1993). Psychology as public philosophy: An illustration with the moral and cultural dilemmas of marriage and marital research. *Journal of Theoretical and Philosophical Psychology, 13*, 124–136.

Fowers, B. J., & Richardson, F. C. (1996). Individualism, family ideology and family therapy. *Theory and Psychology, 6*, 121–151.

Fraser, N., & Nicholson, L. J. (1990). Social criticism without philosophy: An encounter between feminism and postmodernism. In L. J. Nicholson (Ed.), *Feminism/postmodernism* (pp. 19–38). New York: Routledge.

Freedman, J., & Combs, G. (1996). *Narrative therapy: The social construction of preferred realities.* New York: W. W. Norton.

Freeman, M. (1993). *Rewriting the self: History, memory, narrative.* London: Routledge.

Freeman, M. (1995). Groping in the light. *Theory and Psychology, 5*, 353–360.

Freud, S. (1964). Constructions in analysis. In J. Strachey (Ed. and Trans.), *The standard edition of the complete psychological works of Sigmund Freud* (Vol. 23, pp. 255–269). London: Hogarth Press. (Original work published in 1937)

Friedman, S. (1993). *The new language of change: Constructive collaboration in psychotherapy.* New York: Guilford.

Friedman, S. (1995). *The reflecting team in action: Collaborative practice in family therapy.* New York: Guilford.

Fried Schnitman, D. F. (1989). Paradigma y crisis familiar. *Psicoterapia y Familia, 2*(2), 16–24.

Fried Schnitman, D. F. (1994). *Nuevos paradigmas, cultura y subjetividad.* Buenos Aires: Paidos.

Fulford, K. W. M. (1989). *Moral theory and medical practice.* Cambridge: Cambridge University Press.

Gadamer, H.-G. (1975). *Truth and method* (G. Burden & J. Cumming, Trans.). New York: Seabury Press.

Gadamer, H.-G. (1988). *Truth and method* (J. Weinsheimer & D. G. Marshall, Trans.). 2d rev. ed. New York: Crossroad.

Garfinkel, H. (1967). *Studies in ethnomethodology.* New York: Prentice-Hall.

Gauron, E. F., & Dickinson, J. K. (1969). The influence of seeing the patient first on diagnostic decision making in psychiatry. *American Journal of Psychiatry, 126*, 199–205.

Geertz, C. (1973). *The interpretation of cultures.* New York: Basic Books.

Geertz, C. (1983). *Local knowledge.* New York: Basic Books.

Gergen, K. J. (1973). Social psychology as history. *Journal of Personality and Social Psychology, 26*, 309–320.

Gergen, K. J. (1977). The social construction of self-knowledge. In T. Mischel (Ed.), *The self: Psychological and philosophical issues*. Oxford: Blackwell.

Gergen, K. J. (1982). *Toward transformation in social knowledge*. New York: Springer-Verlag.

Gergen K. J. (1985). The social constructionist movement in modern psychology. *American Psychologist, 40,* 255–275.

Gergen, K. J. (1987). Towards self as a relationship. In T. Honess & K. Yardley (Eds.), *Self and identity: Psychosocial processes*. London: Wiley.

Gergen, K. J. (1988a). If persons are texts. In S. B. Messer, L. A. Sass, & R. L. Woolfolk (Eds.), *Hermeneutics and psychological theory* (pp. 28–51). New Brunswick, NJ: Rutgers University Press.

Gergen, K. J. (1988b). The pragmatics of human nature: Commentary on Joel Kovel. In S. B. Messer, L. A. Sass, & R. L. Woolfolk (Eds.), *Hermeneutics and psychological theory* (pp. 400–405). New Brunswick, NJ: Rutgers University Press.

Gergen, K. J. (1988c, August). *Understanding as a literary achievement*. Presidential address to Psychology and the Arts, Annual Meetings of the American Psychological Association, Atlanta, GA.

Gergen, K. J. (1989). Warranting voice and the elaboration of the self. In J. Shotter & K. J. Gergen (Eds.), *Texts of identity* (pp. 70–81). London: Sage.

Gergen, K. J. (1990, June). *Constructionisms*. Seminar presented at the Melbu Conference, Melbu, Vesteralen, Norway.

Gergen, K. J. (1991a, November). *Future directions for psychology: Realism or social constructionism*. Paper presented at the University of Houston, Houston, TX.

Gergen, K. J. (1991b). *The saturated self*. New York: Basic Books.

Gergen, K. J. (1994). *Realities and relationships: Soundings in social construction*. Cambridge, MA: Harvard University Press.

Gergen, K. J. & Gergen, M. M. (1983). Narratives of the self. In T. R. Sarbin & K. E. Scheibe (Eds.), *Studies in social identity* (pp. 254–273). New York: Praeger.

Gergen, K. J. & Gergen, M. M. (1986). Narrative form and the construction of psychological science. In T. R. Sarbin (Ed.), *Narrative psychology: The storied nature of human conduct*. New York: Praeger.

Gergen, K. J. & Gergen, M. M. (1988). Narrative and the self as relationship. In L. Berkowitz (Ed.), *Advances in experimental social psychology* (pp. 17–56). San Diego: Academic Press.

Gergen, K. J., Hoffman, L., & Anderson, H. (1995). Is diagnosis a disaster: A constructionist trialogue. In F. Kaslow (Ed.), *Handbook of relational diagnosis* (pp. 102–118). New York: John Wiley & Sons.

Gergen, K. J. & McNamee, S. 1994, April. *Communication as relational process*. Paper presented at the Relational Practices: Social Construction in Therapy and Organization Development Conference, Taos, NM.

Gergen, K. J. & Semin, G. R. (1990). Everday understanding in science and daily life. In G. R. Semin & K. J. Gergen (Eds.) *Everyday understanding: Social and scientific implications* (pp. 1–18). London: Sage.

Gergen, K. J. & Taylor, M. G. (1969). Social expectancy and self-presentation in a status hierarchy. *Journal of Experimental Social Psychology, 5,* 79–82.

Gergen, M. M. (1988). *Feminist thought and the structure of knowledge.* New York: New York University Press.

Gergen, M. M. (1994). Free will and psychotherapy: complaints of the draughtman's daughters. *Journal of Theoretical and Philosophical Psychology, 14,* 87–95.

Gergen, M. M. (1995). Postmodern, post-Cartesian positionings on the subject of psychology. *Theory and Psychology, 5,* 361–368.

Giddens, A. (1984). Hermeneutics and social theory. In G. Shapiro & A. Sica (Eds.), *Hermeneutics: Questions and prospects* (pp. 215–230). Amherst, MA: University of Massachusetts Press.

Gilligan, C. (1982). *In a different voice.* Cambridge, MA: Harvard University Press.

Giorgi, A. (1990). Phenomenology, psychological science and common sense. In G. R. Semin & K. J. Gergen (Eds.), *Everyday understanding: Social and scientific implications* (pp. 64–82). London: Sage.

Golann, S. (1988). On second-order family therapy. *Family Process, 27,* 51–72.

Goldner, V. (1985). Feminism and family therapy. *Family Process, 24,* 31–47.

Goldner, V. (1988). Generation and gender: Normative and covert hierarchies. *Family Process, 27,* 17–33.

Goodman, N. (1978). *Ways of worldmaking.* New York: Hackett Publishing.

Goolishian, H. (1985, August). *Beyond family therapy: Some implications from systems theory.* Paper presented at the Annual Meeting of the American Psychological Association, Division 43, San Francisco, CA.

Goolishian, H. (1989). *The self: Some thoughts from a postmodern perspective on the intersubjectivity of mind.* Unpublished manuscript.

Goolishian, H., & Anderson, H. (1987a). Language systems and therapy: An evolving idea. *Psychotherapy, 24(3S),* 529–538.

Goolishian, H., & Anderson, H. (1987b). De la thérapie familiale à la thérapie systémique et au-delà. In F. Ladame, P. Gutton, & M. Kalogerakis (Eds.), *Psychoses et adolescence: Annales internationales de psychiatrie de l'adolescence* (pp. 160–173). Paris: Masson.

Goolishian, H., & Anderson, H. (1988). Menschliche systeme: Vor welche probleme sie uns stellen und wie wir mit ihnen arbeiten. In L. Reiter, J. Brunner, & S. Reither-Theil (Eds.), *Von der familientherapie zur systemischen therapie* (pp. 189–216). Heidelberg: Springer-Verlag.

Goolishian, H., & Anderson, H. (1990). Understanding the therapeutic process: From individuals and families to systems in language. In F. Laslow (Ed.), *Voices in family psychology* (pp. 91–113). Newbury Park: Sage.

Goolishian, H., & Anderson, H. (1992). Strategy and intervention versus nonintervention: A matter of theory. *Journal of Marital and Family Therapy, 18,* 5–16.

Goolishian, H., & Anderson, H. (1994). Narrativa y self. Algunos dilemas posmodernos de la psicoterapia [Narrative and self: Some postmodern dilemmas of psychotherapy]. In D. F. Schnitman (Ed.), *Nuevos paradigmas, cultura y subjetividad* (pp. 293–306). Buenos Aires: Paidos.

Goolishian, H., & Kivell. (1981). Including non-blood-related persons in family therapy. In A. Gurman (Ed.), *Questions and answers in the practice of family therapy* (pp. 75–79). New York: Brunner/Mazel.

Grimshaw, J. (1988). Autonomy and identity in feminist thinking. In M. Griffiths & M. Whitfield (Eds.), *Feminist perspectives in philosophy* (pp. 90–108). Bloomington: Indiana University Press.

Groeben, N. (1990). Subjective theories and the explanation of human action. In G. R. Semin & K. J. Gergen (Eds.), *Everyday understanding: Social and scientific implications* (pp. 19–44). London: Sage.

Habermas, J. (1973). *Theory and psychology.* Boston: Beacon.

Hardy, K. V. (1994). Marginalization or development? A response to Shields, Wynne, McDaniel, and Gawinski. *Journal of Marital and Family Therapy, 20,* 139–143.

Hare-Mustin, R. (1987). The problem of gender in family therapy theory. *Journal of Marital and Family Therapy, 26,* 15–27.

Hare-Mustin, R., & Marecek, J. (1988). The meaning of difference: Gender theory, postmodernism, and psychology. *American Psychologist, 43,* 455–464.

Harré, R. (1979). *Social being: A theory for social psychology.* Oxford: Basil Blackwell.

Harré, R. (1983). *Personal being: A theory for individual psychology.* Oxford: Basil Blackwell.

Harré, R. (1995). The necessity of personhood as embodied in being. *Theory and Psychology, 5,* 369–373.

Harré, R., & Secord, P. (1972). *The explanation of social behaviour.* Oxford: Blackwell.

Heidegger, M. (1962). *Being and time* (J. Macquarrie & C. Robinson, Trans.). New York: Harper & Row.

Held, B. S., & Pols, E. (1985). The confusion about epistemology and "epistomology"—and what to do about it. *Family Process, 24,* 509–517.

Hermans, H. J. M. (1995). The limitations of logic in defining the self. *Theory and Psychology, 5,* 375–382.

Hermans, H. J. M., Kempen, H. J. G., & Van Loon, R. J. P. (1992). The dialogical self: Beyond individualism and rationalism. *American Psychologist, 47,* 23–33.

Høeg, P. (1993). *Smilla's sense of snow* (T. Nunnally, Trans.). New York: Dell.

Hoffman, L. (1971). Deviation-amplifying processes in natural groups. In J. Haley (Ed.), *Changing families.* New York: Grune & Stratton.

Hoffman, L. (1975). Enmeshment and the too richly cross-joined system. *Family Process, 14,* 457–468.

Hoffman, L. (1981). *Foundations of family therapy: A conceptual framework for systems change.* New York: Basic Books.

Hoffman, L. (1983). Diagnosis and assessment in family therapy: II. A co-evolutionary framework for systemic family therapy. *Family Therapy Collections, 4,* 35–61.

Hoffman, L. (1985). Beyond power and control: Toward a "second order" family systems therapy. *Family Systems Medicine, 3,* 381–396.

Hoffman, L. (1988). Reply to Stuart Golann. *Family Process, 27,* 65–68.

Hoffman, L. (1990). Constructing realities: An art of lenses. *Family Process, 29,* 1–12.

Hoffman, L. (1991). A reflexive stance for family therapy. *Journal of Strategic and Systemic Therapies, 10(3,4),* 1–17.

Hoffman, L. (1993). *Exchanging voices: A collaborative approach to family therapy.* London: Karnac Books.

Hoffman, L. (1994, October). Panel discussion at the New Voices in Human Systems: A Collaborative Conference, Northampton, Massachusetts.

Holloway, E. L. (1992). Supervision: A way of teaching and learning. In S. D. Brown & R. W. Lent (Eds.), *Handbook of counseling psychology* (2d ed., pp. 177–214). New York: Wiley.

hooks, b. (1984). *Feminist theory: From margin to center.* Boston: South End Press.

Hoshmand, L. T. (1994). *Orientation to inquiry in a reflective professional psychology.* Albany: State University of New York Press.

Hoshmand, L. T., & Polkinghorne, D. E. (1992). Redefining the science—practice relationship and professional training. *American Psychologist, 47,* 55–66.

Hoy, D. C. (1986). Must we say what we mean? The grammatological critique of hermeneutics. In B. R. Wachterhauser (Ed.), *Hermeneutics and modern philosophy* (pp. 397–415). Albany: State University of New York Press.

Hughes, J. (1988). The philosopher's child. In M. Griffiths & M. Whitford (Eds.), *Feminist perspectives in philosophy* (pp. 72–89). Bloomington: Indiana University Press.

Huyssen, A. (1990). Mapping the postmodern. In L. J. Nicholson (Ed.), *Feminism/postmodern* (pp. 234–277). New York: Routledge.

Imber-Coppersmith (Black), E. (1982). The place of family therapy in the homeostasis of larger systems. In L. R. Wolberg & M. L. Aronson (Eds.), *Group and family therapy: An overview* (pp. 216–227). New York: Brunner/Mazel.

Imber-Coppersmith (Black), E. (1983). The family and public sector systems: Interviewing and interventions. *Journal of Strategic and Systems Therapies, 2,* 38–47.

Imber-Coppersmith (Black), E. (1985). Families and multiple helpers: A systemic perspective. In D. Campbell & R. Draper (Eds.), *Applications of systemic family therapy: The Milan method*. London: Grune & Stratton.

Jackson, D. (1957). The question of family homeostasis. *Psychiatric Quarterly Supplement, 3*, 79–90.

Jackson, D. (1965). Family rules: Marital quid pro quo. *Archives of General Psychiatry, 12*, 589–594.

Jackson, D. D. (1968a). *Communication, family, and marriage: Human communication.* Vol. 1. Palo Alto, CA: Science and Behavior Books.

Jackson, D. D. (1968b). *Communication, family, and marriage: Human communication.* Vol. 2. Palo Alto, CA: Science and Behavior Books.

Jackson, S. W. (1992). The listening healer in the history of psychological healing. *American Journal of Psychiatry, 149*, 1623–1632.

Jantsch, E. (1975). *Design for evolution: Self organization and planning in the life of human systems.* New York: Braziller.

Jones, E. E. (1986). Interpreting interpersonal behavior: The effects of expectancies. *Science, 234*, 41–46.

Jones, E. E. (1993). Afterword: An avuncular view. *Personality and Social Psychology Bulletin, 19*, 657–661.

Jordan, J. (1991). The meaning of mutuality. In J. V. Jordan, A. G. Kaplan, J. B. Miller, I. P. Stiver, & J. L. Surrey (Eds.), *Women's growth in connection: Writings from the Stone Center* (pp. 81–96). New York: Guilford.

Joy, M. (1993). Feminism and the self. *Theory and Psychology, 3*, 275–302.

Kaslow, F. W. (1980). History of family therapy in the United States: A kaleidoscopic overview. *Marriage and Family Review, 3*, 77–111.

Kearney, P. A., Byrne, N., & McCarthy, I. C. (1989). Just metaphors: Marginal illuminations in a colonial retreat. *Family Therapy Cases Studies, 4*, 17–31.

Keeney, B. P. (1979). Ecosystemic epistemology: An alternative paradigm for diagnosis. *Family Process, 2*, 17–129.

Keeney, B. P. (1982). What is an epistemology of family therapy? *Family Process, 21*, 153–168.

Keeney, B. P. (1983). Diagnosis and assessment in family therapy: IX. Ecological assessment. *Family Therapy Collections, 4*, 155–169.

Keeney, B. P., & Sprenkle, D. H. (1982). Ecosystemic epistemology: Critical implications for family therapy. *Family Process, 21*, 1–19.

Kelly, G. A. (1955). *The psychology of personal constructs* (Vols. 1–2). New York: Norton.

Kerby, A. P. (1991). *Narrative and the self.* Bloomington: Indiana University Press.

Kitzinger, C. (1987). *The social construction of lesbianism.* London: Sage.

Kitzinger, C. (1989). The regulation of lesbian identities: Liberal humanism as an ideology of social control. In J. Shotter & K. J. Gergen (Eds.), *Texts of identity* (pp. 82–98). London: Sage.

Kjellberg, E., Edwardsson, M., Niemela, B. J., & Oberg, T. (1995). Using the reflecting process with families stuck in violence and child abuse. In S. Friedman (Ed.), *The reflecting team in action* (pp. 38–61). New York: Guilford.

Kjellberg, E., Niemela, B. J., Lovenborn, G., Oberg, T., Olssen, A., & Wessel, A. (1996). The community and the clinicians co-evaluate the clinical work. Presented at The Impact of Conversations and Language on Clinical Work and Research conference, June 13–19, Sulitjelma, Norway.

Kleinman, A. (1986). *Social origins of distress and disease.* New Haven, CT: Yale University Press.

Kleinman, A. (1988a). *The illness narratives: Suffering, healing, and the human condition.* New York: Basic Books.

Kleinman, A. (1988b). *Rethinking psychiatry: From cultural category to personal experience.* New York: Free Press.

Kuhn, T. S. (1970). *The structure of scientific revolutions* (2nd rev. ed.). Chicago: University of Chicago Press.

Kvale, S. (Ed.). (1992). *Psychology and postmodernism.* London: Sage.

Kvale, S. (1996). *InterViews.* London: Sage.

Labov, W. (1972). *Language in the inner city.* Philadelphia: University of Pennsylvania Press.

Laing, R. D. (1969). *Self and others.* New York: Pantheon.

Laing, R. D., & Esterson, A. (1971). *Sanity, madness and the family.* New York: Basic Books.

Laird, J. (1989). Women and stories: Restorying women's self-constructions. In M. McGoldrick, C. Anderson, & F. Walsh (Eds.), *Women in families* (pp. 427–450). New York: Norton.

Lehtinen, U. (1993). Feelings are "patterns in the weave of our life" not a basis for feminist epistemology. *Nordic Journal of Women's Studies, 1,* 39–50.

Leppingston, R. (1991). From constructivism to social constructionism and doing critical therapy. *Human Systems, 2,* 79–103.

Levin, S. B. (1992). *Hearing the unheard: Stories of women who have been battered.* Unpublished doctoral dissertation, The Union Institute, Cincinnati, OH.

Luepnitz, D. A. (1988). *The family interpreted: Feminist theory in clinical practice.* New York: Basic Books.

Lyotard, J.-F. (1984). *The post-modern condition: A report on knowledge.* Minneapolis: University of Minnesota Press.

MacGregor, R., Ritchie, A. M., Serrano, A. C., Schuster, F. P., McDanald, E. C., & Goolishian, H. A. (1964). *Multiple impact therapy with families.* New York: McGraw-Hill.

MacKinnon, L., & Miller, D. (1987). The new epistemology and the Milan approach: Feminist and sociopolitical considerations. *Journal of Marital and Family Therapy, 13,* 139–156.

Madison, G. B. (1988). *The hermeneutics of postmodernity.* Bloomington: Indiana University Press.

Mair, M. (1988). Psychology as storytelling. *International Journal of Personal Construct Psychology, 1,* 125–137.

Marayuma, M. (1963). The second cybernetics: Deviation-amplifying mutual causal processes. *American Scientist, 51,* 164–179.

Maturana, H. (1975). The organization of the living: A theory of the living organization. *International Journal of Man-Machine Studies, 7,* 313–332.

Maturana, H. R. (1978). Biology of language: Epistemology of reality. In G. Miller & E. Lenneberg (Eds.), *Psychology and biology of language and thought* (pp. 27–63). New York: Academic Press.

Maturana, H., & Varela, F. (1980). *Autopoiesis and cognition: The realization of the living.* Dordrecht, Holland: D. Reidel.

Maturana, H., & Varela, F. (1987). *The tree of knowledge.* Boston: New Science Library, Shambhala.

McArthur, T. (Ed.). (1992). *The Oxford companion to the English language.* Oxford: Oxford University Press.

McCarthy, I., & Byrne, N. (1988). Mis-taken love: Conversations on the problem of incest in an Irish context. *Family Process, 27,* 181–200.

McKeachie, W. J., & Kaplan, M. (1996, February). Persistent problems in evaluating college teaching. *American Association of Higher Education Bulletin,* 5–8.

McNamee, S., & Gergen, K. (Eds.). (1992). *Social construction and the therapeutic process.* Newbury Park, CA: Sage.

Mead, G. (1968). *Essays on his social philosophy* (J. W. Petras, Ed.). New York: Teachers College Press.

Mendez, C., Coddou, F., & Maturana, H. (1988). The bringing forth of pathology—radical constructivism, autopoiesis and psychotherapy. *The Irish Journal of Psychology, Special Issue, 9.*

Messer, S. B., Sass, L. A., & Woolfolk, R. L. (Eds.) (1988). *Hermeneutics and psychological theory: Interpretive perspectives on personality, psychotherapy, and psychopathology.* New Brunswick, NJ: Rutgers University Press.

Milford, N. (1972). *Zelda: A biography.* New York: Harper & Row.

Mitchell, W. J. T. (1981). *On narrative.* Chicago: University of Chicago Press.

Morse, S. J., & Gergen, K. J. (1970). Social comparison, self-consistency, and the presentation of self. *Journal of Personality and Social Psychology, 26,* 309–320.

Mueller-Vollmer, K. (Ed.) (1989). Language, mind, and artifact: An outline of hermeneutic theory since the Enlightenment. In *The hermeneutics reader* (pp. 1–53). New York: Continuum.

Murray, K. (1995). Narratology. In J. A. Smith, R. Harré, & L. Van Langenhove (Eds.), *Rethinking psychology* (pp. 179–195). London: Sage.

Nelson, K. (1989). Monologue as representation of real-life experience. In K. Nelson (Ed.), *Narratives from the crib* (pp. 27–72). Cambridge, MA: Harvard University Press.

Neufeldt, S. A., Karno, M. P., & Nelson, M. L. (1996). A qualitative study of experts' conceptualization of supervisee reflectivity. *Journal of Counseling Psychology, 43,* 3–9.

Nicholson, L. J. (Ed.) (1990). Introduction. In *Feminism/postmoderism* (pp. 1–16). New York: Routledge.

Palmer, R. (1984). Expostulations on the postmodern turn. *KRISIS, no. 2,* 140–149. Houston, TX: International Circle for Research in Philosophy.

Palmer, R. (1985). Quest for a concept of postmodernity. *kpíois/Krisis, 3–4*, 9–21.

Palmer, R. (1987). Nietzsche and the Project of Post-Modern Hermeneutics. *kpíois/Krisis: Hermeneutics and Humanism, 5–6*, 3–19.

Parsons, T. (1951). *The social system*. New York: Free Press.

Penn, P., & Frankfurt, M. (1994). Creating a participant text: Writing, multiple voices, narrative multiplicity. *Family Process, 33*, 217–231.

Percy, W. (1996). Shakespeare had it easy. *The New Yorker*, June 24–July 1.

Piaget, J. (1954). *The construction of reality in the child*. New York: Basic Books.

Piaget, J. (1971). *Genetic epistemology*. New York: Norton.

Pittman, B. (1995). Cross-cultural reading and generic transformations: The chronotype of the road in Erdrich's *Love Medicine*. *American Literature, 67*, 777–792.

Polkinghorne, D. (1983). *Methodology for the human sciences: Systems of injury*. Albany: State University of New York Press.

Polkinghorne, D. (1988). *Narrative knowing and the human sciences*. Albany: State University of New York Press.

Polkinghorne, D. (1991). Two conflicting calls for methodological reform. *The Counseling Psychologist, 19*, 103–114.

Potter, J., & Wetherell, M. (1987). *Discourse and social psychology: Beyond attitudes and behaviour*. London: Sage.

Prigogene, I., & Stengers, I. (1984). *Order out of chaos: Man's new dialogue with nature*. New York: Bantam Books.

Reichelt, S., & Christensen, B. (1990). Reflections during a study on family therapy with drug addicts. *Family Process, 29*, 273–287.

Reichelt, S., & Sveaass, N. (1994). Therapy with refugee families: What is a "good" conversation? *Family Process, 33*, 247–262.

Reik, T. (1951). Listening with the third ear: The inner experience of a psychoanalyst. Garden City, NY: Garden City Books.

Rice, A. (1976). *Interview with a vampire*. New York: Ballantine Books.

Rice, A. (1990). *The witching hour*. New York: Ballantine Books.

Richardson, F. C., & Woolfolk, R. L. (1994). Social theory and values: A hermeneutic perspective. *Theory and Psychology, 4*, 99–226.

Ricoeur, P. (1988). *Time and narrative* (K. Blamey & D. Pellauer, Trans.). Chicago: University of Chicago Press.

Ricoeur, P. (1991). Narrative identity. *Philosophy Today, 35*, 3–81.

Roebeck, A. A. (1964). *History of psychology and psychiatry*. New York: Citadel Press.

Rønnestad, M. H., & Skovholt, T. M. (1993). Supervision of beginning and advanced graduate students of counseling and psychotherapy. *Journal of Counseling and Development, 71*, 396–405.

Rorty, R. (1979). *Philosophy and the mirror of nature*. Princeton, NJ: Princeton University Press.

Rosenhan, D. L. (1973). On being sane in insane places. *Science, 179*, 250–258.

Roth, S. A. (1985). Psychotherapy with lesbian couples: Individual issues, female socialization, and the social context. *Journal of Marital and Family Therapy, 11,* 273–286.

Russell, R. L., Broek, P., Adams, S., Rosenberger, K., & Essig, T. (1993). Analyzing narratives in psychotherapy: A formal framework and empirical analyses. *Journal of Narrative and Life History, 3,* 337–360.

Ryder, R. (1987). *The realistic therapist: Modesty and relativism in therapy and research.* New Park, CA: Sage.

Saba, G. (Guest Ed.). (1985). A contextual refocus of systems therapy: An expansion of role, purpose, and responsibility. *Journal of Strategic and Systemic Therapies, 4*(2).

Sachs, O. (1985). *The man who mistook his wife for a hat.* London: Duckworth.

St. George, S. A. (1994). Multiple formats in the collaborative application of the "as if" technique in the process of family therapy supervision. *Dissertation Abstracts International, 55(9A),* 3006–3246.

Sampson, E. E. (1981). Cognitive psychology as ideology. *American Psychologist, 36,* 730–743.

Sandifer, M. G., Hordern, A., & Green, L. M. (1970). The psychiatric interview: The impact of the first three minutes. *American Journal of Psychiatry, 126,* 968–973.

Sarbin, T. R. (1986). Emotion and act: Roles and rhetoric. In R. Harré (Ed.), *The social construction of emotions* (pp. 83–98). New York: Basil Blackwell.

Sarbin, T. R. (1990). The narrative quality of action. *Theoretical and Philosophical Psychology, 10,* 49–65.

Sass, L. A. (1992). *Madness and modernism: Insanity in the light of modern art, literature, and thought.* New York: Basic Books.

Scarr, S. (1985). Constructing psychology: Making facts and fables for our times. *American psychologist, 40,* 499–512.

Schafer, R. (1978). *Language and insight.* New Haven, CT: Yale University Press.

Schafer, R. (1981). Narration in the psychoanalytic dialogue. In W. J. T. Mitchell (Ed.), *On narrative* (pp. 25–49). Chicago: University of Chicago Press.

Schön, D. A. (1983). *The reflective practitioner: How professionals think in America.* New York: Basic Books.

Schön, D. (1987). *Educating the reflective practitioner.* San Francisco: Jossey-Bass.

Schön, D. (1991). *The reflective practitioner: Case studies in and on educational practice.* New York: Teachers College Press.

Schwartzman, J. (1984). Family therapy and the scientific method. *Family Process, 23,* 223–236.

Searle, J. R. (1992). *Searle on conversation* (Compiled by H. Parret & J. Verschueren). Amsterdam: John Benjamins.

Segal, L. (1986). *The dream of reality: Heinz von Foerster's constructivism.* New York: Norton.

Seikkula, J. (1993). The aim of therapy is generating dialogue: Bakhtin and Vygotsky in family system. *Human Systems Journal, 4,* 33–48.

Selvini-Palazzoli, M., Boscolo, L., Cecchin, G., & Prata, G. (1978). *Paradox and counterparadox.* New York: Jason Aronson.

Selvini-Palazzoli, M., Boscolo, L., Cecchin, G., & Prata, G. (1980a). Hypothesizing, circularity, and neutrality: Three guidelines for the conductor of the interview. *Family Process, 19,* 3–12.

Selvini-Palazzoli, M., Boscolo, L., Cecchin, G., & Prata, G. (1980b). The problem of the referring person. *Journal of Marital and Family Therapy, 6,* 3–9.

Selvini-Palazzoli, M., & Prata, G. (1982). Snares in family therapy. *Journal of Marital and Family Therapy, 8,* 443–450.

Semin, G. R. (1990). Everyday assumptions, language and personality. In G. R. Semin & K. J. Gergen (Eds.), *Everyday understanding: Social and scientific implications* (pp. 151–175). London: Sage.

Shapiro, G., & Sica, A. (Eds.). (1984). Introduction. In *Hermeneutics* (pp. 1–21). Amherst: University of Massachusetts Press.

Sherwin, R. K. (1993). Lawyering theory: An overview of what we talk about when we talk about law. *New York Law School Law Review, 37,* 9–53.

Shields, C. (1986). Critiquing the new epistemologies: Toward minimum requirements for a scientific theory of family therapy. *Journal of Marital and Family Therapy, 12,* 359–372.

Shields, C. G., Wynne, L. C., McDaniel, S. H., & Gawinski, B. A. (1994). The marginalization of family therapy: A historical and continuing problem. *Journal of Marital and Family Therapy, 20,* 117–138.

Shotter, J. (1974). What is it to be human? In N. Armistead (Ed.), *Reconstructing social psychology.* Harmondsworth: Penguin.

Shotter, J. (1975). *Images of man in psychological research.* London: Methuen.

Shotter, J. (1984). *Social accountability and selfhood.* Oxford: Blackwell.

Shotter, J. (1985). Social accountability and self specification. In K. J. Gergen & E. Davis (Eds.), *The social construction of a person.* New York: Springer-Verlag.

Shotter, J. (1987). The social construction of an 'us': Problems of accountability and narratology. In R. Burnett, P. McGee, & D. Clarke (Eds.), *Accounting for personal relationships: Social representations of interpersonal links.* London: Methuen.

Shotter, J. (1988). *Real and counterfeit constructions in interpersonal relations.* Paper presented at the Don Bannister Memorial Conference, Metaphors in Life and Psychotherapy, London Institute of Group Analysis.

Shotter, J. (1989). Social accountability and the social construction of "you." In J. Shotter & K. J. Gergen (Eds.), *Texts of identity* (pp. 133–151). London: Sage.

Shotter, J. (1990). *Knowing of the third kind.* Utrecht: ISOR.

Shotter, J. (1991a, May). *Consultant re-authoring: The "making" and "finding" of narrative constructions.* Paper presented at the Houston–Galveston Conference on Narrative and Psychotherapy: New Directions in Theory and Practice, Houston, TX.

Shotter, J. (1991b). Rhetoric and the social construction of cognitivism. *Theory and Psychology, 1,* 495–513.

Shotter, J. (1993a). *Conversational realities: Constructing life through language.* London: Sage.

Shotter, J. (1993b). *Cultural politics of everyday life.* Toronto: University of Toronto Press.

Shotter, J. (1994). Making sense on the boundaries: On moving between philosophy and psychotherapy. In A. P. Griffiths (Ed.), *Philosophy, psychiatry, and psychology* (pp. 55–72). Cambridge, MA: Cambridge University Press.

Shotter, J. (1995a). A "show" of agency is enough. *Theory and Psychology, 5,* 383–390.

Shotter, J. (1995b). In conversation: Joint action, shared intentionality and ethics. *Theory and Psychology, 5,* 49–73.

Shotter, J., & Gergen, K. J. (Eds.) (1989). *Texts of identity.* London: Sage.

Simon, G. M. (1992). Having a second-order mind while doing first-order therapy. *Journal of Marital and Family Therapy, 18,* 377–387.

Simons, H. W., & Billig, M. (1994). *After postmodernism: Reconstructing ideology critique.* London: Sage.

Slife, B. D. (1993). *Time and psychological explanation.* Albany: State University of New York Press.

Sluzki, C. E., & Ransom, D. C. (Eds.). (1976). *The double bind: The foundation of the communication approach to the family.* New York: Grune & Stratton.

Smedslund, J. (1978). Bandura's theory of self-efficacy: A set of common sense theories. *Scandinavian Journal of Psychology, 19,* 1–14.

Smedslund, J. (1988). *Psycho-logic.* New York: Springer-Verlag.

Smedslund, J. (1990). Psychology and psychologic: Characterization of the difference. In G. R. Semin & K. J. Gergen (Eds.), *Everyday understanding: Social and scientific implications* (pp. 45–63). London: Sage.

Smedslund, J. (1993). How shall the concept of anger be defined? *Theory & Psychology, 3,* 5–34.

Smith, D. (1988). *Interpretation theory: Freud and Ricoeur.* Paper presented at the American Psychological Association Meeting, Washington, DC.

Smith, J. A., Harré, R., & Van Langenhove, L. (1995). *Rethinking psychology.* London: Sage.

Snyder, M. (1984). *When belief creates reality.* San Diego: Academic Press.

Snyder, M. & Thomsen, C. J. (1988). Interactions between therapists and clients: Hypothesis testing and behavioral confirmation. In D. C. Turk & P. Salovey (Eds.), *Reasoning, inference, and judgment in clinical psychology* (pp. 124–152). New York: Free Press.

Spanos, W. (1985). Postmodern literature and its occasion: Towards a "definition." *kpíois/Krisis, 3–4,* 54–76.

Speed, B. (1984). How really real is real and rejoinder. *Family Process, 23,* 511–520.

Speer, A. (1970). Family systems: Morphostasis and morphogenesis, or "Is homeostasis enough?" *Family Process, 9,* 259–278.

Spence, D. (1984). *Narrative truth and historical truth: Meaning and interpretation in psychoanalysis.* New York: Norton.

Spolin, V. (1963). *Improvisations for the theater.* Chicago: Northwestern University Press.

Stanfield, S., Matthews, K. L., & Heatherly, V. (1993). What do excellent psychotherapy supervisors do? *American Journal of Psychiatry, 150,* 1081–1084.

Surrey, J. L. (1991). Relationship and empowerment. In J. V. Jordan, A. G. Kaplan, J. B. Miller, I. P. Stiver, & J. L. Surrey (Eds.), *Women's growth in connection: Writings from the stone center* (pp. 162–180). New York: Guilford.

Sylvester, D. (1985). A note in reply to the questionnaire on postmodernism. *kpíois/Krisis, 3–4,* 232.

Szasz, T. S. (1961). *The myth of mental illness.* New York: Hoeber-Harper.

Taggart, M. (1985). The feminist critique in epistemological perspective: Questions of context in family therapy. *Journal of Marital and Family Therapy, 11,* 113–126.

Tannen, D. (1990). *You just don't understand me: Women and men in conversation.* New York: Ballantine Books.

Taylor, C. (1989). *Sources of the self: The making of the modern identity.* Cambridge, MA: Harvard University Press.

Terwee, S. (1988). Need rhetorical analysis lead to relativism? An examination of the views of K. J. Gergen. In W. J. Baker, L. P. Mos, H. V. Rappard, & H. J. Stan (Eds.), *Recent trends in theoretical psychology* (pp. 15–27). New York: Springer-Verlag.

Tjersland, O. A. (1990). From universe to multiverses—and back again. *Family Process, 29,* 385–397.

Tolstoy, L. (1967). On teaching the rudiments. In L. Weiner (Ed.), *Tolstoy on education.* London: University of London Press.

Toombs, S. K. (1990). The temporality of illness: Four levels of experience. *Theoretical Medicine, 11,* 227–241.

Turner, V. (1980). Social dramas and stories about them. *Critical Inquiry, 7,* 141–168.

van der Merwe, W. L., & Voestermans, P. P. (1995). Wittgenstein's legacy and the challenge to psychology. *Theory and Psychology, 5,* 5–26.

von Foerster, H. (1982). *Observing systems.* Seaside: Intersystems Publications.

von Foerster, H. (1984). On constructing a reality. In P. Watzlawick (Ed.), *The invented reality* (pp. 41–61). New York: Norton.

von Glasersfeld, E. (1984). An introduction to radical constructivism. In P. Watzlawick (Ed.), *The invented reality* (pp. 13–40). New York: Norton.

von Glasersfeld, E. (1987). The control of perception and the construction of reality. *Dialectica, 33,* 37–50.

Vygotsky, L. S. (1962). *Thought and language* (E. Hanfmann & G. Vakar, Ed. and Trans.). Cambridge, MA: MIT Press. (Original work published in 1934)

Vygotsky, L. S. (1966). Development of the higher mental functions. In

A. N. Leont'ev, A. R. Luria, & A. Smirnov (Eds.), *Psychological research in the USSR*. Moscow: Progress Publishers.

Vygotsky, L. S. (1986). *Thought and language* (rev. ed.) (A. Kozulin, Trans.). Cambridge, MA: MIT Press. (Original work published 1934)

Wachterhauser, B. R. (Ed.) (1986a). Introduction: History and language in understanding. In *Hermeneutics and modern philosophy* (pp. 5–61). Albany: State University of New York Press.

Wachterhauser, B. R. (Ed.) (1986b). Must we be what we say? Gadamer on truth in the human sciences. In *Hermeneutics and modern philosophy* (pp. 219–240). Albany: State University of New York Press.

Warneke, G. (1987). *Gadamer: hermeneutics, tradition and reason*. Stanford, CA: Stanford University Press.

Watzlawick, P. (1976). *How real is real?* New York: Vintage Books.

Watzlawick, P. (1977). *The interactional view: Studies at the Mental Research Institute Palo Alto, 1965–74*. New York: Norton.

Watzlawick, P. (Ed.). (1984). *The invented reality*. New York: Norton.

Watzlawick, P., Beaven, J. H., & Jackson, D. D. (1967). *Pragmatics of human communication*. New York: Norton.

Watzlawick, P., Weakland, J., & Fisch, R. (1974). *Change: Principles of problem formation and problem resolution*. New York: Norton.

Weakland, J., Fisch, R., Watzlawick, P., & Bodin, A. M. (1974). Brief-therapy: Focused problem resolution. *Family Process, 13*, 141–168.

Weingarten, K. (1991). The discourses of intimacy: Adding a social constructionist and feminist view. *Family Process, 30*, 285–305.

Weingarten, K. (Ed.). (1995). *Cultural resistance: Challenging beliefs about men, women, and therapy*. New York: Harrington Park Press.

White, H. (1980). The values of narrativity in the prepresentation of reality. *Critical Inquiry, 7*, 5–27.

White, M. (1995). *Re-authoring lives*. Adelaide, Australia: Dulwich Centre.

White, M., & Epston, D. (1990). *Narrative means to therapeutic ends*. New York: Norton.

Wile, D. B. (1977). Ideological conflicts between clients and psychotherapists. *American Journal of Psychotherapy, 31*, 437–449.

Wilkins, A. (1983). Organizational stories as symbols which control the organization. In L. R. Pondy, P. J. Frost, G. Morgan, & T. C. Dandridge (Eds.), *Organizational symbolism* (pp. 81–92). Greenwich, CT: JAI Press.

Wittgenstein, L. (1961). *Tractatus logico-philosophicus* (D. Pears & B. McGuiness, Trans.). London: Routledge and Kegan Paul. (Original work published in 1922)

Woolfolk, R. L., Sass, L. A., & Messer, S. B. (1988). Introduction to hermeneutics. In S. B. Messer, L. A. Sass, & R. L. Woolfolk (Eds.), *Hermeneutics and psychological theory: Interpretive perspectives on personality, psychotherapy, and psychopathology* (pp. 2–26). New Brunswick, NJ: Rutgers University Press.

INDEX

Index